THE OBSERVER XIMENES PRIZE

1436 · 1517

PRIZE

REMINISCENCES OF MY LIFE IN THE HIGHLANDS

VOLUME 2

REMINISCENCES
OF MY LIFE IN THE
HIGHLANDS
(1884)

by
Joseph Mitchell

A reprint with a new introduction, corrigenda
and index contributed by
IAN ROBERTSON

VOLUME 2

DAVID & CHARLES REPRINTS

ISBN 0 7153 5300 4

· Volume 2 of *Reminiscences of My Life in the Highlands*
was originally published by the author in 1884

This reprint, which includes a new introduction, corrigenda
and index, published in 1971

© 1971 Introduction, corrigenda and index by Ian Robertson

Printed in Great Britain by
Lewis Reprints Limited, London and Tonbridge
for David & Charles (Publishers) Limited
South Devon House Newton Abbot
Devon

INTRODUCTION

Readers of the first volume of the *Reminiscences* will be acquainted with the sterling qualities of the author whose monument is the Highland Railway which threads its way unobtrusively through the glens north of Perth.

Trained by Thomas Telford, Joseph Mitchell succeeded his father as Chief Inspector and Superintendent of Highland Roads and Bridges. This enterprise and the construction of the Caledonian Canal were twin projects administered by commissioners appointed by act of parliament. The execution of the work was entrusted to Telford whose genius had many facets; his ability to select outstanding men to superintend unprecedented tasks was a notable example.

Fortunately for Mitchell his father had completed the pioneering work by 1824, albeit at the cost of his life. His conscientious example encouraged twenty-one year old Joseph to continue the arduous task undaunted—yet with an ever-increasing awareness of his father's unselfish exertions. Until the death of Telford in 1834 the overall impression is that of a keen young man supporting his mother and younger members of the family, while endeavouring to satisfy his employer and mentor. Thereafter the scene changes to that of a thoroughly experienced civil engineer in private practice seeking to pursue a career in keeping with current developments in the Steam Age.

Contemporaneous with the publication of Mitchell's first volume there appeared *The History of the Highland Clearances* by Alexander Mackenzie, which was quickly followed by Thomas Sellar's refutation, *The Sutherland Evictions of 1814*. Mitchell knew both James Loch and Patrick Sellar, the Duke of Sutherland's commissioner and factor respectively, in their latter years. Doubtless the revival of public interest prompted his recollection of Loch canvassing (unsuccessfully) in Wick during the general election of 1852, when Loch was unable to shake off a mob baa-ing like sheep and carrying a model of a half-burned cottage. Three years later, when travelling through Sutherland, Mitchell was greeted along the whole course of his journey with the quiet but exultant enquiry 'Did you hear the news? Loch is dead.' During a conversation with Patrick Sellar, Mitchell was astonished by the notorious factor's repetition of an ungracious retort he had made to the second Duke of Sutherland who, having realised his parents' blunder, intimated his intention of ultimately reducing the area of the sheep farms leased to Sellar and others.

Describing the plight of Highlanders dispossessed to accommodate the incoming Lowland sheep farmers, Mitchell makes the point that while poor people merely obtained possession from year to year at the landowner's pleasure, leases were invariably given to the larger tenants. He recounts how the late Countess of Sutherland held court on the castle lawn during the summer. She examined and cross-examined acutely and gave fair verdicts, but the crux of the people's problem was neatly summarised by a worthy old man who, despite many supplications, received no more than a verbal assurance that he would not be dispossessed of his home. 'Your hand o' write ye'll no' give and your word is no' worth a damn', he retorted when the countess unyieldingly repeated her formula.

Sheep farming did not invariably prove to be as lucrative as expected and in some parts of the Highlands the sheep gave way to deer and game 'rendering the solitude of these regions still more oppressive'. In Invernessshire Mitchell found in one of his gravel pits a tent of blankets, the only habitation of a woman and her young family. They had been removed off land required for sport, and her husband had gone further down the road in search of employment and a shelter for his family.

The completion of the roads did not bring unalloyed happiness to the Highlands. The patriarchal system ceased, and the chiefs succumbed to the blandishments of southern society, failing to realise that lowland lairds enjoyed greater revenues. In the end many chiefs had to follow their people into exile, having sold their patrimony.

The heritors of Caithness, a county which claims affinity with Orkney rather than with the Highlands, spent some £30,000 on roads constructed on the Macadam system, but the climatic conditions of the county proved insuperable and an appeal was made to the Highlands Roads and Bridges Commissioners. Subsequently Mitchell was able to claim that he had maintained the Caithness roads to the entire satisfaction of the public for a period of twenty-two years. When he initiated the work he could hardly have foreseen that his roads would soon be subjected to stresses other than the forces of nature. In 1859 the Duke of Sutherland's heir bought a Ricketts steam car which probably aroused the interest of the Earl of Caithness who purchased a similar model the following year. Despite Mitchell's protestations, the earl piloted his countess in this three-wheeled iron-tyred vehicle over the 170 miles between Inverness and his Caithness residence near John O' Groats, the brave lady declaring that she was determined to accompany her lord even if the machine exploded. This historic vehicle is well recorded in the engineering journals of the period. The boiler and furnace were at the rear and, of course, required a stoker. There must have been frequent stops for coal and water but, when interviewed, the earl stated 'On the level I got 19 miles per hour'.

In March 1844 the prospectus of the Scottish Central Railway was issued, backed by seventy-five of the most influential members of the nobility residing in the counties of Stirling and Perth and headed by the Marquis of Breadalbane. This project was, however, the brain-child of Mitchell who carried out the parliamentary surveys at his own expense. His plan was to establish a junction with the Edinburgh & Glasgow Railway at Castlecary near Falkirk which would suit either an east coast or a west coast route to London, once that very debatable question had been settled. He resisted pressure from those in favour of the Caledonian scheme and consequently found himself at cross purposes with Messrs Locke and Errington,

and without the whole-hearted support of Breadalbane.   The
position became intolerable and Mitchell resigned.

Retreating to Inverness, Mitchell spent some years battling
with the Aberdeen promoters of the Great North of Scotland
Railway over routes in the north-eastern counties, but eventu-
ally in 1855 he was able to establish his base line between
Inverness and Nairn which enabled the great line over the
Grampians to proceed in 1861.   Twenty-three months later
the line was passed by the government inspector.   Although
certain work had not been completed and engine crews and
station staff were not fully acquainted with their tasks, the
over-enthusiastic managing director of the railway insisted on
commencing full-scale operations forthwith.   The immediate
consequences have been ably reported in the contemporary
local press.   Throughout the entire period Mitchell had been
subjected to great strain resulting in a paralytic stroke from
which he fortunately recovered.   His capable assistants,
William and Murdoch Paterson, whom he assumed as partners
under the firm name of J. Mitchell & Co, were able to maintain
the pace but they and their chief spent a most anxious winter,
which fortunately proved to be comparatively mild, while a
large body of men kept watch over the line and unfinished
water courses.

In his closing chapters Mitchell refers to the construction of
the Dingwall & Skye Railway and the line through Sutherland
and Caithness to Wick and Thurso.   West of Dingwall the
preliminary work was no easy task as hundreds of miles had to
be surveyed in the search for a feasible route.   There are
glimpses of engineers and contractors whose names are part of
railway history.   The tragic Bouch and the fortunate Fowler
were both known to Mitchell.   Fowler, having become a
Highland laird by purchasing an estate in Wester Ross, was on
friendly terms with the third Duke of Sutherland, sharing his
enthusiasm for mechanical engineering.

The duke was rigidly economical, and this foible was readily
exploited by sycophants and countenanced by tactful friends.
By remarking that his bridges were unnecessarily ornate,
Fowler brought upon Mitchell the duke's displeasure.   The
inference that ugly bridges would cost less was an unfair

criticism of the Telford school and of the conscientious masons who so ably executed their plans. In the resultant unpleasant atmosphere, George Loch, who had succeeded his father as the duke's commissioner, introduced Messrs Maclean and Stileman and Messrs Brassey and Falshaw who were instructed to estimate for the Sutherland and Caithness line. Mitchell describes Falshaw as an organiser of great ability whom he had had to compel to execute works on the Inverness & Aberdeen Junction Railway in accordance with the contract. The duke sat on the fence. No other opinion in Sutherland really mattered, but Caithness hearts warmed at the thought of the leading men from the south's concern for them until Mitchell, writing in the press, pointed out that Messrs Brassey and Falshaw's estimate, shorn of all adornment, was £6,500 per mile while his own price was £5,000 per mile. His Grace promptly came down on the economical side of the fence and repudiated the entire business. The matter lay in abeyance for five years when the line was completed according to the plans of J. Mitchell & Co by Murdoch Paterson—ill health and advancing years having compelled Mitchell to retire.

In this volume, as in his preceding work, the author reveals his considerable knowledge of Highland customs and also of the principal families in the North, with perhaps insufficient regard for their feelings. His account of how a funeral cortege proceeded on the last lap of a 7 mile journey minus the hearse, confirms the substance of tales concerning convivial obsequies. In presenting personalities Mitchell appears to relate every favourable point while lamenting any uncharitable and foolish ways. His strictures are reserved for those who treated him unjustly and all such are the subject of pithy Mitchellisms.

Presumably the author did not enjoin his select circle of readers to secrecy and no fortunate recipient of the first volume would thereafter lack company over the winter. Verbal reports of the contents probably circulated with ever decreasing veracity and in certain quarters added fuel to a smouldering fire of resentment. While the heat generated, the author passed peacefully from this world leaving his second volume in the press. The merit of the work mattered little to injured pride, and threats of litigation could only be appeased by its virtual suppression. Consequently much valuable railway history and a practically unknown appraisal of George Hudson, including correspondence revealing Mitchell as a stockholder in the Midland and the North Eastern railways who had declined a directorship, escaped notice.

Probably no more than a smile will be raised by the passages which so excited some of the author's contemporaries, but the tantalisingly short excerpts published in recent histories have aroused interest of a different kind happily met by this present reprint.

CORRIGENDA

Vol I
Page 181

Lines 29–31 and 37. Colonel John Cameron was killed at Quatre Bras while commanding the 92nd Regiment. He was the younger son of Ewen Cameron. The author has confused the Cameron Highlanders with the Cameronians of Lanarkshire origin.

Vol II
Page v

Contents of chapters line 1   After *Clan* read *Mackintosh*

2   line 21 for *Macgillavry of Dumnaglass* read *MacGillivray of Dunmaglass.*

4   line 15 after *Dalvey* read (*Cromdale*)

5   line 17 after *Dalvey* read (*Dyke and Moy*)

31   line 13 after *given* read *in* '*Pencillings by the Way*' and for *H.P.* read *Nathaniel P.*

38   line 36 for *Adams* read *William Adam*

39   line 21 for *Monurghty, Aslisk* read *Monaughty, Asliesk* both in Alves Parish

84   Footnote for *1810* read *1811 census* for *1825* read *1821 census*

88   line 31 The correct title of Stewart's book is given on page 46

89   line 33 for *seven years* read from *1811 to 1816*

97   line 2 for *500 members* read *over 450 ministers*

112   line 9 for *Memorials* read *Journal vol 2 page 247*

131   line 31   There is only one edition of Sinclair's *Statistical Account* but he published an analysis of it in 1826 and in 1831

137   line 26   for *Sir John* read *Sir James*

137   line 32   Mitchell's friend was the fourteenth Earl.

168   line 3   ⎧ The author apparently uses 'South' to
189   line 25 ⎨ distinguish the Aberdeen Railway Co and associated companies from the Great North of Scotland Railway headquarters in Aberdeen.

200   line 27   Probably a sentence has been omitted here. The viaduct cost £5,720 as stated by Mitchell to the British Association at Dundee 1867.

Page 200   line 38   For *1,588 feet* read *1,488 feet*
At Dundee meeting of BA Mitchell explained 'from Perth to Blair Athole the line rises 443 feet and from Blair Athole to Summit it rises 1,045 feet making extreme summit 1,488 feet.' The figure usually quoted is 1,484 feet as shown on the summit board.

232   line 8   For *Ear Wash* read *Erewash*

237   line 22   For *Thomson Fireman & Co.* read *Thompson & Forman*

241   line 1   In 1859 Hudson's industrial connections were finally severed but 1854 marked the termination of his railway career.

246 and 248 onwards   For *H. S. Thomson* read *Harry S. Thompson*

REMINISCENCES OF MY LIFE IN THE HIGHLANDS.

REMINISCENCES

MY LIFE IN THE HIGHLANDS.

CONTAINING

NOTICES OF THE CHANGES IN THE COUNTRY
DURING THE PRESENT CENTURY.

BY

JOSEPH MITCHELL, C.E.,

F.R.S.E., F.G.S., AND M.I.C.E.

With a Narrative of

THE WORKS OF THE CALEDONIAN CANAL,

AND THE

HIGHLAND ROADS, BRIDGES, AND HARBOURS,

CONSTRUCTED UNDER THE

AUTHORITY OF A PARLIAMENTARY COMMISSION.

VOLUME II.

Printed privately for the Author

AT THE GRESHAM PRESS:

UNWIN BROTHERS, CHILWORTH AND LONDON.

MDCCCLXXXIV.

CONTENTS.

CHAPTER I.

PAGE

Extensive territories of the Clan—Æneas, chief in 1745—His Jacobite Lady—The Rout of Moy—Sir Æneas Mackintosh, 23rd chief — Succession of a collateral branch—Alexander, 26th chief—Marriage and early death of the 27th chief—Alfred Donald, 28th chief—Peculiarity of succession—Æneas Mackintosh of Daviot 1

CHAPTER II.

The Clan Fraser—Lord Simon of the '45—Forfeiture and restoration of the estates—The succession of the Strichen branch of the family—Litigation with Fraser of Abertarff—Families of the name of Fraser—The Belladrum estate—Its purchase by Mr. Merry 8

CHAPTER III.

The possessions of the Gordons—The Jacobite Duke, 1715—Lord Lewis Gordon, 1745—Marriage of Alexander, the fourth Duke, to Lady Jane Maxwell—Lady Jane's character and history— Her tomb at Kinrara—The Duke's second marriage—The last Duke and Duchess—Gordon Castle—Dispersion of the estates— The Duke of Richmond 24

CHAPTER IV.

The Duff family—Their shrewdness and accumulations of property —Raised to the peerage—The history of the fourth Earl—His retired residence in Duff House—The late and present Earls . 36

CHAPTER V.

The territory and families of the clan—The Ogilvies, Earls of Findlater and Seafield—The chief of the Grants succeeds to the possessions of the Ogilvies and the title of Seafield—A romantic marriage—The last clan demonstration—The forests of Strathspey—Castle Grant and Balmacaan 44

CHAPTER VI.

PAGE

Visit to Fort George—Description of fortress—Two Yorkshire friends—Visit to Cawdor Castle—A baronial pile of the olden time—The hawthorn tree—A beautiful ravine . . . 54

CHAPTER VII.

Smuggling in the Highlands—Its universal character—An Act to authorize small stills—A morning encounter in Glenmoriston— A cargo from Holland—Two smuggled kegs of brandy . . 60

CHAPTER VIII.

Extract from Journal—Howe of the Elms 63

CHAPTER IX.

The Caledonian Bank—Negotiations preceding its commencement —Appointment of Mr. Waterston, manager—Success of the Bank—Unfortunate entanglement with the City of Glasgow Bank in 1878—Suspension and restoration—St. John's Friendly Society—The Caledonian Hotel 65

CHAPTER X.

Commercial travellers in riding and coaching days—The change made by railways—Anecdotes of the commercial-room . . 75

CHAPTER XI.

Account of the County of Sutherland—Sad death of the Earl and Countess of Sutherland in 1776—Their daughter served heir to the estates—The state of the people—Marriage of the young Countess to the Marquis of Stafford—Clearances and improvements carried out under Mr. Loch, Mr. Young, and Mr. Patrick Sellar—Purchase of the Reay country 78

CHAPTER XII.

Construction of roads and steadings—A contested Wick election— Death of the first Duke—The Duchess-Countess at Dunrobin— The Disruption and refusal of sites—The reclamations of the present Duke 92

CHAPTER XIII.

General remarks on the clearances in the Highlands . . 104

CHAPTER XIV.

PAGE

The Right Hon. Edward Ellice, M.P.—His residence at Glenquoich—His political connections—Purchases Glenquoich and Glengarry—His hospitality 123

CHAPTER XV.

The Great North Road through Sutherland and Caithness—Description of the County of Caithness—Making of county roads—Improvements in this bleak region—Superiority of the peasantry of Caithness—Caithness in the olden times—The Dunbars—The Earldom of Caithness—Thurso Castle and the Sinclairs—The Sinclairs of Freswick—The Trails—Tragic story of the eleventh Earl of Caithness—Mr. James Horne of Langwell—Islands of Orkney 126

CHAPTER XVI.

The Chisholms of Chisholm—Funeral of the Chisholm in 1838—Funeral of the Hon. Mrs. Fraser of Lovat—Vicissitudes of the Chisholm family—Lady Ramsay and her matrimonial relations—Visit of the writer to Dunrobin Castle—The first Duchess of Sutherland 142

CHAPTER XVII.

Early efforts to obtain railway employment—Early surveys—Survey of the Elgin and Lossiemouth Railway—The beginning of the Scottish Central Railway—The winter's engagement and work—Conduct of other engineers—Resignation of appointment 149

CHAPTER XVIII.

Railways continued—Excitement in 1845—Suggested construction of the Highland Railway—Appointment of a committee—Whole stock taken in a week—Objections of landed proprietors—Deputation to the Earl of Seafield—Labour and survey—Anecdote of a cattle dealer—Parliament throws out the scheme—Publication of pamphlet in vindication 158

CHAPTER XIX.

Railway mania—Loss and misery through railway speculation—Difficulties of the Great North of Scotland Railway—Harbour surveys in 1847—Visit to London—Trip to Paris—Dr. O'Leary 166

CHAPTER XX.

Floods in the River Ness—The flood of 1849—Part of town under water—Fall of the old bridge—Narrow escape of the wooden bridge—The breaking of the Canal bank—The works at the outlet of the Ness—The magistrates of Inverness and the Canal Commissioners—Proposed new bridge—Dispute as to kind of bridge—Costliness of suspension bridge erected by Mr. Rendal   171

PAGE

CHAPTER XXI.

Become tacksman of a Highland farm—Its interesting situation— The difficulties of farming—Quit the farm   176

CHAPTER XXII.

Renewed efforts to promote Highland Railway—Effect of pamphlet on public mind—Effort to resuscitate scheme—Interview with the North-Western directors and Mr. Brassey—Construction of line to Nairn—Progress of railway eastwards—Negotiations with the Great North Company—Extension to Keith—Unfortunate accident   179

CHAPTER XXIII.

Extension of Railway to Invergordon—The Highland Railway— Visit to the Duke of Athole—Construction of Line—Banquet at Inverness 188

CHAPTER XXIV.

Abolition of the Commission for Highland Roads and Bridges— Construction of Railway to Bonar—The Sutherland Railways— The Duke of Sutherland—The Sutherland and Caithness Railway 204

APPENDIX.

I. Mr. George Hudson, M.P.   229
II. The Fisheries in the North   252

REMINISCENCES

MY LIFE IN THE HIGHLANDS.

CHAPTER I.

The Clan Mackintosh.

Extensive territories of the Clan—Æneas, chief in 1745—His Jacobite
Lady—The Rout of Moy—Sir Æneas Mackintosh, 23rd chief—
Succession of a collateral branch—Alexander, 26th chief—Marriage
and early death of the 27th chief—Alfred Donald, 28th chief—
Peculiarity of succession—Æneas Mackintosh of Daviot.

I HAVE had frequent intercourse with Alexander, the twenty-
sixth chief of the Mackintoshes. He was an agreeable and
kindly man, though very jealous of his dignity as a chief.
He had long controversies in the local newspapers with his
neighbour Cluny Macpherson, who claimed to be the chief
of the clan Chattan : one of the dignities which the Mackintosh considered appertained to his family.

The Mackintoshes were one of the most powerful clans
in the Highlands. Their territories are detached, but of
considerable extent, being situated near Inverness, at
Moyhall, in Strathdearn, in Strathspey, and in Lochaber.
Their revenues were, sixty years ago, from £5000 to £6000
a year, and are now increased with shootings, &c., to more
than £12,000.

The changes of the family border´ on romance. Their

VOL. II.   2

origin is as mystical as that of most of the other Highland clans, though their existence can be traced as far back as the twelfth century.

Prior to the Battle of Culloden, Æneas, the twenty-second chief, was a captain in the Black Watch, or 42nd Highlanders. At this time the regiment, along with a considerable royal force, was stationed at Inverness, under the command of the Earl of Loudon. The main body of the royal army, under the Duke of Cumberland, was marching northward from Aberdeen. The Highland army, under the prince, was advancing through the central Highlands, along General Wade's military road. As the Highlanders approached Inverness, the prince and a small following were a little in advance. He took up his abode at Moyhall, twelve miles from Inverness, on February 16th, 1746.

The lady of the chief, a daughter of Farquharson, of Invercauld, who had strong Jacobite tendencies (notwithstanding that her husband was in arms for the Government) raised the clan in behalf of the prince, and placed them under the command of a relative, Mr. Macgillavry, of Dumnaglass.

The Earl of Loudon, knowing that the Highland army was approaching Inverness, and hearing that the prince was to sleep at Moyhall on the 16th, conceived the idea of surprising him there and seizing his person. The enterprise required to be carried out with great secrecy, and with this view Lord Loudon placed a cordon of guards around the town to prevent any alarm being given or notice sent. He gave orders that 1500 men should be in readiness for a midnight expedition.

Some of the troopers, prior to their march, were drinking in a public-house kept by a widow Baillie. She overheard their talk and conjectures that they believed the expedition was with the view of proceeding to Moyhall to capture the prince. On this she sent a messenger to the Dowager Lady Mackintosh, who was also a Jacobite, and was then residing in Inverness, to intimate what she had overheard. The old lady immediately despatched one of her maid servants as messenger to Moyhall to warn them of the intended expedition and the danger to which the person of the prince would be exposed. This messenger, after many hairbreadth escapes, arrived in time to give the necessary alarm.

The lady of the chief at Moyhall, without ceremony and in great haste, sent the prince and his followers to a place of safety. She had previously instructed Fraser, the black-smith of Moy, with a few trusty men under his command, to watch the approaches from Inverness.

Fraser concealed his men behind a series of hillocks which exist along the roadside, planting them at various distances as if there were a great body of men, and as Lord Loudon's men approached in the dark, he gave orders to his men at the various distances to fire. The first shot killed Macleod's piper, Macrimmon (said to be the best in the Highlands), Fraser at the same time calling out in the dark with a loud voice on the Macdonalds and the Camerons to advance and protect the sacred person of their prince. The royalists were seized with panic, which passed along the whole body of the troops. They fled in great disorder, trampling on each other; and so complete was their rout and fear that they never stopped till they reached their head-quarters at Inverness. The royalists were disheart-ened and much disgusted at this disastrous repulse.

Immediately after the battle of Culloden a party of soldiers proceeded to Moyhall, seized the high-spirited lady who was the cause of this disaster, and carried her a prisoner to Inverness. The general, on the way back, in his polite and encouraging manner told her "to be hung would be her fate, but from her pluck and spirit she was worthy to be swung from a golden cord and to stand on a mahogany gallows." Such was the brutal comfort ten-dered to his prisoner, so unlike what might be expected from the brave and gallant soldier Hawley was reported to have been.

This lady was afterwards conveyed to Edinburgh, and there detained for two years a prisoner in rigorous confine-ment, and was then liberated. She seems to have suffered much from ill-health, and resided at Invercauld with her relatives, or in Edinburgh, where she died in March, 1774. Her portrait is still preserved at Moyhall, showing much beauty, with an expression of grace and spirit quite in accordance with the character she displayed during these exciting times.

The laird lived, after his military adventures, on his estate at Moyhall, and died without issue in 1770. Thus the direct descent of the chief of the Mackintoshes was again broken, and fell into a collateral branch of the family, ending in Æneas, the twenty-third chief, afterwards Sir Æneas Mackintosh, Bart. He was a captain in the 71st, or Fraser, Highlanders, and served in America during the revolutionary war. He married Margaret Grant, daughter of Sir Ludovick Grant, of Dalvey, in 1785, and died without issue in 1821.

The succession now opened to a very remote branch of the family, in consequence of a deed of entail executed by Sir Æneas Mackintosh. The occupier of a small farm near Inverness, called Castle Leather, had six sons and three daughters. On the death of Sir Æneas, Castle Leather's eldest son succeeded as twenty-fourth chief. This gentleman had gone to Canada, where he resided many years. He returned in 1799 to Scotland, in bad health. Latterly he occupied a small farm near Kirkhill, a few miles from Inverness. As my father lived on the outskirts of the town, I used, when a boy, to see him and his sisters come in on a Sunday morning: the ladies in a cart, and the gentleman riding a farm horse; but as the equipage was not considered dignified, when within a mile of the town they left their conveyance and walked to church. The old gentleman could not have had an income of £100 a year, if so much.

On the death of Sir Æneas, he became, as I have said, the twenty-fourth chief of the clan, and possessor of this fine estate. During his short incumbency as a landlord he was exemplary. He built Daviot House (the Dowager living at Moyhall). He also erected churches and bridges, and effected various land improvements. He died in 1827 without issue, and was succeeded by his brother Angus, the twenty-fifth chief.

This gentleman had settled in British North America, where he acquired land and was a merchant. He had a large family. When his brother Alexander became the chief at an advanced age, he naturally calculated that his own succession was not far distant, and he sent his family to Inverness to be educated, his sons attending the Inverness Academy. After his brother's death, Angus took up his residence at Moyhall. He was a worthy man and much respected. He died in 1833, and was succeeded by his eldest son, my friend Alexander, the twenty-sixth chief.

This gentleman, who commanded a vessel on Lake Ontario, was married in Canada, and for years after his return to Scotland had no family. Suddenly his lady died, and in due time he married again, Charlotte McLeod of Dalvey, by whom he had six children, the sons being Alexander Æneas, Alfred Donald, and Æneas Norman. He bore the character of an excellent landlord, and to his honour and public spirit it must be recorded that he was an active promoter of two schemes of great advantage to the Highlands : viz., the Caledonian Bank and the Highland Railway. Indeed, he offered to give his land gratis for the railway ; but as the other proprietors exacted full payment for their lands, his generous offer was not accepted. He died in 1861, and was succeeded by his eldest son, Alexander Æneas.

This young gentleman was educated at Cambridge, and had the great advantage of foreign travel. The revenues of the estate accumulated during his minority, and on his succeeding to the management, he entered into a succession of extensive improvements, increasing materially the rental of his property, which by last valuation was £12,816. He made extensive additions to Moyhall, converting it into a castellated residence at an outlay of some £20,000. He married Margaret Frances Graham, of Netherby, a lady of great beauty, and had every prospect of a long and distinguished career; but he was seized with a sudden illness and died on the 17th December, 1875.

Alas! how futile are our calculations. In the confidence of youth, he would persist in shooting in inclement weather, and his sudden illness ultimately proved fatal. His death came like an electric shock on the whole neighbourhood and tenantry.

The funeral, which was fixed for December 27th, 1875, was very striking, and was conducted according to the ancient Highland form of the burial of a great chief. The tenantry and clansmen on that day assembled from hill and dale, from Strathdearn and Strathnairn, Badenoch and Lochaber. The Rev. Dr. Macdonald of Inverness conducted at Moyhall the Presbyterian service in the library, at ten o'clock in the morning. The company formed a circle round the coffin, Dr. Macdonald beginning with the beautiful lamentation of Job: "Man that is born of a woman is of few days and full of trouble; he cometh forth like a flower and is cut down, he fleeth also as a shadow and continueth not." The concluding verses were selected from the passage in Thessalonians: "That ye sorrow not even as others who have no hope;" closing with an impressive prayer.

The coffin was borne on clansmen's shoulders, preceded by six pipers playing the solemn dirge, "the Mackintosh's Lament," until it reached the high road, when it was deposited in the hearse, and then the *cortege* proceeded to Inverness. The tenantry from the lower districts met the *cortege* as it approached Inverness, and mingled with some thousands of the inhabitants of the town to express their sorrow at this sad and sudden bereavement.

The family vault is in the churchyard of Petty, situated about six miles from Inverness. On leaving the turnpike, the procession was again formed, the coffin being borne on the shoulders of the tenantry, the pipers again striking up "the Mackintosh's Lament," a dirge expressing deep despair at the loss of the chief, and a sorrowing wail which, in the circumstances, is more impressive than any of the funeral strains common on such occasions. The Rev. Mr. Graham and Rev. Mr. Parminter read the English service with solemn, striking effect. His brother, Alfred Donald, left

Malta, where his regiment was stationed, but was too late for the funeral.

Moyhall, with its gay party, was converted into a house of mourning. The young and beautiful wife was left *enceinte*, and much anxiety was felt by the clan, and in the country, as to the result of the approaching birth. To Alfred Donald, the then heir-apparent, that birth would have a life-long significance. He returned to his regiment at Malta, quietly performing his duties as a lieutenant in the 71st. At last, when the lady was delivered of a daughter, Alfred Donald became owner of the estates and the chief of the clan, with the earnest wishes of the whole northern community that he may long enjoy his good fortune.* He married Miss Richards of Cotterill, a Welsh lady of large fortune, and had one daughter, since dead. The peculiarity in this family is that in eight successions in a century and a half, there are only two instances of a son's directly inheriting the estate from his father. The country people in my early days used to repeat a couplet that,

> " Mackintosh of Mackintosh, the Laird of Moyhall,
> Never had a bairn, and never, never shall."

It is to be hoped that this prophecy will not apply to the present chief.

* How very different was the fate of his poor uncle, Æneas Mackintosh of Daviot. When the old gentleman Angus Mackintosh died, and his brother succeeded to the property and chieftainship in 1833, Æneas Mackintosh became the heir presumptive, and was allotted as a residence Daviot House and farm. He was very much respected by the whole community, a gallant-looking Highlander, and as the heir presumptive of the estate and chieftainship, he for twenty years was seen driving about, and taking his place in society in that character. He married, first a Miss Macleod, of Dalvey, and secondly Louisa, the youngest of the beautiful daughters of Major Macleod, of Knock, in Skye. As stated above, when the chief married Charlotte Macleod, of Dalvey, the honours of Æneas as heir presumptive of the Mackintosh estates ceased. Notwithstanding this serious disappointment he acted loyally towards the family, and was a guardian to the young chief during his minority. He lived latterly in Inverness, and died on April 25th, 1880, universally regretted, his widow and family of five out of nine children surviving him.

CHAPTER II.

The Frasers of Lovat.

The Clan Fraser—Lord Simon of the '45—Forfeiture and restoration of the estates—The succession of the Strichen branch of the family— Litigation with Fraser of Abertarff—Families of the name of Fraser— The Belladrum estate—Its purchase by Mr. Merry.

THE Fraser Clan was one of the most powerful in the Highlands, from its numbers, extent of territory, and the intelligence of its leading men, many being educated gentlemen and proprietors of estates, but all acknowledging and obeying Lord Fraser of Lovat as their chief.

The Frasers occupied almost the entire country from the boundary of the burgh of Inverness, northwards through the fertile districts of the Aird, to Glen Strathfarrar, in Strathglass, thirty or forty miles; the range of country extending from the burgh of Inverness along the south-west side of Loch Ness, nearly forty miles, called the district of Stratherrick, as well as the lands from Fort Augustus, six miles northward, on the opposite side of the lake. They held likewise the estate of Morar in Arisaig.

The clan at the period of the two rebellions of 1715 and 1745 obtained an unenviable notoriety, from the cunning and treacherous character of their then chief, Simon, the twelfth lord.

The eleventh lord, Hugh, married a sister of the Earl of Athole. He died in 1696, leaving four daughters. The eldest, Amelia, by the decision of the Court of Session, was declared heir of line, and was held to be successor to the Lovat estates.

The heir male was Thomas Fraser of Beaufort, the acknowledged male representative of Hugh. His eldest son having died, he and his next eldest son Simon, who was a captain in the army, claimed the chieftainship and estates. Thomas's rights seem to have been disputed, and it being unsafe for him to remain in possession, he fled to Dunvegan in Skye, where he died.

Simon, his son and successor as heir male, was guilty of many lawless acts. He attempted an alliance with the heiress, the daughter of Hugh, but failed, and she fled to her uncle, the Earl of Athole. Disappointed in his attempt, he seized her mother, the Dowager Lady Lovat, and under the guise of a pretended marriage, in a cruel and savage manner perpetrated on her the crime of rape. For this outrage he had, in 1702, to fly from justice, and as he failed to appear at his trial was outlawed by the Court of Session. The estates were then taken possession of by the factors of the heiress, who collected the rents and whose authority was maintained by the Government in the Fraser country.

Simon from his talents and insinuating manners was a great favourite with the clan. They looked upon him as their chief, and despatched a messenger, a Major Fraser, to France to solicit his return. The major reluctantly went, for he had a large family and could not speak any foreign language; but with an intrepid resolution worthy of a better cause he discovered Lovat, who after an exile of twelve years came back to Beaufort and his clan.

His return was most opportune, for by his great efforts at the time in suppressing the Rebellion of 1715, he obtained from the Government in the following year a free pardon for his crimes. He also by long litigations, intrigues, and extensive pecuniary compromises, arranged a settlement with the representatives of Baroness Amelia, the heiress, and thus his claim to the title and estates of Lovat was finally acknowledged and secured.

It is unnecessary further to allude to him (for his history

is already familiar to the public) beyond the fact that his life thereafter appears to have been constantly passed in subtle, savage, and unlawful intrigues, which ended in the Clan Fraser joining the Rebellion of 1745. His proved complicity in that rebellion, notwithstanding all his crafty devices, ended in his ignominious death on the scaffold, and the forfeiture to the Crown of his extensive and beautiful estates, to the consolidating and securing of which his whole life had been so assiduously devoted.

When the rebellion broke out in 1745, his son Simon, the Master of Lovat, then a lad of nineteen, was pursuing his studies at St. Andrews. He was sent for by his father, and directed to join Prince Charlie, which he did on January 17th, 1746, with six hundred of the Fraser Clan. The young chief adhered thereafter to the service of the prince, and was bringing up additional forces to Culloden when they were met by the Highlanders in flight after the battle. The conduct of the Clan Fraser engaged in the battle was so resolute that they were permitted to return to their own country with their pipers playing and their colours flying.

For the part the Master took in the service of the prince, he with forty-three others was attainted for high treason. He soon after surrendered to the Government, and was imprisoned in Edinburgh Castle for eight months, but in April, 1750, he received a free pardon.

He became an advocate in Edinburgh in 1752, but as his tastes were for a military life, he very soon abandoned the bar. He was offered a regiment in the French service but declined it.

Subsequently he raised on his father's forfeited estates a regiment numbering 1800 men (in 1757), to which he was appointed colonel by the Government. He went with it to America, where he distinguished himself at Louisburgh and Quebec. In 1762 he was raised to the rank of Brigadier-General of the Forces, and went to Portugal. On his return he was appointed Colonel of the 71st Regiment of Foot, with which he performed eminent service during the American War.

He became M.P. for the county of Inverness, and was constantly re-elected and continued in Parliament till his death. For his eminent services the Government, by special Act of Parliament, restored to him in 1774 the forfeited estates of his family, subject to a fine of £21,000. He married Miss Bristow, and died suddenly in London without issue in February, 1782.

His immediately younger brother Alexander, a brigadier-general in the Dutch service, died a bachelor at Dunma-glass in Stratherrick, in August, 1762, so that the estates of Lovat fell in terms of General Fraser's entail of 1774 to the Honourable Archibald Campbell Fraser, his half-brother, and youngest son of the beheaded Lord Lovat.

He was born in 1736, and served heir to the estates in 1782. In early life he assumed the name of Fitz-Simon, and seems then to have distinguished himself as a sports-man. He acted for many years as British Consul at Tripoli and Algiers, where he was engaged in important negotia-tions, and in this capacity he continued till 1774.

He married, in 1763, Jane Fraser, sister of Sir William Fraser of Ledclune, and had five children, all of whom predeceased him. He is reported to have been somewhat eccentric, but was an able man of the world, and interested himself greatly in local affairs and improvements after he became proprietor of the estates. During the French War, he was colonel of the local militia in Inverness, and as a boy, I recollect him, an old man in military uniform, attending in his carriage an inspection of the corps.

His eldest son was M.P. for the county and Colonel of the Fraser Fencibles, with whom he served in the Irish rebel-lion. He died in 1803 at Lisbon, aged thirty-eight. He left an illegitimate son, who on the death of his father was brought up and educated by his grandmother, an object of solicitude and affection.

When the Honourable General Fraser obtained a grant by Act of Parliament of the estates of Lovat in considera-tion of his eminent services to the State, he executed a deed of entail and succession of his property in favour of his brother, the Honourable Archibald Campbell, failing whom in favour of the Laird of Strichen, who was considered to be the next male heir of the house of Lovat.

The Honourable Archibald Campbell Fraser, all his own children having predeceased him, executed ten deeds of settlement, and confirmed the decision of his brother, the general, in the settlement of the estates of Lovat on the Laird of Strichen as the legal heir male of Thomas of Knockie, the second son of Alexander, sixth Lord Lovat. Knockie was granted to this Thomas by his father in 1557, who also left Ardachie to his third son James.*

* Thomas of Knockie, although the holder of a very small patrimony, seems to have been a very astute man, and had a clear perception of his own interests. He became tutor-at-law in 1576 to his nephew Simon, eighth Lord Lovat (according to Highland custom), and of course in that capacity had all the influence and power over the Lovat clan and territory.

Up to this time the Lovats had no connection with Strichen. The estate of Strichen was possessed by a William Chalmers, who died in possession, but who had an elder brother abroad. He (William Chalmers) left on his death to his widow, Isabel Forbes, a life-rent of the estate. She married thereafter Thomas Fraser, son of Fraser of Philorth, who assumed the title of Strichen, and had by Isabel Forbes two daughters—Catherine and Violet. The Chalmerses, unwilling to part with their inheritance, resisted this arrangement, and called in Gordon of Gight to their side, with a view to recover the estate.

In October, 1576, Gordon and Fraser met at Old Deer, in the hope of effecting a compromise of this dispute. The conference led to violent accusations and recriminations on both sides, and ended by Gordon drawing his sword and killing Fraser on the spot. To revenge her husband's murder, Isabel Forbes, then a second time a widow, imparted her wrongs to Fraser of Knockie. He sympathized with her complaints and became himself the suitor of the lady, and out of gratitude for his sympathy and services she became his wife. He immediately thereafter purchased all the claims of the Chalmers family.

He then entered into a solemn contract with Catherine and Violet Fraser, with consent of Alexander Fraser of Philorth, that they should serve themselves heirs to their father's estate of Strichen, and "thereafter divest themselves of the said estate in favour of himself and his heirs male lawfully begotten or to be begotten between him and the said Isabella Forbes their mother. The plea was that, as their mother had a life-rent of the estate, they had no means of obtaining a dowry or 'tocher,' except the expectation of the lands after the death of their mother."

In consideration of these stipulations, Alexander Fraser of Philorth

Singularly enough of all the offshoots of the Lovat family who have estates in the Fraser country, Knockie and Ardachie are the smallest, the latter being even now quoted in the valuation roll at £338 per annum. It has often been wondered how, with so many distinguished and gallant relatives in his immediate neighbourhood, General Fraser should have entailed the estate on the family of Strichen in Aberdeenshire, which dated their connection with the chief from so remote and obscure an origin.

The principal families, until a recent period, were as follows :—Struy, Belladrum, Moniack, Newton, Auchnagairn, Culduthel, Torbreck, Gorthleck, Balnain, Ness-side, and Foyers; the proprietors all independent, educated gentlemen, offshoots from, and many of them nearer relatives than Fraser of Strichen to, the Lovat family.

On the death of the Honourable Colonel Fraser in 1815, Thomas Alexander Fraser, the Laird of Strichen, then a minor, succeeded to the Lovat estates in terms of the entail. They were very extensive, as already explained, and as the young proprietor did not come into legal possession till 1823, a very considerable accumulation of rents must necessarily have accrued.

Perhaps no proprietor entered life with so fair a prospect of long continued usefulness and happiness. When he was

was to be paid 12,000 marks for the transfer of his rights; Catherine, 5000 marks for " tochering " and providing of her in honourable marriage; and Violet Fraser 3500 marks: Thomas of Knockie and his wife becoming bound to sustain the young ladies "in meat and clayth untill their lawful marriage."

A document of the Sheriff of Aberdeen finds the selling of the lands of Strichen by the young ladies profitable to them. And in order that there might be no doubts of the rights of Thomas Fraser of Knockie, a judicial ratification by Catherine and Violet Fraser of their transference of the estate was made after Violet became of age in December, 1592.

The estate of Strichen having been lawfully secured by Thomas of Knockie, it has descended in regular order of succession to Thomas Alexander Fraser of Lovat and Strichen, who on the 3rd November, 1823, was served nearest and lawful heir of the house of Lovat, he being the descendant of that Knockie who acquired the estates of Strichen.

c

twenty-three years of age he married a young and beautiful
wife, the daughter of Lord Stafford of Norfolk. He was the
representative of an ancient house, and his clear rental at
that time could not be much under £20,000 a year, while
his vast territories represented every variety of beautiful
scenery as well as every kind of sport peculiar to a great
Highland estate.

Although in terms of the entail both of the general and
colonel, the Lovat estates fell to the Laird of Strichen,
Thomas Frederick Fraser, the illegitimate grandson, was
naturally cherished by the old colonel and his lady as the
only blood representative of their dearly loved son and heir,
who had been so prematurely cut off in the midst of his distinction and usefulness. Colonel Archibald, accordingly,
by will left him the estate of Abertarff, which he had acquired, also the lands and house known as the "Crown"
in Inverness, and his personalty, a moderate but goodly
inheritance; so that there was no reason why these legal
and illegal descendants of the house of Lovat should not
have lived in harmony.

They, however, entered into a series of litigations of the
most extended and protracted character, which have only
ended with the death of Lord Lovat, the heir of entail; it
thus appearing as if these descendants of Lord Simon of
Lovat had inherited with their estates his litigious and
contentious spirit.

The cause of these lawsuits, besides others relative to
the estate, arose from a custom then common throughout
the Highlands, of the tenants constructing such buildings
and making such improvements as they required, and being
paid melioration for them at the end of their leases. Lord
Lovat, the heir of entail, maintained that this should be
sustained by the heir of the personality.

It is unnecessary to enter into the details of these questions, which to all appearance might have been settled in
a few months by any honest referee. But bitter lawsuits
were commenced and carried on for upwards of forty years,
which neither improved the revenues of the litigants nor
the amiability of their tempers. These contentions have

ended, as most such end, by Abertarff being nearly ruined,
while the estate of Abertarff, left him by his grandfather,
and which was to fall to Lovat on Abertarff's death (he
having no male heir), was found to be chargeable with the
whole meliorations paid to tenants as well as Abertarff's
legal expenses, amounting almost to the entire value of the
estate, £60,000.

Besides these Lovat had other lawsuits with the Chisholm
and surrounding proprietors.

One of these litigations was of a specially vexatious
character in the shape of a claim to the estates of
Lovat by a clergyman from New York, who asserted that
he was nearer in descent than the Laird of Strichen, so
that, whether he had a just claim or not, his presence in
Inverness, and his lawsuits before the courts for a good
many years, were most unpleasant, and a disturbing draw-
back to the enjoyment of the Lovat inheritance.

Another litigation was his claim to the forfeited peerage
of Lovat. Although the estates were entailed on him by
General Fraser and his immediate successor, Colonel
Fraser (both sons of Lord Simon), the Laird of Strichen
failed to establish his descent and right to the Lovat
peerage. But the Laird of Lovat was a Whig; and on the
accession of the Whigs to office, among their adherents
rewarded for their support was Thomas Alexander Fraser.
He was made a Peer of Great Britain, under the title of
Lord Fraser of Lovat.

Some few years after his succession to the estates, Lovat
seems to have lived in a style becoming his rank and
wealth. He was frequently seen driving into Inverness
with four spirited horses in his carriage, his beautiful
bride by his side. But all at once the four horses were
reduced to two, his superfluous retinue was dismissed, and
his affairs were placed and continued, till his death, in the
management of an eminent firm of Writers to the Signet
in Edinburgh, under whose administration rigid economy
was established. There is no doubt that he had accumulated very serious and heavy debts. Whether these debts
were incurred by necessity or imprudence remains a

mystery; the outer world has no right to know further than that they were honourably met.

He sold his original heritage of Strichen for £140,000, and he effected insurances on his life, which, his estate being entailed, seriously affected his annual income and the benefit to the locality from the revenue of his valuable estate. He planted a good deal, and improved to a certain extent; and with the enormous increase in the value of Highland property, he died, leaving a gross rental of £28,000 a year. He was reckoned a hard man, rigid for his rights, but attentive to the local business of the county. He was most exemplary as a family man, and much loved by his dependants.

I have enlarged on his career as an evidence of the curse of entails, both to the heir and the general public, and the misery brought on by the perpetual lawsuits in which he was engaged during his whole life.

Lord Lovat was a witness against the Highland Railway, and was astonished at the presumption of the promoters of the Caledonian Bank. His lordship was a strict Catholic, and appeared to be (as most honest Catholics are) much under the influence of the priests. He erected a chapel a few miles from Beaufort, and the priest who officiated there acted as chaplain to his lordship.

Some twenty-three years ago there was a priest, a Mr. Mackenzie, at Inverness, a superior and intelligent man. He frequently dined with me. He told me he was asked to remove to Strathglass, on which I expressed my surprise that he should leave the charge he then held in Inverness, where he was so much esteemed, to bury himself in the solitude of that sequestered glen amongst a rude and uncultivated peasantry. He said it was quite true, but priests were like soldiers, their duty was to go where their bishops ordered them. The bishop in this case flatteringly told him it was important in the interests of the Church to have at the ear of a British peer an intelligent and sensible confessor and director, and as a favour he asked him to go, and of course he went.

Poor fellow, he met with a tragic end. He was attending

some Catholic Mission at Dingwall in January, 1856, and was dining after it with a party of Catholic gentlemen. There was roast beef at dinner. The cook had pulled aconite-root from the garden instead of horse-radish to make sauce for the beef. Aconite being a deadly poison, those who partook of the beef were at once affected. One recovered, but three of the party were dead in two hours. Poor Mackenzie was one of the number. This sad tragedy created a great sensation all over the district at the time.

The fortress of Fort Augustus had become in these peaceful times an unnecessary appendage and expense to the Government, and they resolved to dispose of it. It being in the centre of his estate in that locality, Lord Lovat became the purchaser for £4000. At his death the public were surprised to learn that he had directed it to be conveyed to a fraternity of Benedictine monks, to be converted into a monastery.

Although I love the romance of Catholicism with its long history, its convents, its monasteries, its beautiful cathedrals, its enthusiastic missionaries, its superstitions, and its wonderful organization, yet I am bewildered at this transition, recollecting as I do the fortress in its pristine shape with its garrison of veteran soldiers, the awe-inspiring governor, and other officials—the galley on the lake with its commander, a lieutenant in the navy, my old friend Captain Gwynne.

Poor Lord Lovat, a few years before his death, became weak in intellect, and a Protestant clergyman in the neighbourhood told me with great glee that at Beaufort he broke an image of the Virgin, destroyed some pictures of saints, and was on his way one Sunday to the parish church of Kirkhill, when he was followed and taken back. This showed, it was said, that he was at heart a Protestant; but I fear the bequest of Fort Augustus for a monastery was no evidence of a change in his religion. He died in June, 1875, and was buried at Eskadale, according to the rites of the Catholic Church, with great pomp and ceremony, some 1500 people attending; the Catholic priest passing an eulogium on his character, as if he were the greatest patriot and most liberal of landlords.

The present lord is an amiable and kindly country gentleman; he is Lord-lieutenant of the county, and was raised by his father from being a lieutenant to be colonel of the Inverness-shire Militia. This caused the resignation of the senior officers of the regiment, and a great scandal at the time. This power is now taken from the Lord-lieutenants of counties.

I have enumerated some twelve families, independent proprietors, and offshoots of the Lovats, who, within my memory, have sold their estates chiefly to strangers, and their families have in a great measure ceased to exist in the Highlands. Indeed, there are very few tenant farmers now, if any, in the rank of gentlemen on the Lovat estates, and I doubt whether Lord Lovat can at present, from no fault of his own, raise 100 men from his estate to fill the ranks of his regiment. Where, therefore, is the Clan Fraser that old Lord Simon used to be so proud of, and from which General Fraser raised, while the estates were forfeited, the 78th Regiment, mustering 1800, to which he was appointed colonel? Is this change the result of civilization?

The Frasers must have been a great clan in the olden time, for when King Charles II. landed in Scotland in June, 1650, the then Captain Alexander Fraser, son of the Lord Lovat of that time, came to the north with a Lieutenant-colonel's commission; he embodied the Frasers, who mustered at Inverness 800 men in full armour, where they joined the king's camp. King Charles's defeat at the battle of Worcester, and Cromwell's establishing a fort at Inverness, checked the warlike tendencies of the clan.

The last Lairds of Culbokie, Torbreck, Fingask, and Belladrum, became planters in the West Indies, and returned enriched.

I recollect, when a boy, Belladrum driving four horses in his carriage, living in splendour, and exercising among his neighbours a liberal hospitality. It was said he had an income of £30,000 a year from his slave estates. He built a handsome house, and planted extensively—in fact, made Belladrum a spacious and beautiful residence. Gradually, however, the revenues from the West Indies decreased, and ultimately ceased, and at last the home estate of Belladrum was mortgaged and for sale. It was purchased by a Mr. Stewart, an East India merchant, for £65,000, but as there was a deficiency in the acreage delineated on the plans, Stewart retained £15,000 of the purchase price. This was the subject of a lawsuit. Fraser gained it, and with his usual hospitality had a great feast on the occasion, but Stewart, who was a keen litigant, appealed, and the decision was reversed. This ultimately ruined Fraser, and he retired to his estates in the West Indies, where in a few years he died.

Stewart thus became the possessor of Belladrum for £50,000. He held the estate for some twenty years, and during that period sold timber to the extent of £30,000. In 1857 he disposed of Belladrum for £83,500 to Mr. Merry, a great iron-master from Glasgow, who resided there during the summer months.

The changes in this district are very marked. Almost all the barons of the Aird, relations, proprietors, and adherents of the clan, gentlemen of independent means, have sold their estates ; Culbokie, in the upper end of Strathglass, to Sir Dudley Coutts Marjoribanks, Bart., now Lord Tweedmouth, who has erected a splendid mansion at Guisichan, and appropriates it as a shooting residence during the autumn. Struy, Eskadale, Belladrum, Newton, Culduthel, Ness-side, Gorthleck, Foyers, Abertarff, have all changed hands, and the changes amongst the tenantry are likewise very numerous. There is scarcely an educated gentleman farmer in the whole of that great estate.

The Frasers of Torbreck were the descendants of Fraser of Phopachy. The Phopachy of Lord Simon's time was an astute man of considerable influence in the locality. In Lord Simon's adversity Phopachy befriended him, and on his lordship's succession to the Lovat estates, in 1716, Phopachy was appointed his chamberlain, and was much eulogized for his fidelity and talent ; but the two seem to have quarrelled, for Lovat writes in April, 1729 : "As to Phopachy I believe he is quite mad, or really possessed with the devil, for as I came home last night from the king's advocate's house (Culloden) I got a letter, of which the enclosed is a copy, by which you will see what a situation I am in with that villain ; but," he continues, " I bless God I never was in my life guilty of a base or villainous action, so I do not fear this wicked calumny; but I think much shame that a monster called Fraser should endeavour to give a scandalous impression of me to the world."

Robert, the son of this man, succeeded to the wadset of Phopachy, which Lord Lovat redeemed, although the family possessed it for one hundred and fifty years.

James, one of Robert's sons, went to the West Indies, and acquired a considerable fortune ; and in 1758 he returned to Inverness, and purchased the lands of Torbreck, Balifeary, and Merkinch—the former being part of the lands of the Castle of Inverness, granted to Lord Huntly, and sold by him to the Baillies, and from them acquired by Mr. Fraser.

Alexander, his son, and the second Laird of Torbreck, held the estates for many years ; he was a prudent, judicious man, and lived in good style. I remember him, as a boy, coming to church on Sundays in his grand coach, exciting awe among the lieges by his dignified bearing as he descended from it.

When the basin of the Caledonian Canal was in progress some speculative people thought the Merkinch lands adjacent would become of great value, and they applied to Torbreck for a building feu of this land. This he granted for 999 years ; but the feuars complained of the heavy feu duty—more than half was remitted in consideration of the time being limited to 199 years.

He died in 1823, and was succeeded by his son Robert, who was very handsome in person, but thoughtless and not very prudent. He was an officer in the army, stationed with his regiment at Dunbar. He there met the daughter of the Earl of Lauderdale, Lady Ann Maitland, who fell desperately in love with him. They eloped, and it is related of the fair lady, in her excitement on arriving at an inn, hotly pursued, she threw herself under the bedclothes, and, Torbreck vainly endeavouring to unloose his riding-boots, she, nervously impatient, called out, "Jump in, Bob, boots and all." Under the circumstances the pursuers thought it prudent to desist from further interference.

Lady Ann lived at Torbreck; she was pretty and possessed engaging manners. Torbreck, in order to provide a handsome dwelling for his young wife, purchased some 200 acres of wooded land, and erected the present house, called Ness Castle; but after her ladyship's death he got into pecuniary difficulties, and his estates were sold in 1834; and he himself died in 1847, leaving a son and two daughters.

I have mentioned that the property of Belladrum was purchased by Mr. Merry, the great iron-master, in 1857. Although Belladrum was constructed and adorned by Mr. Fraser, Mr. Merry enlarged, almost reconstructed, and beautified the house, and furnished it with every modern luxury and convenience. The gardens and grounds, naturally beautiful, were laid out with great taste and on an extensive scale.

Mr. Merry was M.P. for Falkirk, a man of great wealth, and for many years a distinguished votary of the turf. He succeeded to iron and coal works in Ayrshire and Lanarkshire, which he enlarged and extended.

In 1872 he resolved to convert them into a Limited Liability Company. The price he fixed on as the value of the business was £1,500,000. Reports by eminent mining engineers and accountants who had investigated the affairs of the company, showed that for ten years prior to June, 1872, the average profits of the firm were £125,000 per annum.

The prospectus bore: "That if the result of the last year of the firm's experience is taken as a criterion, the profits, pending the extinction of the debenture debts in six years, would amount to 18 per cent.; thereafter the profits would yield 27 per cent.," and Mr. Merry for the first ten years guaranteed 10 per cent. on the capital paid up. The public seemed to appreciate the advantages of these great profits, and made application for the stock to the extent of from five to six millions.

The company was duly formed and in operation; the iron and coal trade was at this time most flourishing; but somehow or other, the stock which should have borne a great premium, mysteriously floated at and about par, a price supposed to arise from some misrepresentation of the value of the works. In the meantime 10 per cent. was paid on the stock called up, as guaranteed.

On the 24th August, 1874, a meeting was held of the shareholders, when Mr. Merry offered to remit £150,000 of the purchase price, if the shareholders would waive his guarantee of 10 per cent. for ten years; this was reluctantly agreed to.

At a subsequent meeting on the 13th January, 1875, the directors reported that there were great deficiencies in the minerals, and satisfied Mr. Merry on that point. He offered in consequence, and they accepted his offer, to remit £450,000 for these deficiencies.

The shareholders were very indignant at this proposition; they immediately appointed a committee of investigation, which sat for three weeks pursuing their inquiries, when all at once Mr. Merry's agents intimated that he was prepared to have the works reconveyed to him, and that Mr. Merry, up to the date of transfer, would pay to the shareholders, besides the dividend they had received, 5 per cent. on all their advances. This honourable proposition was at once accepted by the shareholders on the 25th May, 1875, and so the works were transferred to their original owners.

The public was at this time in a state of excitement by questions of misrepresentations in several joint stock companies, the proceedings of one of which, the Canada Oil Company, were being discussed before the law courts, when the conduct of M.P.'s, and persons of position and distinction, who had become directors, was impugned.

Whether it was the fear of some such inquiry in his case

or not, immediately on the company being formed Mr. Merry fell into a nervous state of health, from which he never recovered, and he died in 1876.

Mr. Merry acted towards the shareholders very honourably in this matter ; but no explanation of the discrepancies in the valuation was ever made.   Mr. Merry died, notwithstanding the losses he must have sustained in this transaction, leaving a fortune sworn under £750,000.

CHAPTER III.

Dukes of Gordon.

Motto—" By Courage not by Craft."

The possessions of the Gordons—The Jacobite Duke, 1715—Lord
Lewis Gordon, 1745—Marriage of Alexander, the fourth Duke, to
Lady Jane Maxwell—Lady Jane's character and history—Her tomb
at Kinrara—The Duke's second marriage—The last Duke and
Duchess—Gordon Castle—Dispersion of the estates—The Duke of
Richmond.

THE Earls of Huntly, afterwards Marquises and Dukes
of Gordon, were great feudal lords, for several centuries
distinguished in Scottish history. They were not strictly
Highland chiefs or heads of a clan, although they possessed
extensive territories in the central Highlands.

Their chief and most valuable possessions were on the
border counties of Kincardine, Aberdeen, and Banff. On
the banks of the Dee, immediately above Aberdeen,
they owned the beautiful property of Durris, containing
16,659 acres, and yielding now a revenue of upwards of
£10,000 per annum. In Aberdeenshire they possess
69,660 acres, chiefly in Huntly and Strathbogie, yielding a
present revenue of £24,747. In Banffshire their acreage
is 160,000, with a rental now of £24,000. Besides these
properties they possessed extensive estates in Strathspey,
Badenoch, and Lochaber—these latter were strictly Highland, including the great mountain of Ben Nevis, and
a large tract of country on the banks of the river Lochy
and the Caledonian Canal.

It may be readily conceived how vast was their influence from being the possessors of such an extensive tract of country, extending from the east coast of Aberdeenshire to the Linnhe Loch on the west coast of Inverness-shire. In feudal times the Dukes of Gordon commanded on their east-coast estates a great force of cavalry and gentlemen on horseback, who were at all times at their service.

Duke Alexander was a Roman Catholic, and was out in the Rebellion in 1715. He made a narrow escape—indeed, had it not been from the great influence of his relative, John, Earl of Sutherland, his honours and estates would in all probability have been forfeited. He married a daughter of the distinguished Earl of Peterborough, Henrietta Mordaunt; and on the death of her husband in 1728, she trained up her family in the Protestant faith, and the family continued Protestants thereafter.

Cosmo George (called Cosmo after his godfather, the Duke of Tuscany), her eldest son, was only eight years of age on the death of his father. He married, in 1741, Lady Catherine Gordon, only daughter of William, second Earl of Aberdeen; by whom he had Alexander, fourth Duke of Gordon; two other sons, Lord William and Lord George Gordon; and three daughters. He appears to have been abroad during the Rebellion in 1745-46 and took no part in it. He died at Amiens on the 5th of August, 1752, at the early age of 32. His widow thereafter married a General Morris and lived till 1774.

Although Cosmo George, the third duke, took no part in the Rebellion of 1745, his brother, Lord Lewis Gordon, joined the Prince, and was a follower of his fortunes throughout. He was present at the Battle of Culloden, but escaped abroad immediately after. He died unmarried, in 1754, at Montreuil in France. He had a very romantic career, and it is of him that Dr. Alexander Geddes wrote the famous song—

> " Oh send me Lewie Gordon hame,
> And the lad I daurna name ;
> Although his back be at the wa,
> Here's to him that's far awa."

Alexander, the fourth Duke of Gordon, and son of Cosmo George, succeeded his father, when only nine years old, and he lived up to 1827, in possession of the honours and estates of his house for the long period of seventy-five years. He is reported to have been handsome in person, a keen sportsman, accomplished and well educated, and had a taste for mechanics, and I have seen many specimens of his workmanship on the turning-lathe. He was also a draughtsman and musician, particularly fond of Scotch music, and was the patron of Marshall, the composer of many charming Scottish melodies. During the greater part of his career there was little progress or improvement in the country; he seems to have been more of a great feudal lord and man of fashion than a statesman or improver.

In his twenty-fourth year he fell in love with Jane Maxwell, the "Flower of Galloway," one of the most beautiful women of her time, as portrayed in Reynolds's magnificent portrait still preserved in Gordon Castle. This union prognosticated great happiness, for it combined high rank, talent, beauty, and wealth. But, alas, the Fates decreed otherwise. As a girl, Duchess Jane had become strongly attached to a young officer, who returned her affection with chivalrous enthusiasm. He was suddenly ordered abroad with his regiment, and soon after was reported killed. The lady was overwhelmed with grief and sank into a state of lethargic listlessness, refusing to be comforted. The Duke of Gordon came forward soon after as her suitor, and her family conceived that the offer of a person of such high and distinguished rank should not be abruptly refused. Jane Maxwell was persuaded to become Duchess of Gordon. While in Berwickshire and on their marriage tour, a letter was received by her Grace, addressed to her in her maiden name, from her early lover. It was to intimate that he had not been killed as was reported, and that he was on his way home, and soon he hoped to meet her, and by their marriage consummate their long anticipated happiness. The young duchess, distracted by this intelligence, fled from the house, and after long search was found prostrated by grief, lying listlessly by the side of a burn.

She seems soon to have forgotten this blow to her early affections, for she entered very soon after into all the excitement of fashionable life, indeed became a leader of fashion, not only in Edinburgh but in London. In the latter place her dinners and assemblies were of the most brilliant character, and were much frequented by many of the distinguished orators, statesmen, and wits of the time. She exhibited wonderful tact in securing for her daughters noblemen of the highest rank. One became Duchess of Richmond, another Duchess of Bedford, the third Duchess of Manchester, and the fourth Marchioness of Cornwallis. Her only surviving son, George, Marquis of Huntly, entered the army early in life. To assist him in raising his regiment, the 92nd Highlanders, it is reported of her that she headed a recruiting party in the Highlands, and at the fairs, dressed in plaid and Highland bonnet with sword in hand, she held a shilling in her teeth, and every handsome Highlander she saw in the crowd she enlisted by placing it in his mouth. No gallant Highlander, then or even now, could resist such an inducement to serve his king and country from so fascinating a personage.

The union of the noble duke with Jane Maxwell, notwithstanding her fascinations and beauty, does not seem to have been happy, for latterly they lived much apart, she chiefly in the south. She died in London in 1812, in the Pulteney Hotel; her body lay there in state for nearly a week, about which a contemporary lady, as quoted in the *North British Review*, wrote as follows—

" There was something peculiarly revolting in the kind of mockery of state which attended her remains. The idea of her lying in state at such a place as the Pulteney Hotel seems in itself preposterous, and from the great want of judgment and attention with which the body was exposed, for above a week after her death, to the curiosity of all who thought fit to go into the hotel, it became quite indecent. It is said that the whole was done, not only without the consent, but without the knowledge of the duke, who by no means approved of the proceedings when he heard of the expenses of £2000 which they brought upon him. I shall not waste much compassion on him. It was his part to give what orders he thought right about the funeral, and see that they were performed, nor was this last mark of attention too much to have given to one whom his own conduct, perhaps more than anything else, contributed to make her what she was. A melancholy instance of gifts neglected and talents misapplied."

Among the many sweet and sequestered spots in the wide territories of the duke, the duchess, in her pride of life and with her taste and tact, selected, and had erected for herself, a villa at Kinrara, on the banks of the Spey. It is situated on an elevated mount, in the midst of woods of weeping birch, and commands extensive views of the valley and its cultivated lands with the windings of the river. On each side are the magnificent mountains (the Cairngorms on the south), partially clad with the grim pine forests peculiar to the district. Here she used to spend some weeks in the autumn with her gay friends, and here she fixed on a site for her final resting-place—a more lovely or sequestered spot does not exist in the Highlands. According to her wish she was buried at Kinrara, and a granite monument has been raised there to her memory.

> " Fair in Kinrara blooms the rose,
>   And softly waves the drooping willow ;
>   Where beauty's faded charms repose,
>   And splendour rests on earth's green pillow.
>
>   And oft amidst the festive scenes,
>   Where pleasure cheats the midnight pillow ;
>   A sigh shall breathe for noble Jane,
>   Laid low beneath Kinrara's willow."

The duke spent the latter part of his life at Gordon Castle. His affection seems to have been alienated from the duchess and settled on a village maid named Jane Christie, who was betrothed to a young man in her own rank, but the intended marriage with whom was broken off in consequence of the attentions of the duke. Eight years after the death of Jane Maxwell he elevated this young woman to the dignity of Duchess of Gordon ; he seemed to have been much attached to her. In a letter dated August 7th, 1820, and quoted by the Rev. Moody Stuart in his " Life of the last Duchess of Gordon," he writes : " You no doubt have heard of the step I have taken, for which I know I am much blamed; but my conscience approves, and I trust I shall have no cause to repent it." In another letter regarding her health he speaks of her with much affection and anxiety—

" My spirits have been much distressed since I had the pleasure of seeing you. The duchess's state of health becomes more serious every day and I dread the consequences. She grows weaker and can take no nourishment. God only knows how it may end. I am very unhappy about her. Her kindness and attention to me are beyond my powers of expression, and I can say, upon every occasion but one, she has always conformed to my wishes; and that one is rather to her credit, and must give all those who know the circumstance a high opinion of her.

" I must now, however, explain myself. After my marriage I wished to bring her home to Gordon Castle, and have urged her since; but she has always refused, saying, that were she established at Gordon Castle, she is sure that my friends would not come to the castle, and she should never forgive herself if she were the means of preventing any of my friends from visiting me as they have always done. Excuse me for giving you this detail on what only concerns myself; but being aware of your friendship I open my mind to you, knowing you will feel for me in my present distress.

" Yours most affectionately and truly,

" GORDON."

The duchess's illness proved fatal; she died in July, 1824. The duke erected a monument to her memory, where she slumbers among her kindred in a churchyard on the banks of the Spey. The duke died in 1827, and was buried beside the remains of his ancestors in the family mausoleum in Elgin Cathedral.

On the death of his father the Marquis of Huntly

D

assumed the duties of his high position as lord of the great
territory of his family in the northern counties. The
marquis was born in 1770, and entered the army as ensign
in 1790. In 1792 he was captain in the 3rd Guards, with
whom he served in Holland. Having raised the 92nd
Gordon Highlanders, he went with them to Gibraltar. In
Ireland he served during the Rebellion. In 1809, in the
Walcheren expedition, he commanded a division of the army.
Afterwards he became Colonel of the 42nd Highlanders, and
subsequently Colonel of the 3rd Foot Guards.

He was thus essentially a soldier, and with some considerable experience of war. Although not very perfectly
educated, he was generous, affable, and high-spirited. He
was very handsome, of distinguished presence, and his
graceful deportment indicated the very *beau ideal* of a
British nobleman. To all ranks he was frank and kind ;
he was called the " Cock of the North," and high and low
revered and loved him. He was the most perfect chairman of festive meetings ever known, and was often solicited
to preside. In that capacity his readiness, lively wit,
and good humour have never been surpassed. People often
wondered that he never took part in the debates of the
House of Lords, but to this, although a keen politician, he
had an insuperable objection. It is said the late Lord
Liverpool proposed at one time that his Grace should move
the Address on the opening of Parliament, but the duke
objected. He said he would venture to entertain all their
lordships if they would adjourn to the City of London
Tavern, but he could not undertake the same duty in the
House of Lords.

He married in 1813 Miss Brodie, the daughter and
heiress of Mr. Brodie, a younger son of the Laird of Brodie,
who had returned from India with a large fortune. The
lady had been simply and religiously brought up, partly by
her maiden aunts in Elgin. It was feared the union might
be unhappy, although it proved the reverse, for such was
his generous nature, that although all his life a soldier, a
man of the world, and a man of fashion, he gave in to her
religious proclivities, and ultimately she got him to join in

and promote all the benevolent and educational schemes she established for the benefit of her people.

Gordon Castle, the chief seat of this distinguished family, is one of the finest ducal mansions in Scotland. The park is vast, swept on the west by the rapid Spey, bounded by the horizon, and studded with gigantic trees. The house, of various styles of architecture, is no less than 568 feet in length, built of freestone, with the ancient tower in the centre; and the interior contains every arrangement which might be expected from the refinement and taste of a long line of educated and wealthy proprietors. Here his Grace dispensed his hospitalities, of which the following lively sketch was given by an American writer, H. P. Willis, in 1833—

" The immense iron gates surmounted by the Gordon arms, the handsome and spacious stone lodges on either side, the canonically fat porter in white stockings and gay livery, lifting his hat as he swings open the massive portal, all bespoke the entrance to a noble residence. The road was edged with velvet sward, and rolled to the smoothness of a terrace walk; the winding avenue lengthened away before, with trees of every variety of foliage; light carriages passed me driven by ladies and gentlemen bound on their afternoon airing; keepers with hounds and terriers, gentlemen on foot idling along the walks, and servants in different liveries hurrying to and fro, betokened a scene of busy gaiety before me. I had hardly noted these varied circumstances before a sudden curve in the road brought the castle into view, a vast stone pile with castellated wings; and in another moment I was at the door, where a dozen powdered footmen were waiting on a party of ladies and gentlemen to their several carriages.

" I passed the time till sunset looking out on the park. Hill and valley lay between my eye and the horizon; sheep fed in picturesque flocks, and small fallow deer grazed near them; the trees were planted, and the distant forest shaped by the hand of taste: and broad and beautiful as was the expanse taken in by the eye, it was evidently a princely possession. A mile from the castle wall the shaven sward extended in a carpet of velvet softness, as bright as emerald, studded by clumps of shrubbery, like flowers wrought elegantly in tapestry, and across it bounded occasionally a hare, and the pheasants fed undisturbed near the thickets.

" This little world of enjoyment, luxury, and beauty lay in the hand of one man, and was created by his wealth in these northern wilds of Scotland. I never realized so forcibly the splendid results of wealth and primogeniture.

" I was sitting by the fire, when there was a knock at the door, and a tall, white-haired gentleman of noble physiognomy, but singularly cordial address, entered with a broad red ribbon across his breast, and welcomed me most heartily to the castle. The duchess, a tall and very handsome woman, with a smile of the most winning sweetness, received me at the drawing-room door, and I was presented to every person present.

" Dinner was announced immediately, and the difficult question of precedence being sooner settled than I had ever seen it before in so large a party, we passed through files of servants to the dining-room. It was a large and very lofty hall, supported at the end by marble columns. The walls were lined with full-length family pictures, from old knights in armour to the modern dukes in kilt of the Gordon plaid; and on the sideboards stood services of gold plate, the most gorgeously massive and the most beautiful in workmanship I have ever seen. There were among the vases several large coursing cups, won by the duke's hounds, of exquisite shape and ornament. The Jacobite songs, with their half-warlike, half-melancholy music, were favourites of the Duchess of Gordon, who sang them in their original Scotch with great enthusiasm and sweetness. The aim of Scotch hospitality seems to be to convince you that the house and all that is in it is your own, and you are at liberty to enjoy it as if you were, in the French phrase, *chez vous*. The routine of Gordon Castle was what each one chose to make it. The number at dinner was seldom less than thirty, but the company was continually varied by departures and arrivals: no sensation was made by either one or the other. A carriage drove to the door, was disburdened of its load, drove round to the stables, and the question was seldom asked, 'Who is arrived?' You are sure to see at dinner; and an addition of half a dozen to the party made no perceptible difference in anything."

Notwithstanding this charming picture of aristocratic life, the duke was at this time in great pecuniary difficulties. It turned out that Duke Alexander his father had left his estates heavily burdened, and the legal advisers of the family recommended that the whole should be placed under trust for the sale of large portions with a view to relieve the rest. Consequently the trustees had limited his Grace to a fixed sum for the expenses of his establishment until these transactions were concluded. Although this allowance befitted his ducal rank, yet the duchess and he felt it a great privation to be deprived of the means of contributing as their generous dispositions wished to many benevolent and charitable objects which they were anxious to promote.

And now comes the cruel part of this proceeding, the dismemberment of this ducal territory. The fine estate of Durris, in Kincardineshire, was sold for £100,000. And in 1828 and 1830 part of the Badenoch estate was bought by Sir George Macpherson Grant, and the greater part of Kingussie by Mr. Baillie of Bristol. The Lochaber estates were purchased by the Earl of Aboyne, and were re-sold to Lord Abinger and Mr. Walker and others. These estates seem to have been disposed of at a most unfortunate time; the prices received were probably not one-third of their present value, and their sale very much severed the family from its Highland connection, of which the duke was always so proud.

Early in 1836 his Grace's health began to fail. He removed to his London residence in Belgrave Square, where he died on the 28th of May, aged sixty-six. The Government ordered the body to be conveyed to Scotland in a ship of war, in honour of the deceased; and he was buried in the family vault in Elgin Cathedral in the midst of universal sorrow. Thus has terminated the distinguished family of the Gordons, who for centuries maintained great sway in the north, and held a prominent position in the history of their country.

The late duke, although not distinguished as a statesman, possessed every good and kindly quality. He was a generous landlord, a warm-hearted friend, and the promoter of every good and benevolent object within the sphere of his influence. As he was the last of his race, perhaps he was among the best. Monuments have been erected to his memory in Aberdeen, Badenoch, and Elgin, indicating the sentiments of respect and love of the inhabitants of the districts where he was best known.

The worthy duchess after the funeral retired to Huntly Lodge, the residence which had been assigned to her, and where she continued to reside till her death, which took place on the 31st of January, 1864, in her 70th year. Her whole time was devoted to works of piety and charity.

On the death of the duke the title became extinct, and the estates descended to his Grace Charles, Duke of Richmond, in right of his wife, the eldest sister of the late Duke of Gordon.

For nearly one hundred years while the estates were possessed by the two last Dukes of Gordon no great improvements had been made. The tenants lived at easy rents and in rough comfort; but such a mode of life was incompatible with the progress of the times. Duke Charles of Richmond was a man of business, tact, and sense; and when his Grace entered into possession, he found many parts of these estates in a very neglected condition. He secured at once the services of an eminent agriculturist, Mr. Thomas Balmer, whom he appointed his commissioner, and by whose advice and under whose direction he re-arranged the whole properties. New houses and steadings were built, drains and fences were made, extensive plantations formed, and everything put in complete agricultural order. His Grace, who enjoyed the estates for upwards of twenty-four years, had the satisfaction of seeing the whole of these improvements completed, so that there has been comparatively little work for the present proprietor to do.

The Highland estate of Glenlivet was the most difficult portion to deal with. It was a nest of old smugglers. By the absurd excise laws, which confined the distilling of whisky to capitalist distillers, no good whisky could be got except smuggled, and Glenlivet was very prominent for the quality of its smuggled whisky. In fact they drove a thriving and adventurous trade, but well suited to the taste of idle and daring Highlanders. The smugglers had to be rooted out, and a number of poor crofters removed; but the duke handled the business with great delicacy. He pensioned some, gave others better crofts and houses, and, in short, managed matters so adroitly that no complaint or grievance was heard in regard to the changes he adopted. The result is that this splendid inheritance now yields, notwithstanding its serious curtailment, a gross revenue of £49,760 per annum.

It is gratifying to notice, although the old family and time-honoured title of the Dukes of Gordon is extinct,* the spirit and patriotism of the family are still maintained in a marked degree by the present duke. His Grace, instead of spending his time in the blandishments of his high rank and wealth, has become a distinguished statesman, and, at the present time, devotes his nights and days to laborious and disinterested labours in the service of his country.

* Her Majesty has lately added the title of Gordon to that of Richmond.

CHAPTER IV.

The Earls of Fife.

The Duff Family—Their shrewdness and accumulations of property
—Raised to the peerage—The history of the fourth Earl—His retired
residence in Duff House—The late and present Earls.

The distinguished families in the North of Scotland appear generally in early times to have fought for and obtained
their position and estates very much by the power of the
sword.

The acquisitions and progress of the Duff family exhibit
a marked contrast to the acts of their lawless and unscrupulous neighbours. It is reported that, notwithstanding
the turbulent times in which they lived during five or six
generations, the Duffs were a family of shrewd, clear-headed,
far-seeing men, who turned their attention to mercantile
business, and exercised their talents in that channel at a
period when the country was exhausted by the civil wars of
the seventeenth century. Having thus always the command
of money, they readily availed themselves of the opportunity
of profitable investments.

From a succession of bad harvests at the end of the
seventeenth and the beginning of the eighteenth century,
and from the disasters of the Darien scheme, which caused
widespread ruin all over Scotland, there was, throughout
the country, a great depreciation in the value of land, then
the chief capital of the country.

The Duffs seem to have taken advantage of these sad
calamities, and readily turned them to profitable account,

by securing bargains on very favourable terms. They dealt largely in wadsets and mortgages which were never redeemed, or were foreclosed, or their rights of reversion purchased ; they thus with facility acquired many of their estates, which they thereafter legally held. They are reported to have been men of good conduct, just, perhaps hard in their dealings, but honourable ; and some were religious, strictly fulfilling their engagements.

The family claim descent from Macduff, the Thane of Fife, but this is a myth, although generally conceded. They have descended however from a sufficiently remote period from a succession of prosperous men, as above described, and their pedigree can be traced in regular line from the fourteenth and fifteenth century, an evidence of antiquity with which they may be well content.

William Duff of Dipple was the lineal descendant, and succeeded as male heir in 1718 to the then accumulated fortunes of the Duff family. In early life he was engaged with his uncle as a merchant in Inverness. He was prudent and sagacious, much esteemed, and like the rest of his race turned his ready money largely to account in the purchase of wadsets. He acquired in Morayshire the estates of Dipple, Pluscarden, Oldmills, Coxton, Quarriewood, Aldroughty, Mosstowie, Sheriffmill, Inverlochty, and others.

He married, first, Ellen Gordon, daughter of Sir George Gordon of Edinglassie, by whom he had one son, William, elevated to the peerage, and four daughters. He married, a second time, Jane, daughter of Sir William Dunbar of Durn, and had a son, who died in infancy. Some of the four daughters were married to men of position. One Henrietta, an excellent and charitable person, remained unmarried.

He seems to have lived in Elgin during the last seventeen years of his life, and carried on mercantile business, but was occupied principally as a private banker. He died in 1722 aged sixty-eight years ; but, as said, in 1718, by the death of his nephew, William Duff of Braco, he succeeded to the whole estates of the principal branch of the

Duff family, which he is reported to have left clear, besides £30,000 in money, a large sum for that period.

William Duff, his only son by his first marriage, succeeded his father in his accumulated possessions. He was elected Member of Parliament for the county of Banff in 1727 ; managed to get created a Peer of Ireland on the 28th July, 1735, by the title of Lord Braco of Kilbride; and on the 26th April, 1759, he was elevated to the dignity of the Earl of Fife and Viscount Macduff, the patent being limited in both cases to him and the heirs male of his body.

He also was a careful manager of his affairs, and purchased considerable estates in the counties of Aberdeen, Banff, and Moray. He married, first, Lady Jane Ogilvie, second daughter of his neighbour, the fourth Earl of Findlater, by whom he had no issue. He married, a second time, Jane, daughter of Sir James Grant of Grant, Bart., by whom he had a family of seven sons and seven daughters. Two of these sons died unmarried ; to the third son, Alexander, he left the estate of Echt, in Aberdeenshire ; to George, the fifth son, the estates of Milton and Inverlochty and Barmuckity in Morayshire; to Ludovick, the sixth son, the estate of Blervie ; and to Arthur, the seventh son, who died unmarried, the estate of Orton.

The daughters of this second marriage, except Lady Catherine, who died unmarried, were married to men of position and property in the country, viz., Duff of Hatton, Sir William Gordon of Park, Keith Urquhart of Meldrum, Robert Duff of Logie and Fetteresso, Thomas Wharton, whose son succeeded to Orton, and James Brodie of Brodie.

Although the earl was a great economist he was evidently a man of refinement and taste, fond of architecture, and he laid out large sums in buildings. Soon after his accession to his estates in 1724 he built the new castle of Balvenie, and thereafter, between 1740 and 1745, he erected Duff House, close to Banff, from the designs of Adams the architect—a palatial structure. This building cost no less a sum than £70,000. He died in September, 1763, and was buried in the mausoleum at Duff House.

James, the second Earl of Fife, born in 1729, succeeded to the honours and estates on the death of his father. He was Member of Parliament for the county of Banff for twenty years, from 1754 to 1774, and sat for the county of Elgin from 1780 to 1784. He is reported a man of great talent, and nearly doubled the possessions of the family by the judicious purchase of estates.

He planted about 14,000 acres of moor; he was a great agriculturist and improver of land; and such was at that time his political influence that it is said he was able to return in 1774 the members for the counties of Aberdeen, Banff, and Moray.

In accordance with the proclivities of his family he largely invested in land in Morayshire and elsewhere. He acquired the beautiful estate of Innes, near Elgin, from Innes of that ilk in 1767; also the estates of Inchbroom, Dunkinty, and Leuchars.

In 1777 he acquired, by excambion from the Duke of Gordon, the lordship of Urquhart, the estates of Ardgay, Leggatt, and part of Kintra; also the estates of Spynie, Monurghty, Aslisk, Rosehaugh in the parish of Spynie; and in Aberdeenshire, Dalgetty and Braemar; and by the death of his brother Ludovick he succeeded to the estates of Blervie.

He married Lady Dorothea Sinclair, daughter of the ninth Earl of Caithness, by whom he had no issue. He died at his house Whitehall, London, on the 20th January, 1809, aged eighty, and was interred in the mausoleum at Duff House.

He is reported as having been kind and hospitable to his tenants, the principal of whom he entertained at his own table when he visited his different estates. He was reckoned a hard man, but this may have arisen from his being very exact and precise in all his pecuniary transactions.

In one instance, however, it is recorded of him that in the year 1783, a season of famine, he deducted 20 per cent. from the rents of his Highland tenants; and he sold his own grain, and imported cargoes from England for the poor at a loss to himself of £3000.

The estates which he had purchased, as well as a large sum of money, he placed in trust to be accumulated for the acquirement of additional lands in the locality. The entailed estates and the Irish titles descended to his immediately younger brother, Alexander Duff of Echt.

Alexander, the third Earl of Fife, succeeded to the estates and honours when he was sixty-eight years of age. He had been a member of the Faculty of Advocates, and married at Careston in 1775, Mary, eldest daughter of George Skene of Skene and Careston. Succeeding to the Duff estates so late in life he effected no great changes.

He had four children : James, the fourth earl; Alexander, a general in the army, who resided at Dalgetty Castle, in Aberdeenshire, father of the fifth earl; and two daughters.

The eldest son, James, entered the Spanish army during the Peninsular campaigns, was appointed major-general, was wounded in the battle of Talavera in 1809, and severely wounded at the storming of Mategora, near Cadiz, in 1810. On the death of his father he succeeded, on April 7th, 1811, to the entailed estates and honours of the family ; but having a taste for lavish expenditure, his careful uncle, the second earl, placed the funds and fee simple estates he himself had acquired under trust, as I have said, for his next succeeding heirs, so that James, the fourth earl, on his accession, succeeded merely to the entailed estates.

On his return from Spain, James, the fourth earl, took a prominent part in fashionable society, led a gay life, was much about the Court, and an intimate companion and friend of George IV., by whom he was created a Peer of the United Kingdom in 1827 by the title of Baron Fife.

The ballet ladies of the opera were in great favour at this time with the gay part of the fashionable nobility and gentry, and it was not uncommon for them by their attractions and beauty to secure for themselves rich and noble husbands. It is said of Lord Fife that he presented a fair *danseuse* with a diamond necklace which cost £700. She returned it with a message that if it was a friendly gift, it was too much; but if he expected any return, it was too little.

Of course a life in such society involved him in heavy debts, and large sums had to be borrowed on life insurances.

At last, tired with the dissipation and frivolity of this sort of existence, and worried, no doubt, with the debts he had incurred, he suddenly retired to Scotland in 1828, and placed his affairs under trust. He resided at Duff House, and there lived the life of a recluse. He denuded himself of all his equipages and servants, and in two rooms of that splendid mansion spent his time much in solitude.

Having frequently to pass through Banff during Lord Fife's sojourn there, I never missed an opportunity of visiting the beautiful gallery of paintings at Duff House, which the noble lord, in a most liberal manner, threw open, along with the grounds and park, to the public at all times. These paintings consist of a large collection of the old masters, as well as many of the eminent modern painters ; they are unique, and many are of the highest merit, indicating the taste and culture of the former lords.

The old lady, Lord Fife's solitary domestic, acted as cicerone, and on one occasion showed me the two rooms in which his lordship resided. His bedroom had a small French bed against the wall, with two book-shelves, containing the newest publications, to which he could stretch without trouble. His solitary dinner was for the first few years procured from the inn. To his neighbours and friends who called on him he was gentlemanly in his bearing and an intelligent man of the world, and to the poor he was most liberal and kind. Indeed, in the locality he was a universal favourite.

He married early in life (1799) Maria Caroline Manners, second daughter of John Manners, of Grantham Grange, and sister of Louisa, Duchess of St. Albans, but she died in December, 1805, without issue.

In 1827, by the death of his uncle, he succeeded, in addition to the old Duff estates, to the valuable properties of Skene and Careston.

For upwards of twenty years he lived a secluded and solitary life. Notwithstanding the anticipations of his predecessor, raised by his early wasteful and spendthrift habits, he was able from this mode of life to clear off all his encumbrances and leave to his immediate relatives a sum of upwards of £50,000.

He died in March, 1857, and was buried in the family mausoleum at Duff House.

James, the fifth earl, succeeded his uncle, and entered into possession, not only of the entailed estates, but also of the estates placed by the second Earl under trust to be accumulated and entailed; the united rentals of which, according to the public returns of 1873, amount to between £70,000 and £80,000 per annum.

But as if in mockery of the wise bargains and accumulations of his ancestors, the early Duffs, this nobleman, in anticipation of his succession, entered on his inheritance with a debt of some £300,000, a heavy burden incurred by life insurances.

He was born in 1814, and married in 1846 Lady Agnes Georgina Hay, daughter of William George, seventeenth Earl of Errol. This lady is said to have had expensive tastes, and to have assisted very materially in increasing the burdens on the property. She died in December, 1869, and was buried in the mausoleum at Duff House. She left one son, Viscount Macduff, born on November 10th, 1849, and four daughters, all of whom were married.

The only public act of this earl was taking shares to the extent of £30,000 in the Highland Railway, and although it has yielded to him a good return, his subscribing that sum so early tended to promote that work, the construction of which has proved so beneficial to the whole Northern Highlands.

Lord Macduff was elected member for the county of Elgin in 1873, and his appearances in Parliament and the North have been highly creditable, and give indication that he will become a most useful and efficient public man. Lord Fife has transferred to his son the administration of the whole of his vast estates, which have always been managed judiciously and with great consideration for the interests of the tenants.

Taking advantage of the present law of entail, Lord Macduff has disentailed the whole of these estates, and thus, by lessening the charges for interest and insurances, will very materially lessen—if not in due time entirely extinguish—the debts that have been incurred by his father on this splendid property.* Lord Macduff, anticipating the modern legislation of the Government, has abandoned the rights of hypothec, which consisted of giving a preference to the landlord for his rent over any other creditor. He also conceded game privileges to his tenants prior to the Hares and Rabbits Bill being brought in by the Government, and in general by his urbanity of manners and kindness and liberality to his tenants has secured for himself universal affection and esteem.

* Since the above was written, Lord Macduff has succeeded to the earldom.

CHAPTER V.

The Clan Grant.

The territory and families of the clan—The Ogilvies, Earls of Findlater
and Seafield—The chief of the Grants succeeds to the possessions of
the Ogilvies and the title of Seafield—A romantic marriage—The
last clan demonstration—The forests of Strathspey—Castle Grant
and Balmacaan.

PERHAPS no clan in the Highlands has produced so many
men of mark as the Clan Grant. In every rank in life and
in every profession they have acquired and secured a
distinguished and prominent place.

The main territory of the chief is situated in Strathspey,
beginning near the celebrated rock from which the clan
takes their motto, "Stand fast Craigellachie," and extending downwards along the banks of the Spey to the village
of Rothes, and hence across to Elgin. The chief holds,
also, a large estate extending about nineteen miles on the
west bank of Loch Ness, including the beautiful and
picturesque valley of Glen Urquhart.

Adjoining and intermixing with the territories of the
chief are the estates, on the right bank of the Spey, of Sir
J. P. Grant of Rothiemurchus, late Deputy-Governor of
Bengal, of Sir G. Macpherson Grant of Ballindalloch, of
the late Miss Macpherson Grant of Aberlour, and of Mr.
Grant of Arndilly; and on the left bank, that of Mr. Grant
of Elchies; while adjoining the Glen Urquhart estate lies
the beautiful property of Mr. Grant of Glenmoriston. All
these territorial families in the olden time constituted

part of the clan, and were understood to be subject to the feudal rule of the chief of the Grants.

Besides the ancient territorial property of the Grants in the Highlands, the family of the chief succeeded in 1811 to the large estates of the Earl of Findlater, in Banffshire, as also to the title of the Earl of Seafield.

The Earls of Findlater, Ogilvie by name, were an ancient house. James, the fourth Earl of Findlater, succeeded his father in 1711. He was an eminent lawyer, and held high office in the State. He was created in June, 1701, Earl of Seafield, before his father's death, and is particularly distinguished by having moved in the House of Lords, in June, 1713, for leave to bring in a Bill to dissolve the union between England and Scotland, which was refused by a majority of four only, the peers present being equally divided—the proxies were thirteen for, and seventeen against, the motion.

He was succeeded by his eldest son James, fifth Earl of Findlater and second Earl of Seafield, and left, besides, a daughter Margaret, who married Sir Ludovick Grant of Grant, Bart. His son Sir James Grant of Grant, Bart., born on May 19th, 1738, married in 1763 Jane, daughter of Alexander Duff of Hatton, in Aberdeenshire, and had issue seven sons and six daughters. Lewis Alexander, the eldest, became imbecile; Alexander, the second son, died in 1772; and James Thomas, the third son, who was a judge in India, died in that country in 1804: Francis William, the fourth son, therefore became the heir presumptive to the Grant estates.

Reverting to the house of Findlater, the sixth Earl of Findlater married Lady Mary Murray, daughter of the Earl of Athole, and he, dying on November 3rd, 1770, was succeeded by his only surviving child, James, seventh Earl of Findlater and fourth Earl of Seafield. He married at Brussels, Christina Theresa, daughter of Count Murray of Melgam, but had no issue.

At his lordship's decease on October 5th, 1811, the earldom of Findlater became extinct, and the other title of that house reverted to his cousin Sir Lewis Alexander Grant of

E

Grant, Bart., who thus became fifth Earl of Seafield, and who also succeeded to the Findlater estates. He assumed the name of Ogilvie in addition to his family name.

He was born on March 27th, 1767. In his youth he studied for the Bar, was very promising, and sat as M.P. for the county of Elgin, in 1796. He was of a nervous temperament, and before he succeeded to the estates, was, as stated, afflicted with mental disorder, from which he never recovered, although he was never violent nor required to be confined.

Sir Lewis Alexander Grant, being thus imbecile, and unfit to manage his estates, his next brother and heir, Colonel Francis William Grant, was appointed curator-at-law to him, and administered the estates of Findlater and Grant up to 1840, when the earl died, and Colonel Francis William succeeded to the earldom and estates.

When Francis William Grant was appointed curator to his brother, the Court of Session did not then require such strict accounting as at present; but by an Act subsequently passed, curators are now required to lodge their accounts with the Accountant of Court every year for the purpose of being properly examined and duly audited. Previous to that time there was no such rule, so besides the expenditure required for the support of the earl, lands were bought, political contests were carried on, improvements were made, money borrowed, and the management was conducted very much as if the colonel had been absolute proprietor of the estates. The consequence of this mode of administration has ended in a very complicated lawsuit of count and reckoning between the present earl and his younger brothers, extending from 1811 to 1840, and which is likely to be unsettled for many years.*

The father of these two last earls, Sir James Grant of Grant, Bart., was distinguished for every good and amiable quality. General Stewart of Garth, in his " Sketches of the Character and Manners of the Highlanders of Scotland," describes him "as the best friend, husband, father, and Christian of the district, to which he was an honour and a

---

* Since the above was written the suit has been compromised.

blessing." He lived in his feudal residence of Castle Grant in Strathspey, surrounded by miles of natural pine forests, for which Strathspey has ever been celebrated. He was the *beau ideal* of a patriarchal chief, took great interest in his clan, and owing to his kindly and amiable disposition (which has been the characteristic of the family for generations) he was universally beloved. He raised among his dependents for the Government two regiments—one a Fencible regiment in 1795 and disembodied in 1799, and the other, during the last French war, the Inverness-shire militia ; this regiment formed part of the garrison of Portsmouth, where they were quartered for five years.

In 1814, on the termination of the war, this regiment was sent to Inverness to be disbanded, and I, then a boy at school, recollect seeing it on parade with intense admiration and wonder. The regiment was fourteen hundred strong, composed of fine, well-disciplined stalwart Highlanders. Francis William Grant was the colonel, and Cumming Bruce of Dunphail, the major ; both dashing officers, then in the prime of life. The astonishment of us juveniles was specially directed to the large regimental band, discoursing music and exhibiting instruments which had never before been seen in Inverness, and which excited the wonder and admiration of the natives.

There is a romance about the marriage of Colonel Grant. While at Portsmouth in command of his regiment he met with an accident, which nearly deprived him of life. Riding along the street his horse suddenly took fright, and he was thrown violently on the ground. He was conveyed in a state of insensibility to the house of a surgeon in the neighbourhood, Dr. Charles Dunn. There he lay for a long period, suffering from the effects of his accident. In the course of his illness and convalescence he was attended by Dr. Dunn's eldest daughter, Miss Mary Anne Dunn. She nursed him with such tenderness and assiduity that she won his affections, and on his recovery he declared his attachment, and they were married on May 20th, 1811. She was beautiful and accomplished, and invariably carried out with grace and dignity the duties devolving upon her as representing the position of the Countess of Seafield although she died a few months before her husband succeeded to the earldom. She had six sons and one daughter. The earl married, a second time, Louisa Mansell (the countess who reigned at Cullen on the occasion of the visit of the Highland Railway deputation in 1845). She now lives as dowager countess at Grant Lodge in Elgin.

The administration of the Grant and afterwards of the Findlater estates was conducted very much on a patriarchal principle, under Sir James Grant and the Colonel, his son. The proprietor and his factors seemed to take a paternal interest in the well-being of the tenants, and they promoted very effectively the young men of the clan by their interest and influence in high quarters. The factors were devoted to their chief, and regarded his interest and honour entirely in the administration of their duties. Mr. John Fraser, a clever and intelligent man, and a devoted servant, was chief factor, and was known as cashier ; for there were no "Commissioners" in those days. There were few banks in the country, and in order to encourage the tenants in economy and saving (not to ascertain their wealth and increase their rents), Mr. Fraser was authorized to receive money on account of the chief, for which good interest was paid, and bills from Sir James and Colonel Grant were reckoned throughout the district as secure as the Bank of England. The result was that Mr. Fraser ultimately became unconsciously a banker on a very considerable scale.* Perhaps nowhere in the Highlands at any period was there so happy, contented, and virtuous a tenantry as during the incumbency of these two proprietors. Many of the tacksmen were educated gentlemen and retired officers in the army, thereby infusing a higher tone among the people than was found in most other parts of the Highlands. Hence, as has been said, the offshoots of the Clan Grant have been distinguished above those of almost any other clan for the high positions they have acquired in all parts of the outer world.

* This system was put a stop to in 1847, when there was a run on many of the proprietors at the period of the potato famine.

Although great improvements have been carried out on these estates during the period alluded to, the happiness and comfort of the people were at this time a special object of these proprietors. They seemed to feel that the welfare of the inhabitants of the land should be their first consideration, and to be imbued with the sentiment that " property has its duties as well as its rights."

I may mention here an incident as a last expression of the feudal spirit and attachment of the clan for the honour of the chief and his family. In 1820, before the first Reform Bill was passed, the election of burgh members in Scotland was in the hands of town councils; and in the course of an election that year at Elgin, strenuous efforts were made by allies of the Fife family to secure a majority in the Liberal interest, which then, as now, in Scotland accorded with the popular wish—the political influence of the Grants, from their great territorial possessions in the neighbourhood, being at that time paramount both in the town and county of Elgin.

Grant Lodge, in Elgin, was then the winter residence of the junior members of the family of the chief, and in his absence his daughters, Lady Ann Margaret and her sister, resided there. Lady Ann, a genuine scion of the house of Grant, entered with much spirit into the election contest. A wavering dignitary in the council had been spirited across the sea into Sutherlandshire to prevent his voting, and the opponents of the Grant party deemed it necessary for the success of their cause to control the family influence and to confine her ladyship and her sister within the precincts of their residence. A vigilant watch was kept on the ladies, and their appearance outside the grounds of the lodge was the signal for the hooting and jeering of the populace. Lady Ann had too high a spirit quietly to brook the indignity offered to her person and family, and on Saturday night she despatched a messenger on horseback to Strathspey to make her friends aware of her enforced confinement. The messenger arrived at Cromdale church before the congregation dispersed ; her letter was read from the pulpit by the minister, himself a zealous clansman. He exhorted

the male portion of his hearers to proceed to Elgin at
once, and suggested that they might provide themselves
with weapons of defence on their way through the woods
of Knockando. The messenger sped also to Congish, the
residence of Captain Grant, the local factor, whose love for
the honour of the Grant family was his highest consideration. At once he entered into the movement, and was
joined by Captain Grant of Birchfield. The fiery cross was
not raised as of old, but the tidings were soon spread
throughout the Strath, and a rendezvous of Strathspey men
was fixed within a mile of Elgin for the following morning.
At the place and hour appointed, upwards of a thousand
clansmen assembled, chiefly Grants, armed with every
variety of weapon, formidable, at any rate, in appearance.

Intelligence of this hostile demonstration preceded the
Grants to Elgin, and instead of resistance or continued dis-
respect to the inmates of Grant Lodge, a course was taken
attributed by the Highlanders to cowardice, but evidence of
the prudence and tact of the town authorities. The Highlanders were received in the kindest manner possible, and
permitted to march through the town to Grant Lodge un-
molested. They were there assured of the perfect safety
and liberty of the fair inmates, who expressed gratitude for
their loyalty, and entertained them to a sumptuous repast.

The matter was reported to the Government of the day,
and it required all the influence of the Grant family to prevent a public investigation. So ended the last demonstration
of love and affection in the Highlands by a clan for their chief.

Francis William, Lord Seafield, died on the 30th July,
1853, and was succeeded by the present earl, born on the 4th
September, 1815. He married, on the 12th August, 1850,
Caroline Stewart, youngest daughter of Lord Blantyre.
They have one son, Ian Charles, Lord Reidhaven, born in
October, 1851.

The present earl,* since his succession to the estates, has
displayed great judgment and prudence in their administration. Formerly the vast forests in Strathspey, which

* Since this was written the earl has died, and been succeeded by
his son.

produced the finest timber in Great Britain, were managed very primitively and unprofitably. The timber was cut down in the forest, and afforded very considerable employment to the tenants, whose horses dragged it down to the river side, where it was formed into rafts. The tenants were paid by tickets from the wood department, and the amount due to them was placed by the factor to the credit of their rents; consequently the real value of the timber was néver known. About three hundred people were employed in the forests, and a lot of rough Highlanders acted as floaters, for the timber was all floated down the Spey to the sea at Garmouth. Since the accession of the present lord, the management of the estates has been under the Honourable Thomas Bruce, who has changed this system by the advice and under the direction of an eminent forester, Mr. Brown. All the timber is now sold standing, and the returns are kept distinct.

The territories of this family are very extensive. In the counties of Banff, Inverness, and Moray the gross revenue in 1872 and 1873 amounted to £74,000. The chief has four residences—Cullen House, in Banffshire; Castle Grant; Balmacaan, in Glen Urquhart, Inverness-shire; and Grant Lodge, in Elgin.

The family residence of Castle Grant is in the midst of an extensive park and forest of magnificent trees, commanding wide-spread views of Strathspey and the surrounding Cairngorm mountains. The north-west front, built in the fifteenth century, is three sides of a quadrangle, a fine feudal, turreted castle. The hall and staircase are spacious, in which are arranged very curious old Highland armour, and the arms and colours of the old Inverness-shire militia. The old hall or dining-room is handsome; 47 feet by 27 feet, and proportionately high. Throughout the different rooms there are fine paintings, some by the old Italian masters. In the last century an artist of the name of Watt seems to have visited the Strath and painted thirty portraits of gentlemen of the clan. The portrait of the ancestor of Grant of Kincorth would pass very readily for the late laird. There is a full-length portrait of a piper, who is said to have played continuously from Inverness to Castle Grant and on his arrival to have fallen dead, thus sacrificing his life to the enthusiasm of his profession. These native portraits are hung in the hall, and are curious and characteristic.*

Cullen House is one of the most magnificent residences in Scotland. When I visited it in 1845, it was of vast extent; there were seven drawing-rooms, but it had no distinctive architectural features. It has since, by the present lord, been modernized, made architecturally picturesque, and contains every recent luxury and comfort.

It was the seat of the Earls of Findlater, who, besides their other great talents, seem to have been extensive patrons of the fine arts, for the different rooms contain a valuable collection of ancient Italian and modern pictures. The grounds and gardens are beautiful, and on an extensive scale.

Balmacaan, where his lordship chiefly resided, is a residence with every modern comfort; has no architectural features, but is situated in one of the most charming and picturesque glens in the Highlands.

Lord Seafield, unfortunately for the country, has a diffidence peculiar to the family, and does not take the prominent part in public affairs which his good sense and judgment would warrant. No man has done more for the Highlands. Besides great improvements in his estates, he has been an active promoter of the railways through the Highlands, subscribing more than £50,000, and otherwise undertaking obligations for their prompt completion. No doubt he has a good return for his investment, besides the facilities of communication throughout his extensive estates.

Fewer changes of the tenantry have taken place on his estates than on other Highland properties, and although a great portion of the original tenantry remains, yet the modern system of land tenure and increased rents is gradually being adopted instead of the patriarchal, and deer

---

* The modern administration and the necessities of an increased rental has expatriated all gentlemen farmers and tacksmen, and there are now no gentlemen tacksmen of the clan whose portraits could be added to the old gallery in the hall.

forests and shooting-lodges form now a considerable item in the revenues of the Seafield property.

At each of the residences of Lord Seafield the influence of Lady Seafield is felt in acts of benevolence and charity. She takes an active part in the education and improvement of the young, and her gentle and kindly manner has secured for her universal regard among the numerous dependants of the family.

CHAPTER VI.

Extracts from Journal.

Visit to Fort George—Description of fortress—Two Yorkshire friends
—Visit to Cawdor Castle—A baronial pile of the olden time—The
hawthorn tree—A beautiful ravine.

Sept. 11*th*, 1837.—Having business at Nairn in connection with the harbour, I arranged to accompany some
friends who were visiting me, and to take Fort George on
the way.

The fortress is situated on a level point of gravelly land,
projecting about one mile into the sea. It is twelve miles
from Inverness, and one mile from the village of Campbelltown.

The chief approach to the fort is imposing. The approach is through two sets of outworks before reaching
the principal drawbridge and gateway, and in case of
attack there would necessarily be some hard fighting before
these outworks could be carried.

The timber bridge across the moat or ditch is about
fifty paces in length, with two drawbridges, and the walls
of the fortress are not less than fifty feet in height. There
is a moat all round the fort, and by opening sluices the
fort is encircled by the sea.

The red stone of the walls, the white painted wood-work
of the bridges and railings, contrast pleasantly with the
closely shaven green grass of the ditch and works. The
entrance gateway is a handsome piece of architecture; and
the grim visage of the cannon on each side, pointing at
you as you approach, would be anything but a pleasing
welcome to an enemy.

The hollow clank of your footsteps as you pass along the covered archway, and the precise, vigilant attention of the guards, constantly mounted fifteen strong, give you as you pass a peculiar sensation of the strength and military character of the place.

The ramparts are said to be three-quarters of a mile in circumference and from sixty to seventy feet wide. Beneath there are bomb-proof cellars, each capable of holding forty men, and there are enough of them to hold all the men required to defend the fort.

After passing the gateway, you enter on a handsome esplanade. Fronting you is the residence of the Governor, with the houses of the principal officers of the garrison. Behind is a large square, and several ranges of three-storied houses for the soldiers. In fact, it looks like a well-arranged, handsome little town, having the chapel and spire at its further extremity facing the principal entrance.

We saw one solitary officer lounging about, apparently delighted to see strangers. A residence here must be a very dull existence for the officers, except in autumn to those who may have the privilege of shooting; to the men it is little better than a prison.

The sanitary condition of the fort is a disgrace to the Government. The water is bad, and the fort is lighted with little oil lamps; in fact, water, light, and drainage remain the same as when the fort was built, more than a hundred years ago.*

This fortress is said to be the most regular and perfect in Great Britain, according to the rules of Vauban and other eminent military engineers.

It was built in 1726–28, General Skinner being the engineer, and it is most creditable to his constructive skill; but from the long range of our present artillery, with the surrounding heights, it would, as a place of defence, be comparatively useless in the present day. It served its purpose when it was built.

---

* Improvements have been made during the last few years in the drainage and water supply.

It is now used as a depôt for the training of our militia, and there is generally stationed here a regiment of the line.

Fort George was intended to be built at Inverness, but the story goes that Mr. Hossack, then Provost, objected to its being placed there. He had several pretty daughters, and did not wish them to be fascinated by the agreeable red coats, who would necessarily inhabit the fortress.

Cawdor Castle.

September 13th.—Returned to Inverness in the evening of the 13th. Had a visit from two Yorkshire friends, both rich iron-workers in Rotherham, kind-hearted, clear-headed " John Bulls," charmed with our mountains and mountain air, and not objecting to our " mountain dew."

Knowles, a great reformer, complained of the aristocracy in England, who, he says, " form a distinct and separate class, often despising the very people who are the strength and sinew of England, and by whose industry they mainly derive their revenues. What is worse," he says, " each class as it approaches the higher looks down on those who are next to it, until it reaches even to the mechanic, thus creating in all ranks jealousy and discontent."

Knowles has (1837) great confidence in the Reform Bill. The freeman will soon die away, which will secure at all times the popularity of the House of Commons. Tory Government cannot exist except on Reform principles. He has great faith in the good sense of the people of England. He is not afraid of their running into excess or extremes as in France. He is of opinion that the orderly, intelligent mechanic is perfectly capable of judging correctly in politics.

The aristocracy may affect to despise the judgment of artisans, as leading to anarchy; but they are mistaken. Knowles has lived all his life among them, and knows them well. But this is a digression; although the views of an intelligent, clear-headed master of workmen.

September 15th.—Arranged a trip with my Yorkshire friends to Cawdor Castle, the seat of the Thane of Cawdor.

Of all the baronial castles of the olden time, it is perhaps the most entire in the Highlands. It overhangs a mountain stream, is surrounded by a moat, and you cross a draw-bridge, and enter the gateway with a portcullis fortified. Within there are two small courts, the outer and inner.

The entrance door is of thick oak, studded with nails, and inside is an iron-grated door. The kitchen is a long, narrow, arched dungeon, cut out of the rock, with an ample fireplace at one end and a draw-well at the other.

A turnpike-stair leads to the banqueting hall, which is spacious, having a music gallery at one end and amplitude of chimney at the other, the entablature, curiously carved, bearing the date of 1510.

Above, the rooms, according to modern ideas, are narrow and uncomfortable. One bedroom is hung with tapestry, covering the bare walls. In this there is a bed hung with crimson velvet curtains, and lined with silk embroidered with silver, but sadly faded. The family seem to have preserved most of the old furniture and mirrors. The carpentering of the flooring is very rude.

The room containing a bed, called by legend King Duncan's bed, was burnt down about fourteen years ago.

Below, in one of the arched dungeons of the castle, there grows a hawthorn tree, close to which is an iron chest. Tradition says that this chest filled with gold was placed on an ass's back, and he was allowed to stray where he liked, the Laird of Cawdor having made a vow to build his castle where the ass halted. He stopped at this tree, and he must have been an animal of good taste, for a more charming spot could not have been selected.

In front of the castle, looking east, is a nicely kept square lawn, surrounded by rows of stately chestnut-trees, upwards of a hundred feet high, forming, as it were, a solid wall of foliage on three sides. It partly conceals the size of the park; but the great interest of the castle is that it indicates the mode of life of our aristocracy centuries ago. The turreted castle, and the daisied banks of natural grass and magnificent surrounding trees in the park, are all very charming.

Ascending the hill-side close to the castle, there is a deep and beautifully wooded ravine with a mountain burn, and through this gorge there are very pleasant walks.

The Earl of Cawdor comes here to shoot in the autumn. He is a great planter, and has the reputation of being a kind and considerate landlord. The Messrs. Stables, father and son, have together been upwards of seventy years in charge, and during all that time have been much esteemed in the district. The revenue of the estates is £7882 a year. The castle may be seen by the public; and the family, to their no small inconvenience, kindly permit visits even during their sojourn in the autumn.

The Macpherson Family.

At the northern end of this estate lies the farm of Ardersier, tenanted at the close of last century by a Mr. James Macpherson. In his youth he travelled on the Continent with the heir of Cawdor, and had afterwards been appointed to the position of factor on the property. Marrying in 1777, he was blessed with a numerous off-spring of eight sons and eight daughters, who all lived to grow up in the paternal home. Of the eight sons, seven entered the service of their country, five obtaining commissions in the army and two in the navy. The record of the bravery of these young officers is striking. The eldest in the engagement at Alexandria in 1801 was wounded; but, binding the wound with his scarf, continued in the fray till, as he was charging the enemy, he received a death wound, and fell back into the arms of a fellow officer, an old school-fellow. The third son, a captain in the 78th, was killed in Java. The fourth, a commander in the navy, was wounded at Algiers and again at Aboukir. The fifth died from exposure in service, expiring the very night he reached home. The sixth, in the 93rd, was wounded at New Orleans; and the seventh, after serving in the campaign of 1815, was so severely wounded in New Zealand that he was compelled to retire from active service.

The second son, Duncan, had not only a distinguished

career himself, but was the father of two sons who continued and increased the military prestige of the family. He obtained a commission in a West Indian regiment, and joined his corps on the day before his fourteenth birthday. He exchanged into the 35th, and served with them in Egypt and the Peninsula; afterwards he was transferred into the 78th and distinguished himself at the battle of Maida, where he was severely wounded. He retired from the army to the old home at Ardersier, of which he became tenant at the death of his mother. There his sons, James and Herbert, were born. They both entered the army— the elder the Company's service, the younger the 78th Highlanders.

During the mutiny of 1857, Colonel "Mac," as the future Sir James was then called, did splendid work in aiding Sir John Lawrence to train, drill, clothe, and organize into regiments 20,000 Sikh soldiers who took the place of the Sepoys who had mutinied. His zeal and energy were very great. He was rewarded by various military appointments, being Quarter-master-General of the army under Lord Clyde, and finally at the close of the war becoming Commissary-General.

The younger brother, Herbert, has had even a more brilliant career. Serving with his regiment, he won the Victoria Cross on the march to Cawnpore under Sir Henry Havelock. Joining the Bengal Staff, he commanded one of the famous Goorkha regiments, with which he did good service on the North-west frontier. During the Afghan war he was one of the Generals of Division. His distinguished service led to his being selected to command the Indian Contingent in the Egyptian expedition, where his corps aided materially in the final operations of the army. It may be a matter of question whether, notwithstanding the progress of this century, a farmhouse like the Mains of Ardersier is now the nursery of any such family as that of James and Duncan Macpherson. The House of Cawdor must look back with pride to the distinguished careers of the descendants of their former factor.

CHAPTER VII.

Smuggling in the Highlands—Its universal character—An Act to authorize small stills—A morning encounter in Glenmoriston—A cargo from Holland—Two smuggled kegs of brandy.

THE Highlands have long been famous for excellent whisky. Prior to 1745, however, there does not seem to have been much whisky manufactured. Brandy appears to have been the more common spirituous drink in the Highlands.

Indeed, before the roads were made the revenue from the customs, except at Inverness (and even there), was very small. Almost up to 1825 all the whisky drunk in the Highlands was smuggled.

Of course there were excisemen—and formidable authorities they were—in every district. They occasionally had encounters with smugglers, but they seemed to possess very little power to repress illicit distillation, as the people were in favour of the smugglers. In the south of Scotland certain large capitalists, favourites of the Tory Government, had the power and license to distil whisky; but as it was from raw grain and harsh in flavour, it was almost wholly exported into England to be rectified into gin. In fact, the Highlands were wholly supplied, as I have said, with smuggled whisky.

The Highlanders seem to have liked the idle, risky, and adventurous trade, and they felt they had the public sympathy in their favour. There was a romance about it. The still was generally placed in some secluded spot, in the ravine of a Highland burn, or screened by waving birch and natural wood, so that the smoke of the fire could scarcely be observed. There were scouts placed around, often three or four savage-looking men, sometimes women and boys. I have witnessed such a wild and romantic scene, a fit subject for an artist.

So general was smuggling that at Inverness there were two or three master coppersmiths who had a sign above their shops of a whisky still, indicating their employment. I recollect the mysterious manner in which my mother got her supply of whisky, and in perfect safety, although the collector of Excise lived some six doors away. Everybody declared " small still " or smuggled whisky was the only spirit worth drinking. The Highland smugglers baffled the Government.

At last, an Act was passed to authorize small stills to be established in the Highlands, so that good whisky might be legally manufactured and procured. This, with heavy penalties, and stationing a " Revenue cutter " at Inverness and one on the west coast, whose armed men traversed the country, helped at last to put an end to smuggling. But it was the very business that suited a Highlander. I recollect a Highland laird drinking, " Cheap barley, and success to smuggling."

One morning as I was driving up Glenmoriston before breakfast, and taking a turn in the road of that beautiful valley, I saw before me at some little distance about twenty-five Highland horses tied to each other, and carrying two kegs of whisky each. They were attended by ten or twelve men, some in kilts and all with bonnets and plaids, and carrying large bludgeons. When they saw me approach two of them fell back until I came up with them. They scrutinized me sharply and said, " It is a fine morning, sir ; " to which I responded. Then one turned to the other and said, " Ha rickh shealess ha mach Mitchell fere rate— mohr ; " the literal translation of which is, " You need not mind ; it is the son of Mitchell, the man of the high roads."

He then turned to me and said, " Would you took a dram ? " and on my assenting he took out of his pocket a

F

round tin snuff-box, then common, but without the lid, holding about a large wine-glassful, and filled it with whisky from a bottle which he took from his side-pocket.

After some kindly greeting and talk and drinking my dram, I passed on, the other men politely touching their bonnets as I left. This was another scene for an artist, and is not likely to be seen again.

Almost all wines, spirits, and foreign commodities supplied to the Highlands were smuggled, chiefly from Holland.

I recollect, while visiting a tacksman on the west coast, being brought to a cave where a whole cargo of kegs of foreign spirits was piled up. The last cargo from Holland "run" in the Moray Firth was in 1825, brought by one Donald MacKay, the fishermen of Campbelltown assisting.

I happened, with a friend, to be visiting an official of the fort, who had a cottage on the moor outside; and on our admiring the brandy (although being lads, twenty-one years of age, my friend and I were no great judges), he said if we liked we might have a supply; it was part of the cargo lately "run" on the adjoining beach. His gardener placed two kegs (which with others were buried in the garden) in my gig, in which they were triumphantly carried to Inverness, notwithstanding the proximity of the abode of the collector of Excise.

This smuggling adventure was not found profitable by MacKay, a considerable portion having been seized by the Excise. No further cargoes have since been "run" in that part of the Moray Firth..

CHAPTER VIII.

Extract from Journal—Howe of the Elms.

Aberdeen, January 2, 1838.—Dined with my friend Mr.
Rhind, a merchant here. He was a humorist, and told
various stories characteristic of Morayshire, of which
county he is a native.

There was a Mr. Stewart present, another Morayshire
man, and they recounted sundry reminiscences of their
early life. Stewart said, "Did ye ken the Howe of the
Elms?" "That I did," said Mr. Rhind; "an awful place
for ghosts and witches. Many a time when a boy has my
hair stood on end, when in the gloaming I have had to pass
the Howe."

·"It is a deep hollow," he said, "thickly wooded with elm
trees, dark and dismal. The country folk peopled it with
all sorts of supernatural beings.

"I remember a story told of an adventure of an acquaintance of mine, one Sanders Manson, while he was
passing through that dismal glen. Manson had been in
Elgin, enjoying himself with some drouthy neighbours over
the ale then celebrated for its potent quality in that ancient
and goodly burgh. To reach his home he had to pass the
Howe (hollow) of the Elms. It was near Christmas, and
he had been in town making various purchases prior to that
period of festivity. Among other things he bought a bottle
of barm, or yeast, for a Christmas browst of ale, a common
practice among the peasantry at that season. He put the
bottle of yeast in the outside pocket of his coat, and set out
on his homeward route.

"As he approached the Howe of the Elms, feeling rather

uncomfortable he commenced whistling, and assumed an air of courage; but his hair began to rise, he more firmly grasped his stick, and walked on at an increased pace.

" As he got to the middle of the Howe he heard a hissing noise close to his ear, which appeared constantly increasing. At last there was a loud report, and he felt struck on the back as if he had been shot. On this occurring he roared out, and betook himself to his heels.

" In due time and in great trepidation, and covered with perspiration, he reached his house, at the door of which he loudly knocked, and exhausted with fear and fatigue he fell helpless on the ground.

" ' What!' cried his alarmed wife as she opened the door — ' what ails ye? What is the matter with ye, Sanders?'

" 'Oh Lord! Oh Lord!' he replied. 'I'll no live ony time; its a' up wi' me. Guid forgie me for all my sins. Oh, Jenny, woman, dear Jenny, I am elf shot. As I came through the Howe Satan o'ertook me, an' wi' an awful report shot me through the back. The blood, ye see, is pouring down, and it's no likely I can hold out lang. Oh dear, oh dear, I am a dead mon!'

" On getting Sanders conveyed into the house, and examining into the cause of this alarming catastrophe, it was found that this elf-shooting arose from the bottle of barm, or yeast, which, having begun to expand from the heat of his body, forced out the cork just as he passed the Howe of the Elms, and the blood which he imagined was pouring down his back was nothing more than the yeast exuding from the bottle when the cork had been forced out."

CHAPTER IX.

The Caledonian Bank—Negotiations preceding its commencement—
Appointment of Mr. Waterston, manager—Success of the Bank—
Unfortunate entanglement with the City of Glasgow Bank in 1878
—Suspension and restoration—St. John's Friendly Society—The
Caledonian Hotel.

AMONG the measures of progress in which I took great
interest at this time was the establishment of the Caledonian Bank, now a very valuable and useful institution.

Mr. George Monro, a lawyer in Edinburgh, a native of
Inverness, and an old schoolfellow of mine, finding that
the North of Scotland Bank, established in Aberdeen in
1836–37, had proved eminently prosperous, thought that a
similar local bank would prove equally successful in Inverness. He pressed me into the service, and we had many
conferences and communications on the subject.

Banking before then in the North of Scotland had been
carried on by branches from the great banks in Edinburgh,
and south country shareholders reaped the profits. In
Inverness we had branches of the Bank of Scotland, the
British Linen Company, the Commercial, and the National
Bank of Scotland. The agents were gentlemanly men,
who, unfortunately for themselves, were required to find
very heavy securities for their intromissions.

The lairds at this time were always needy, and the
farmers and traders had little or no capital. Hence great
risks were taken by the agents, which led in my recollection to the detriment or ruin of almost every agent in
Inverness during fifty years.

The security required from the agents has since been

much modified. Still, the patronage of dispensing money
not their own, and the insinuating pressure of needy but
influential people, are apt to give the agents undue importance. After the Reform Bill in 1832 we had two Tory
and two Whig banks, which were found oppressive to many
dependent voters.

The project of a new bank, therefore, was felt to afford
a monetary and social relief, and it was astonishing how
readily it received the general support of the community.

When the prospectus was published, an influential committee was appointed, and I was induced to take an active
part in promoting the scheme from a conviction (for I did
not want money accommodation) that it would be a great
boon and advantage to Inverness and the northern counties.
In July, 1838, I was in Aberdeen, and Mr. Paterson, the
manager of the North of Scotland Banking Company, requested a conference with me.

He stated that his directors intended to establish a
branch of their bank in Inverness, and to have directors
there, and he hoped I would agree to be one; indeed, the
idea was so far matured, that they had prepared the bank-
note, which he showed me—a very pretty picture entitled
(if I remember right) " The Great North of Scotland and
Inverness Banking Company."

I told him the Inverness people were arranging to have
a bank of their own, and that I did not think the project
of his directors was practicable ; at any rate, that I could
not support it.

After considerable negotiation, nothing came of this pro-
posal except that it stimulated the Inverness people to
redouble their efforts to establish a bank for themselves.
The committee had meeting after meeting for this object, and
I had to take the labouring oar in all the communications,
Colonel Ross, an elderly gentleman, signing as chairman.

I find in my journal of the 9th and 10th November, 1838:

" Numerous meetings of the Bank Committee ; and as
the time draws near for the election of Directors, the forma-
tion of the institution creates no small excitement.

" A preliminary meeting is fixed for the 19th, to arrange

the business for the general meeting of shareholders, to be held on the 20th."

Mr. Ross, Berbice, a member of the committee, a retired West India planter, and I, were deputed to wait on the Laird of Mackintosh to request that he would act as chairman at our first meeting.

We proceeded to Moyhall. The chief was very cordial, and agreed to comply with our request. The acting committee, consisting of about fifteen members, called in about a dozen of the largest shareholders to attend our preliminary deliberations. Some of these. indicated a disposition to be troublesome. They said they thought every person who had even one share ought to be present.

We remarked that this would be tantamount to a general meeting, which was unsuited for fixing preliminaries, and to that we could not agree.

Those objecting therefore retired, and held a general meeting of shareholders at the Caledonian Hotel, and said they would communicate to the committee their matured views.

I confess I felt very uncomfortable. The meeting of the opposing shareholders was numerously attended. Several persons were excited, and my heart began to fail me lest all our labour and efforts should be lost. At last the deputation from the outside meeting arrived.

Our minutes were read to them, and by a singular coincidence it was found that they almost entirely coincided with those which the outside shareholders had framed. Our proceedings were consequently approved of. We balloted for directors, and I was astonished and gratified to find my own name at the head of the list.

The general meeting of the shareholders was held next day, The Mackintosh in the chair. The resolutions proposed were unanimously approved of and passed.

Immediately after, the directors held a meeting to consider the certificates of candidates for the managership. I stated to the Board that, when in Aberdeen lately, I had been introduced to a Mr. Clark, who was manager of an Insurance Company, and who, I understood, was the projector of the North of Scotland Bank in Aberdeen. Mr.

Clark appeared very intelligent, and well versed in the subject of banking. In my interview with him, he expressed high approval of our undertaking. He pointed out the vast benefit it would be to the whole North; that in a few years our deposits would be half a million, with which we would have the power properly to develop the agriculture and fisheries in the country, and which would yield besides very profitable returns to the shareholders. He enlarged on his belief that the soil might be made doubly productive.

Mr. Clark himself had made successful experiments with artificial manures on a small scale, and he thought much might be done by improved modes of agriculture (this was before artificial manures were thought of or used in the North). I stated that I thought, from all I saw and heard of this gentleman, he was well qualified to be our manager.

Ultimately it was agreed that I should write to him suggesting that he should apply for the appointment. Mr. Clark in due course stated that on his communicating my letter to his directors they said they could not lose his services, and they increased his salary to such an amount as to render it unnecessary for him to entertain the proposal I had made.

Our Board, although excellent men, were not very well instructed in the business we had undertaken; but they thought that, as Mr. Clark would not accept the appointment himself, he might, under the circumstances, give us the benefit of his advice and experience in selecting the best manager out of the seventeen applications we had received. Accordingly Mr. George Munro, the law agent, and myself were instructed to proceed to Aberdeen to go over the applications with Mr. Clark, and to fix on the person whom we considered most competent for the office.

A whole day was spent in reading the certificates and discussing the merits of the different candidates; ultimately Mr. Charles Waterston was selected. The Board approved of our recommendation, and requested an interview with Mr. Waterston, with a view to his appointment.

Mr. Waterston replied that the affairs of the bank for which he then acted (the Darlington) were such that he could not leave for three months. The directors had therefore no alternative but to appoint (in my absence) a Mr. Gray from Glasgow. This gentleman went south to establish agencies in London and elsewhere ; but on his way back to Inverness he was taken suddenly ill at Perth, where he died.

This placed the directors again in a dilemma, the day being fixed for opening the bank for the transaction of business.

Mr. Ross, whom we had appointed chairman of the Board, kindly undertook the duties of manager *pro tem.* We had, fortunately, experienced subordinate officers, but the whole affair was one of much anxiety. Very soon, however, the three months elapsed, and Mr. Waterston accepted the office of manager.

I paid daily visits to the bank ; and one morning, on entering, said to Mr. Ross, " How thankful I am we shall soon have our manager, and be relieved of this serious anxiety and responsibility."

"Not so soon, my friend, as you imagine," said Mr. Ross, showing me a letter he had that morning received, intimating that the coach in which Mr. Waterston was travelling south for his family had been upset near Dumfries, and that Mr. Waterston had his leg fractured, and was not likely to be fit for duty for at least six weeks. Here was another disaster, which in due time was got over. Mr. Waterston recovered, and entered on his duties on the 25th May, 1839.

These mischances were at the time sources of no small anxiety to the directors. The original Board was constituted as follows :—

> Joseph Mitchell, Esq., Civil Engineer.
> John Ross, Esq., of Berbice.
> Captain D. Macpherson, Collector of Customs.
> Neil McLean, Esq., Land Surveyor.
> Andrew Belford, Esq., Solicitor.
> Colonel John Gray Ross, of Strathgarve.
> Patrick Grant, Esq., Sheriff's Clerk, W.S.
> Robert Smith, Esq., Solicitor.

Alas ! all are now gone but myself.

As Mr. Clark had predicted, the bank has been a great boon to the northern counties. Many a rich farmer and trader can date the beginning of their fortune from the facilities afforded them at the Caledonian Bank.

Mr. Waterston has presided over the affairs of the bank since its opening, now forty years ago; and such is his ability and tact that from the beginning he seemed to have secured the confidence of the entire northern public.

Many a widow and orphan has reason to bless his disinterested advice; and the man who saw no extrication from his muddled affairs, after a conference with him has returned to his family with a clear vision of his business and a light heart.

Moreover, the Caledonian Bank has become a nursery for bankers. The young men bred under Mr. Waterston have obtained distinguished positions in almost every part of the world.

The numerous shareholders have to rejoice in the success of this establishment, the value of their capital being nearly tripled, and their last dividend 12 per cent., with a bonus of 2 per cent. The deposits by last balance were £1,139,903, with a surplus fund or rest of £75,000.

I was a director for upwards of thirty years, and although we had difficulties and differences of opinion during that period, this establishment has been one of continued prosperity and success. It is a satisfaction to me to reflect that I afforded a helping hand to promote it, and to carry on so successfully this very important and useful institution.

1882. The above was written about five years ago. Soon after Mr. Waterston tendered his resignation, and thereupon the shareholders, in consideration of his eminent services, unanimously voted him his salary of £1200 a year for life. The directors proceeded immediately to look out for a successor. A deputation went to Edinburgh in the hope of finding an efficient man; but after waiting for a considerable time and meeting with difficulties, they begged of Mr. Waterston to resume his duties. To remove his objections they would make the duties less onerous to him by appointing the accountant assistant-manager, and make Mr. William Waterston, his son, secretary; Mr. Mactavish, the efficient secretary, who had been in the bank for forty years, retiring on a pension of his full salary for life. These changes were very unpopular with the public outside the bank, and created much speculation and discontent; but a catastrophe of a much more serious nature occurred in the failure of the City of Glasgow Bank. It seems a shareholder, holding four shares of that bank of £50 each, had got some advances from the Nairn agent of the Caledonian Bank; and his security for his advance was the City of Glasgow Bank shares, which, although merely a security, were unfortunately registered in the name of the Bank. The liquidators of the City of Glasgow Bank, and the other banks in Edinburgh whom they seem to have consulted, considered this a good opportunity for extending their base of security, and dragging in the whole shareholders of the Caledonian Bank as creditors of the City of Glasgow Bank. Accordingly, their credit being damaged by various paragraphs in the newspapers and the threats of the liquidators to apply to the Court of Session to stop the register transfers of the Caledonian Bank, a run was caused on the deposits, and the directors had nothing for it but to shut their doors, the Edinburgh banks being prepared and offering to send agencies to supply the services of the Caledonian Bank. This, of course, created dismay and distress throughout the northern parts of Scotland, the more so as the Caledonian Bank was falsely rumoured to be insolvent. Of course Mr. Waterston's reputation as a banker suffered, and he had to undergo the odium of minute investigations. It turned out, on the report of competent neutral accountants, that the capital of the company was intact, as well as the rest of £75,000. In due time, however, it was found that the claim of the City of Glasgow Bank would not amount to above £11,000; and by a circular of the leading noblemen and gentlemen and men of business throughout the district it was agreed that the Caledonian Bank should resume business, which was done in July, 1879, and the business is now conducted under the efficient management of Mr. E. H. Macmillan. The bank is now in good credit, performing the business of the country, and the deposits by last account amounted to £806,104, and are gradually increasing.

St. John's Friendly Society of Freemasons.

Another local institution in which I took an interest is the St. John's Mason Lodge, although I was never very profound in masonic mystery.

It appears, when there was little communication between Inverness and the outer world, this lodge was a centre for social meetings of the gentlemen of Inverness and its neighbourhood.

It is an ancient institution, but its minutes and property were lost in the Rebellion of 1745. To improve their place of meeting, a grant of money was obtained in 1780 from the "Commissioners of the Forfeited Estates" to assist in erecting a new hotel and lodge; hence the existence of the Caledonian Hotel, of which the Masons were the proprietors in 1825-26.

The respectable citizens, in addition to the occasion of the annual dinner, used to meet in masonic array once a month, generally about thirty in number, spending a very agreeable evening in social intercourse and song.

The Caledonian has always been a favourite hotel in the Highlands. The completion of the new roads in 1822 so increased the intercourse of the country that additional accommodation became necessary, and the lodge laid out £2000 in enlarging and improving the building.

Soon after the Reform Bill of 1831, the political agents discovered that the tenant of so large an establishment had considerable political influence among the tradesmen-voters, and hence they became a controlling influence in the lodge; and the tenants, besides paying a very low rent, obtained a large portion of the surplus funds for such improvements, repairs, and decorations as they themselves were entitled and quite able to make.

Seeing the improper use to which the surplus funds

were applied, I proposed that they should form a fund, with such additions as might be contributed, for the benefit of the widows and orphans of members.

This was resisted at first by the law agents ; but ultimately the members saw the importance of it, and a Friendly Society was established on December 27th, 1842, of which I was convener.

This society, by the surplus rents and large contributions from the members themselves, has since very much improved and enlarged the hotel. The value of the property is now estimated at £10,276, with a rental of £860 per annum. The society is at present enabled to give an annuity to twelve widows of £40 per annum—a great boon to many of them.*

My Marriage.

The 2nd of February, 1841, was an important day for the happiness of my life. I was then united to the youngest daughter of James Dunsmure, Esq., Secretary to the Board of Fisheries. This Commission of the Board of Fisheries was established for the encouragement of fisheries throughout Scotland. It was well known that the shores of the northern counties teemed with every variety of the finest fish, and our Dutch neighbours had for centuries been fishing in these waters with the most satisfactory results. The Board was accordingly established, consisting of twelve of the principal and most influential citizens of Edinburgh, and Mr. Dunsmure acted as their secretary ; and owing to his talent, industry, and enterprise, the services of the Board turned out eminently successful. Their duties were to grant bounties for the encouragement of the fisheries, and to establish the Dutch system of curing and, if possible, improve upon it, which was done, and such an impetus was given to the trade in 1825 that the Government thereafter thought it unnecessary to con-

* 1882.—Since the above was written the society has again enlarged this hotel, at an expense of £6000. It is now one of the finest and most luxurious hotels in the kingdom.

tinue the bounties. As engineer to the Board, for erecting harbours along the coast, I had much and constant intercourse with Mr. Dunsmure, and very frequently enjoyed his hospitality. Hence my acquaintance with his daughter, whose affections I had the good fortune to secure. Mr. Dunsmure was a man of classical attainments, and I could not help noticing the admirable manner in which he and his wife devoted themselves to the training and education of their family — six in number. From the day of my marriage, for nearly forty years, my union was a source of great happiness, such as comes to the lot of few men.

My marriage day was not very propitious. We had a storm of high wind, snow, and rain, and in this war of the elements we reached the Queen's Ferry, where a sailing boat awaited us at the pier. There was a steamer at the Ferry, but in storms, at that time, it never seemed to be used. As we got on board, my friend the skipper said, "I see ye he got yen of the Miss Dunsmures wi' you." "Yes," I said, "she is no longer Miss Dunsmure; she is my wife." "God bless me. Ye manna pass the Ferry without our rejoicing. I wish you all happiness. Charlie Peterson, hoist the flag!"—which was done in our honour, for the Dunsmure family were great favourites with the boatmen.* Next day we reached Perth, where my brother Alexander had kindly invited us to take up our quarters with him. The snow and rain were still raging, and there was no alternative than to remain a week with him, until the storm had ceased and the roads were cleared. After a cold and unpleasant journey I placed my bride in her future residence, and from that day her gentle manner, her sweet temper, her good sense, and intellectual culture and accomplishments, rendered Viewhill, to her family and friends, the home of harmony and love to the day of her death.

---

* Mr. Dunsmure for several years in the autumn months rented a villa at north Queen's Ferry, and of course the family were well acquainted with the boatmen.

CHAPTER X.

Commercial travellers in riding and coaching days—The change
made by railways—Anecdotes of the commercial-room.

In the course of my journeys I frequently met commercial
travellers. Many of them were very intelligent men, and
some have since risen to wealth and eminence in their
business, such as Sir James Lumsden, the late Lord Provost of Glasgow, and Sir Andrew Orr, who was also Lord
Provost of Glasgow, and with whom I maintained friendly
acquaintance all my life.

In 1824 the roads in the Highlands had just been completed, and the transition from horseback to gigs for
commercial travellers had not been generally adopted,
particularly among some of the elderly members of the
fraternity.

I recollect a few "riders," as they were called, coming
about that time to Inverness, and they travelled, indeed, as
far north as Tain. They were portly old gentlemen, with
rubicund faces, wore top-boots, blue coats with brass
buttons, rode good horses, did their business in no hurry,
had saddle-bags behind for their cloths and patterns, and
carried large heavy whips.

They were familiar with the good inns on the road, and
generally arranged to reach what was reckoned the best
of them on a Saturday night. In the north, Richardson's,
at Nairn (he being an Englishman), was a favourite house.

The roads having been made, and the inns improved,
gigs became common in the north, and in a few years
the old "riders" disappeared, except occasionally where

coaches ran. Younger men succeeded the old travellers, although a few of the masters and elderly "gents" from habit took, and seemed to like, a journey on the road now and then.

The young men seem to have been an inferior race in intelligence, although sharp enough in business. Their chief conversation was the quality of their horses and their adventures at the inns. They had, however, a very jolly life.

Now all is again changed. The railways have superseded both riders and gigs. The complaints in the commercial-room are now the unfair conduct of stationmasters, who insist on payment beyond a second-class fare for the full weight of a cart-load of patterns which these gentlemen now carry.

Extract from Journal.

October 29, 1837. After my portmanteau, great-coat, &c., were safely deposited in my bedroom, I descended to the commercial-room of the Tontine in Glasgow. There were nine or ten travellers there. One old gentleman sat in an armchair by the fireside; the others talked to and treated him with respect and consideration. Mr. Glendinning was his name, and there were frequent appeals to Mr. Glendinning's decision. He was a venerable-looking gentleman, of mild and kindly aspect, and gave his opinion in a measured and Johnsonian style.

Some of the persons present were rough, others appeared shrewd and intelligent. Some were at tea, some at supper, some drinking whisky toddy, and some were writing letters.

An East Lothian man sat in one corner, doing nothing and saying nothing, but occasionally taking a pinch of snuff. The conversation was varied, including such subjects as the temper, disposition, and attributes of the Queen; the safety in general of investments of capital in business; and the value of stock distributed in small quantities to dealers throughout the towns, which stock yielded 10 per cent., and was turned over three or four times a year. Judiciously managed, no investment could be more profitable or more safe.

On another occasion, at four o'clock, dinner was served at the *table d'hôte*, old Mr. Glendinning presiding. We always seem to have the luck of meeting here. The dinner was excellent, about fourteen gentlemen were present, and we had a goodly allowance of wine.

We had a motley assembly from all parts of Great Britain, besides two Paddies. We had a variety of toasts, old " Glen," who was in the chair, patronizingly drinking wine with, and taking notice of, all around the table.

One Aberdeen man was asked to propose either a toast or give a sentiment—a fashion common in those days. He scratched his head and said "he didna ken fat to gie." However, he said, thinking a little, " I'll gie ye ' Absent freens.' "

" Oh ! by the powers," said one of the Paddies, " it is me that will drink *that* ; here's to ' Cash and Credit.' " This was received with great applause, and we had some more Irish wit. We sat till seven, when most of the gentlemen went out again to business.

About nine they began to reassemble, with some additions. At nine precisely, old " Glen " ordered in pipes and his glass of brandy and water ; a good many followed his example ; some smoked cigars.

We soon got enveloped in smoke, which seemed to have a soporific effect, for we all, one after another, moved off to our respective bedrooms, about eleven o'clock.

CHAPTER XI.

Sutherlandshire.

Account of the County—Sad death of the Earl and Countess of Sutherland in 1776—Their daughter served heir to the estates—The state
of the people—Marriage of the young Countess to the Marquis of
Stafford—Clearances and improvements carried out under Mr. Loch,
Mr. Young, and Mr. Patrick Sellar—Purchase of the Reay country.

SUTHERLAND is the most northern county, except Caithness, on the mainland of Scotland. In his book on the
Sutherland improvements Mr. Loch describes it as bounded
on the west for the distance of forty and a half miles by the
Minch, an arm of the Atlantic Ocean, which separates it
from the islands of Harris and Lewis; on the north, for a
distance of fifty miles, by the Northern Ocean; on the east,
for a distance of thirty-seven and a half miles, by the ridge
of high mountains which divides it from the county of
Caithness; on the south-east, for a distance of thirty-two
and a half miles, by the Moray Firth; and on the south
and south-west, for a distance of fifty-two and a half
miles, by the Dornoch Firth, the river Oykel and lesser
streams, which separate it from the county of Ross. It
is intersected on the south-east by four valleys and
their rivers—Kildonan, Strath Brora, Strathfleet, and the
Oykel.

The county contains thirteen parishes, and the population was, in 1810, 23,689.

The most direct route into the county prior to the construction of the roads was the Meikle Ferry, four miles
from Tain, across the Dornoch Firth, and the Little Ferry

across Loch Fleet. The boats used for crossing these ferries were of the most wretched description, and there were no landing-piers or roads of approach, beyond such bridle-paths or footways as sufficed for the limited intercourse that existed with the county.

There was another approach across the river Oykel, about six miles from the head of the Dornoch Firth. Here, at a place called the Kyle, were held the great cattle markets ; and here the drovers from Caithness and Sutherland crossed to the South.

Except certain fertile spots in the valleys, and a considerable extent of imperfectly cultivated arable land on the eastern seaboard, the whole shire was one uninterrupted succession of wild mountains, valleys, and deep morasses. The intercourse between one part of the county and another was confined exclusively, or nearly so, to the enterprise of those who could travel on foot, or on horseback ; and even this mode of communication, except to the natives, who were brought up to such toil and exertion, was almost impracticable.

Of this extensive county, containing an area of 1,840,000 acres, deducting 32,000 acres for salt - water lochs, the greater part in 1809 was owned by two great chiefs, the Earl of Sutherland and Lord Reay. The original territory of the Earls of Sutherland extended to nearly 800,000 acres, that of Lord Reay to about 400,000, and the remaining 600,000 acres were held by sundry smaller proprietors.

The Lord Reay who died about the end of last century was mentally incapable of managing his own affairs, and the earldom of Sutherland was under trust during the minority of the young Countess, who was only a year old when her parents died in 1766.

The Countess's grandfather, the sixteenth Earl of Sutherland, was married in 1734 to Lady Elizabeth Wemyss, eldest daughter of the third Earl of Wemyss, and had an only son, William, the seventeenth Earl, who was born in 1735. He married, in 1761, Mary, eldest daughter and co-heiress of William Maxwell of Preston, and both parents dying, as I have said, in 1766, left an only daughter, the Countess Elizabeth. Her father and mother died under very sad and distressing circumstances.

The Earl is reported to have been a man of various accomplishments and much beloved for his amiable and benevolent disposition. Being in delicate health he was advised to sojourn for a short period in Bath, where it was hoped, under the influence of a more genial climate, his health might be restored. He was accompanied there by the Countess, and, after a short residence, they were seized with a malignant fever, which proved fatal, both having died within an interval of ten days. They were buried in the Abbey Church of Holyrood in Edinburgh. On the monument erected to their memory it is stated : " that his Lordship died at the age of 32, the Countess at 26. They were not less ennobled by their shining virtues than by their high rank. Their humane disposition and amiability had greatly endeared them to all orders of society.

> ' They were lovely in their lives,
> And in their death they were not divided.' "

The infant Countess was fortunate in the guardians and trustees who were appointed to protect her interests and administer her estates. They were John, Duke of Athole ; Charles, Earl of Elgin ; the Honourable James Wemyss of Wemyss ; Sir David Dalrymple of Hailes, better known as Lord Hailes ; Alexander Boswell of Auchinleck ; and John Mackenzie of Delvin, writer to the signet.

Their duties were onerous and of no ordinary character, for claims were set up by Sir Robert Gordon of Gordonstown, and George Sutherland of Forss in Caithness, each for the estates of Sutherland, on the ground that a chief of a clan must be the male representative. This view was affirmed by the Court of Session, and the case was appealed to the House of Lords. There was a fierce contention, for the stake was great, and Sir Robert Gordon was admitted to be the heir male. It is said that the interests of the young Countess were promoted by Lord Hailes, a judge of the Court of Session, who drew up her ladyship's appeal.

The litigation extended over six years, but the House of Lords brought to bear on this case the ancient law of Scottish descent, whereby titles and estates descended to heirs female, and the estates were finally awarded to the daughter of the deceased Earl.

From this period the Sutherland estates seem to have been managed by factors under the direction of these trustees, and until some years after the beginning of the present century the inhabitants of Sutherland, like those of the neighbouring Highlands, lived a half wild and uncivilized life. It is possible that the Sutherland Highlanders were even less improved than their neighbours, seeing that for a long period of years the greater part of the people were deprived of the supervision of their legitimate chiefs. They were left very much to their own devices, excepting for the influence of such control as the neighbouring tacksmen and clergymen had over them, or that of the sheriffs when they were appointed to administer the law.

The tacksmen were large tenants having extensive tracts of country, and possessing large herds of cattle and some sheep, but they were ignorant of the modern modes of agriculture, and cultivated their lands in a rude and imperfect manner. They had sub-tenants under them, who, in consideration of their lands and crofts, paid a small money rent and certain dues in kind, and rendered otherwise various onerous and oppressive services.

The peasantry in general throughout the county had held their farms in the valleys or on the hillsides from time immemorial; they were members of the clan, and knew no other country but Sutherland. They each possessed from two or four to twenty milk cows—in some cases as many as thirty—with a proportionate following of younger cattle; and the tenants of the separate valleys or other well defined districts grazed their cattle in common. They cultivated, each for his own family, a sufficient extent of barley and oats, along with potatoes after that root was introduced.*

* General Stewart of Garth.

In midsummer, when the grass was rich on the mountain slopes, and the cows yielded a copious quantity of. milk, they migrated and lived in temporary huts called shealings, where for six weeks they made butter and cheese. It was somewhat like the harvesting in the Low country. It was a change and period of enjoyment and rejoicing.

There were then no Game Laws, and no objection was taken to a shot at a stag or a moorfowl. The rivers and sea teemed with fish as they do now, and afforded a plentiful supply for food. Hence in general the people lived comfortably and well in their way. They provided for their own poor and dependents, although, no doubt, from want of forethought they experienced distress in backward seasons and long winters. They built their own houses and provided their own clothes. With these primitive habits and tastes of course they did not improve, and there was very little inducement for them to extend their agricultural work beyond what their simple necessities required. The proceeds of the sale of their cattle paid their rents.

Their sentiments and tastes were warlike from early tradition, and they were always ready for any military enterprise or adventure at the advice or command of their chiefs. At the end of the last, and the beginning of the present century, they were strict in their religious observances, as, indeed, they are up to the present time. The tacksmen, being persons of a superior class, commanded respect and obedience. Many of them had acquired experience of the world as officers of the army. They acted as informal magistrates, settling the disputes and differences that sometimes arose.

Such was the state of the aboriginal inhabitants throughout Sutherlandshire, when it was resolved to break up the old system and remodel the agricultural arrangements of the county. At this time also (1809) the Marquis of Stafford,* who in 1785 married the Countess of Sutherland,

---

* George Granville, second Marquis of Stafford, was born January 9th, 1758, and married the Countess of Sutherland September 4th, 1785. He was created Duke of Sutherland in 1833, and died the same year. The Duchess-Countess died January 29th, 1839, aged seventy-four years.

the heiress to these estates, agreed on her part to accept from the Government, as was done in other parts of the Highlands, half the expense of opening up the country by means of roads, and this great work was carried on and completed in the three succeeding years.

The noble marquis seems to have succeeded about the same time to estates in Staffordshire and Salop in England, the leases on which, extending in most cases over three lives, had fallen in. He found that the system of agriculture which had been adopted on these estates was rude and ancient, and he forthwith adopted measures which produced a complete change, and carried out plans of improvement which not only increased the rentals, but to a great extent improved the condition of the people.

The principal improvements in England consisted in the construction of roads, planting trees, and building about thirty-seven new, and repairing eight old, farm steadings, at a cost of from £1500 to £1600 each, and in building cottages, draining, enlarging, and regulating the size of the farms, and introducing the Norfolk system of agriculture, which was the best then known.

" These works," Mr. Loch says, " were carried out with the greatest consideration for the feelings and interests of the people, and appear to be very readily seconded by them."

" In effecting these necessary changes," continues Mr. Loch, " wherever the old tenant was removed—which was done as seldom as possible—he was, unless he took a farm elsewhere, accommodated with his house and his best grass crofts for his life, and in every case at a low and inadequate rent.

" Whenever it was possible to treat with the person beneficially interested in the lease, and whose continuance

George Granville, second duke, was born August 8th, 1786. He succeeded to the English estates in 1833; to the Scotch honours on the death of his mother in 1839. He married Henrietta Elizabeth Georgina, third daughter of George, sixth Earl of Carlisle, and had by her, who died October 27th, 1868, a large family. The third and present duke succeeded his father in 1861.

in the farm was incompatible with the new arrangements of the land, his interest was purchased for an annuity, or a sum of money to enable him to look for and stock a farm." Few, however, accepted this arrangement; Mr. Loch does not say why.

Mr. Loch goes on to say that the noble Marquis was liberal in assisting to establish schools where necessary; that the character of the many cottagers on the estate was an object of solicitude. Without any interference with the manner in which the man might choose to occupy himself, his regular and decent behaviour was made the subject of care and attention.

He (Mr. Loch) enlarges on the worthy and beneficent acts of charity exercised by the noble Marquis, inasmuch as no less than 13,000 persons were served in 1819 with 14,003 loaves of bread, and a pint of beer to each; also 12,750 quarts of rich soup and 14,134 quarts of milk, as allowances to the poor. This has been and is a custom of the great families in England, but it is stated as an evidence of the liberality of the noble Marquis on his English estates.

Such were the arrangements for the improvements in England, carried out under the immediate direction of Mr. James Loch, the Marquis's commissioner.

Quite different was the treatment experienced by the people of Sutherland. The Sutherland estates were, unfortunately for the people, remotely situated, and were then with difficulty accessible. They contained a vast population,* and when the clearances and improvements were determined on, it does not appear that either the Marquis himself or Mr. Loch had ever visited the county with the view of inquiring into the character of the inhabitants and the nature of their holdings, or their rights with regard to the occupancy of their crofts.† It is to be

* Population of Sutherlandshire in 1810 was 23,629; and in 1825, 23,840.

† In the memoirs of the Duke of Sutherland, written by Mr. Loch in 1834, it is stated that soon after the Marquis's union with the Countess of Sutherland in 1785 they visited Sutherlandshire; but ex-

feared that their opinions were formed from the character
of the squatters found on the English estates, whom Mr.
Loch represents as a very poor, and in many instances a
profligate, population.

The improvements and changes in Sutherland were
placed under charge of Mr. William Young, of Maryhill,
in Morayshire. He was a man of independent means, and
had obtained a distinguished reputation in his own county
for enterprise in agricultural and general improvements.
Mr. Peter Sellar, an able and active young lawyer, also
from Morayshire, was employed as factor and law agent
on the estates.

Mr. Young found this great county in a state of nature,
and his enterprising spirit at once perceived how it might
be turned to profitable account by establishing arable farms
of various sizes, according to the nature of the country,
and following the example of the Highland proprietors in
the southern counties by converting the hill ground into
sheep farms.

Such a process, however, involved the removal of large
numbers of the population. These people had fixed modes
of life; they had for generations occupied the same lands,
and could see no advantage in any such change as that
proposed. Even the tacksmen, many of them old officers,
educated men of the world, demurred to the disturbing
influence of these proposed improvements.

Mr. Young told me he at once saw that this was the
great impediment to the changes contemplated and thought
necessary; and he suggested to his noble constituent that
instead of ruthlessly clearing the people off their lands, as
had been done in the southern Highlands, he should afford
them facilities for emigration. He advised that an agent
should be sent to Canada to purchase land and build
houses for their reception, giving them a free passage and
other assistance, but the Marquis objected to incur this
large expense.

cepting this visit it does not appear that the Marquis visited the county
until some time after the improvements had been commenced and
were far advanced. They were begun in 1812.

Curiously enough, Mr. Loch does not seem to have tried in Sutherland the same conciliatory mode of treatment adopted in England towards the tenants there. It was resolved to remove the people, even without their consent, and place them on crofts along the sea coasts of the county. Notice of removal was therefore promptly given by Mr. Sellar, the law agent, and the people were in dismay. They could not believe that they were to be forced to leave the homes of their fathers. But their opposition was of no avail.

Some, it is reported, were removed to distant parts before their crops were reaped, and had to drive away their cattle and little furniture, and to build new houses on the localities pointed out to them. Others were forced to occupy the lots or crofts provided for them along the sea coasts, particularly at Brora and Helmsdale, where, with facilities to build a house, and a grant of from one to three acres of land, together with any profit fishing would afford, it was contended they might earn a comfortable and satisfactory living. Many accordingly went to the seaside; others who had the means emigrated to America; while not a few removed to Caithness, Ross-shire, and more southern counties.

The plan of the coast settlements was inconsiderate, for many of the people were expected to earn a living as fishermen who had never seen the sea; and to those younger men who had acquired a knowledge of fishing there was then no market for the fish caught. Even to this day, with the facilities of communication which exist, the markets are yet so uncertain, that pauperism reigns throughout the mass of the population settled along the sea coasts of this part of the county. Yet Mr. Loch persisted in this plan, for in his account of the Sutherland Improvements, published in 1820, there is a map showing the whole county divided into sheep farms, and all around the coasts are marked with "crofts for *small* tenants."

Mr. Sellar, as I have said, acted as law agent, and was resolute in carrying out his instructions. The Highlanders were passive and obstinate, and naturally so, for they knew not where to go, unless they accepted the alternative of becoming fishermen. I have heard described many scenes of a painful character in regard to these clearances, some of which were not effected without military force.

A great outcry was raised throughout the country. Complaints of Mr. Sellar's actings were made, and the Sheriff Substitute was ordered to investigate the whole matter. He reported against the conduct of Mr. Sellar. The Sheriff Principal, Mr. Cranston, afterwards Lord Corehouse, supported his substitute. Mr. Sellar was tried at the Spring Circuit of 1816 at Inverness on a charge of culpable homicide, an old bed-ridden woman, it was alleged, having died in consequence of being turned out of her cottage. Mr. Sellar was acquitted, and received an eulogium from the presiding judge, Lord Pitmelly. It is unnecessary to go into the question now.

In those Tory days the people were of no account. The whole of Scotland was ruled by a clique supported by the landed aristocracy. The Lord Advocate was supreme. A judge had then much in his power. Lord Cockburn, in an article in the "Edinburgh Review" of October, 1821, in regard to juries, says, "The forty-five persons at each circuit (jurymen) thus summoned by rotation are recommended to appear in court on the day of trial; and when they do so, *the presiding judge at his own discretion specifies which fifteen of them are to form the jury* for the trial of the case. This is in Edinburgh. *In the country circuits he names the forty-five also.*" Fortunately the law is now altered.

Whether the poor people in the above case got fair play is very doubtful. It was strongly maintained throughout the country that they did not. Indeed, the Government at that time had the means of commanding a conviction, and could ill afford a verdict to be given against the panel. It would have implicated not only the noble proprietors of Sutherland who sanctioned these proceedings, but also all the leading Highland proprietors throughout the country, who were equally guilty of wholesale evictions.

The chiefs and proprietors claimed an absolute right to their properties (on the Duke of Newcastle's principle of doing what they liked with their own), although that absolute right was contested, and doubtful, in an historical point of view; for the claims of the people composing the Highland clans to a share of the territorial patrimony were ancient and continuous, and gladly acknowledged by the chiefs till the middle of the eighteenth century. Until that time the power of a chief did not consist in the amount of his revenue, but in the number of his clansmen.

There was then no Poor Law, as in England, by which an able-bodied man could claim in his parish support or work. Even now in Scotland, although a Poor Law has been made and the sick and helpless are entitled to relief, yet an able-bodied man cannot claim the privilege of support or work from his parish, as in England. If he fails from want of work, he must either starve or declare himself a pauper, and denude of all furniture and property he possesses.

Immediately after the trial both the Sheriffs were dismissed from their offices, and the clearances went on under Mr. Loch, who became sole manager of the Sutherland estates, and shortly afterwards M.P. for the Northern Burghs.

It is a painful episode, and created a great sensation at the time. It is quite clear that the noble Marquis, and particularly his wife, the chieftainess of Sutherland, meant that by these changes the people should be benefited. But they were absentees, and unfortunately the administration of the estates was placed under the control of men who had no sympathy with apparent idleness, and did not understand the peculiar sentiments and feelings of the Highland people.

General Stewart of Garth, author of "The Manners and Habits of the Highlanders," is very indignant at the treatment of the people in Sutherland. He eulogizes them. He feels certain that, advised by their own chiefs and people, whatever improvements were fixed on could have been carried out without the removal of so valuable a population.

To show the character of the people he states that "the last Earl of Sutherland, at the request of Mr. Pitt in 1759,

agreed to raise a Fencible Regiment, and in a space of nine
days after receiving the letters of service he assembled 1100
men on the lawn at Dunrobin.

" These men were equipped and organized, and with the
Earl at their head they marched into Perth in 1760, an
object of admiration to all who·saw them for their muscular
strength and martial bearing. No less than 260 of these
men were 5 feet 11 inches in height. They continued
embodied for four years; and when in 1763 they marched
back to Sutherland and were reduced, it was found that
during that period not a single individual had been punished,
nor did any one by his conduct disgrace his corps, kindred,
or district."

In like manner in Lord Reay's country a regiment of
800 men was raised in 1792, and placed under the command of Colonel George Mackay of Bighouse. The
General reports that their conduct, discipline, and behaviour were meritorious. They returned to Scotland and
were reduced in 1802.

Then, again, in 1800 a regiment of 600 men, afterwards
increased to 1000, was raised on the Sutherland estates,
Major-General W. Wemyss of Wemyss colonel. General
Stewart says none of the Highland corps is superior to
the 93rd Regiment. "I do not make comparisons in point
of bravery, for if well commanded they are all brave; but
it is in their well-regulated habits, of which so much has
been already said, that the Sutherland Highlanders have for
twenty years preserved an unvaried line of conduct. The
Light Infantry company of this regiment has existed for
nineteen years without having a man punished. This
single fact may be taken as evidence of good morals."

In the meantime Mr. Young proceeded with his improvements. During his short reign of seven years he effected
great changes. He saw the great Post Road completed
from the southern to the northern borders of the county,
and helped by his ingenuity in constructing the great Fleet
Mound. This road became the base of a number of roads
which he constructed into the interior valleys, Kildonan,
Strath Brora, Strathnaver, and Strathfleet. Harbours

were erected at Helmsdale and Brora, where fisheries were established. Farms were laid out and substantially enclosed, farm-steadings everywhere were built, the most improved system of agriculture introduced, and encouragement given for the settlement in the county of skilled labour of every description.

In 1818 the mail-coach ran through the county to the towns of Wick and Thurso, in Caithness.

From the boundary of the county at Bonar Bridge I have explained that a road was constructed by Lairg and Aultnaharra through the interior to Tongue, the residence of Lord Reay; and his lordship availed himself of Mr. Young's advice to rearrange and improve the estates according to the system then prevailing in the Highlands. Mr. Young in 1816 retired from his duties. He told me that he felt it a disagreeable service, but he retired with the entire approval of the noble proprietors, who, to the end of his life, had the highest opinion of his judgment and knowledge.

After the retirement of Mr. Young, Mr. Loch assumed the control of the whole Sutherlandshire estates, and converted still further the mountain districts into sheep farms.

His sphere of influence and action was also in 1828 largely increased by the Marquis of Stafford's acquiring for £190,000 the extensive territory of Lord Reay,* consisting of four parishes on the western side of the county.

---

* Alexander, eighth Baron Reay, born 1775, married April 8th, 1809, Marion, daughter of Colonel Gall, and widow of David Ross, eldest son of Lord Ankerville, Ross-shire, a Lord of Session; and by her, who died in 1865, he had George Alexander Carr, who died in 1811, and Eric, ninth baron, born in 1813, and who died June 2nd, 1875. It was this lord who sold the property, which was said to be much encumbered. The title then went to a cousin, Baron Mackay of d'Ophermert, a Minister of State and Vice-President of the Privy Council of the Kingdom of the Netherlands, who was succeeded by Donald James (born December 22nd, 1839) March 6th, 1876, as eleventh Baron Reay. The eleventh baron has left Holland to reside in this country. He married a few months ago an heiress in the South of Scotland, Mrs. Mitchell of Stow.

This, with the estate of Bighouse adjoining, and sundry other small properties, has enlarged the Duke's estates in Sutherlandshire almost to a principality. According to the agricultural returns, the whole area of his possessions is 1,200,000 acres, and the area of the county is 1,840,000 acres. The gross valuation of all Sutherland just completed (August, 1879) is £89,153; rental of other properties in the county about £8000.

NOTE.—Of course these clearances were long before my time, but I had them fully described to me by Mr. Young and others, and I annex a letter quoted from the *Inverness Courier*, written by a Mr. J. Campbell, who was a party to the eviction he describes :

"We have received a letter from Mr. J. Campbell, The Moss, Lairg, who calls in question certain statements made by Mr. Purves at the Commission, and says that he (the writer) was himself witness of a cruel scene at a place called Aberscross, in Strathfleet. Three crofters, he says, resided near the present Mound Wood. The wife of one of them, named Macdonald, was about to give birth to a child. The factor, along with half a dozen servants, went to burn down the houses.

"'They burned the rest of them ; and this crofter's was the last. He pleaded hard to be left in the house till his wife was well. The factor did not heed him, but ordered the house to be burned over him. The crofter was in the house, determined not to quit until the fire compelled him. The factor told us the plan we were to take—namely, to cut the rafters and then set fire to the thatch. This we did, but I shall never forget the sight. The man, seeing it was now no use to persist, wrapt his wife in the blankets and brought her out. For two nights did that woman sleep in a sheep cot, and on the third night she gave birth to a son. That son, I believe, still lives, and is in America. That is only one instance. I could give many more did space permit.'"

CHAPTER XII.

Sutherlandshire.

Construction of roads and steadings—A contested Wick Election—
Death of the first Duke—The Duchess-Countess at Dunrobin—The
Disruption and refusal of sites—The reclamations of the present
Duke.

MR. LOCH, in his account of the changes and improvements (for which he takes the whole credit and responsibility), shows in a map attached to his book the area of
the county, and how the farms and crofts have been laid
out. About the same period that these arrangements were
carried out, roads were constructed to the extent of 350
miles in every direction throughout the county. New inns
were built, where accommodation of a superior character
has always been provided. Steadings and houses were
erected for the accommodation of the stranger tenants
from the south, and such of the native tacksmen as had
the means of adopting and carrying out the altered system
of agriculture enforced. An entire stop was put to poach-
ing on the rivers and moors and taking the mussels on the
seashore, and now a large revenue is derived from the
salmon fishery, the deer forests, and moors throughout the
county.

To the old Castle of Dunrobin, with its quaint gardens
on the seashore, the Marquis built additions such as to
render it suitable as a summer residence. The second
Duke erected the present magnificent palace and improved
the grounds. It is now one of the finest architectural
structures in Scotland, and Sutherland is, for every pur-

pose of rational enjoyment, as improved and enlightened a county as any in Great Britain.

The large sheep farmers and tacksmen have displayed talent and judgment in the improved management of their stock, and many have acquired fortunes. The smaller tenants are also thriving and comfortable, and to the peasantry that remain there is no want of work. But the sudden and arbitrary manner in which the poor people were cleared from their holdings remains to this day a blot, whether justly or unjustly, on the fair fame of the Sutherland family.

The noble proprietors, however, placed entire belief in the action of Mr. Loch. In the face of all the opinions and protestations against these proceedings he retained their implicit confidence. He was a man of iron will, and seemed to carry out his views with despotic authority.

He cultivated the friendship of the clergymen of the county, and gave them various concessions and advantages. He corresponded with them and others privately on the proposed changes of farms and boundaries, and on the character of applicants, and thereby astonished his factors with his apparent local knowledge. He seemed to possess the absolute disposal of farms and control of the extensive works carried on throughout the county. He had, after 1825, three factors under him : Mr. George Gunn at Golspie, Mr. Horsburgh at Tongue, and Mr. MacIver * at Scourie, all men of talent and integrity.

With all Mr. Loch's authority and power for doing good on so large a scale he was certainly not popular.

I recollect being at Wick in 1852 during an election, when he was canvassing the voters. He and some of his friends were making a house-to-house visitation. A

---

* These gentlemen had salaries of £600 a year, with a residence and some other perquisites; but as there were no resident proprietors on the estates, their hospitalities were a great tax on their means. Indeed, Mr. Gunn's house had more the character of an hotel than a private residence, and it could not be avoided. Hence poor Gunn got into difficulties before his death. He was very gentlemanly, much liked by the people, and was much in the confidence of the family, almost constantly dining at the castle when the family were there.

H

number of the people followed them, preceded by a man
dressed in a peculiar manner as a ground officer bearing a
drawn sword, and behind four men carrying a board on
their shoulders, on which was fixed the model of a half-
burned Highland cottage.   When he entered a house they
stopped till he came out, and followed him all over the
town, the mob imitating the baa-ing of sheep.   It was a
painful and degrading spectacle.

At the time of his death, in 1855, I happened to be
travelling through Sutherland when the news arrived, and
along the whole course of my journey through the county
I was asked in quiet, exulting whispers, "Did you hear the
news ?   Loch is dead ! "

Mr. Loch was Member of Parliament for the Northern
Burghs, and a Commissioner for the Caledonian Canal, the
Highland Roads, and the Board of Fisheries.   He was
highly esteemed in the south for his practical business
talent.   He was one of the Whig clique in Edinburgh who
managed the politics of Scotland when the Whigs were in
power.

To the noble house of Sutherland he was a faithful and
attached servant in managing their vast estates and
immense monetary transactions.   He opposed successfully,
on behalf of Lord Stafford, the first bill for the Liverpool
and Manchester Railway; and ultimately, to protect the
interests of the Bridgewater Canal, secured two permanent
seats at the Railway Board (now the London and North
Western) with a holding of stock of £200,000, which soon
after increased to £400,000.   In private life he bore an
exemplary character.   But to this day in the North he
bears a bad reputation for the share he had in the clearances of Sutherland.

The Marquis of Stafford was created Duke of Sutherland
in 1833.   He died the same year at the age of seventy-five,
and was buried in Dornoch Cathedral with great pomp and
ceremony.   The large sheep farmers and tenantry erected
a herculean statue as a memorial to his memory on Ben
Bhraggie.

The Duchess-Countess after his death paid a yearly visit

in autumn to Dunrobin. She was proud of her great county and its improved condition, and took much interest in the welfare of the people that remained.

When at Dunrobin, in accordance with the custom of the chiefs of old, she used every Monday to hold a court on the lawn in front of the castle. There the people were invited to lay their grievances and complaints before her, and there her factors and officers attended to explain and give an account of their stewardship.

Many anecdotes are told of the proceedings at these primitive courts. The lady read the petitions of the people, listened to their stories, and adjusted their differences. She examined and cross-examined both parties in a dispute most acutely, and then and there in each case gave such directions or such summary verdicts as seemed most just to her own highly cultivated and intelligent mind.

On some of these occasions curious scenes naturally occurred, one or two of which may be chronicled here. There was an old salmon fisher in the village of Brora, Alexander or Sandy Urquhart by name, who was a great favourite with the Duchess, and whose outspokenness she greatly enjoyed. He had for several Mondays in succession approached her in her chair of justice with a petition— or what Ritchie Moniplies calls a " bit sufflication "—for (I think) some lease or letter which would give him additional security of tenure in his house or "holding" at Brora. The Countess had always put him off with promises that he was quite safe, that he would never be disturbed in his possession.

This, however, did not satisfy Sandy, and he continued to appear before her, strongly urging her to give him a written document to make matters quite secure. Again and again he besought her for the coveted letter, but her answer was still the same—"Don't trouble yourself, Sandy; it is all right, you are all safe"—till at last poor Sandy gave up his case in despair, and exclaimed, scratching his ear as he left her presence, " Weel, weel, my Lady, your hand o' write ye'll no give, and your word is no worth a d——n."

Sometimes the guests who happened to be in the castle

attended this kind of court, standing round the Countess's chair; and this on one occasion gave rise to an amusing scene.

Some repairs had been done to the manse of Rogart by James Douglas, a plasterer in the village of Golspie. The then minister of the parish was the Rev. John Mackenzie. Douglas rendered his bill to the minister, who declined payment on the ground that manses were the property of the "heritors," who were bound to maintain and keep them in repair—"the heritors" in this case being, of course, the Countess of Sutherland.

He then tendered it at the Dunrobin office, where again payment was refused by the factor on the ground that he had not ordered the repairs to be done. Between the two, the poor tradesman was likely to lose his money altogether, so he resolved to apply direct to head-quarters on the next Monday morning.

Now it so happened that this same Rev. Mr. Mackenzie preached before the Countess on Sunday in the church at Golspie, and, according to invariable custom, he was asked to dine at Dunrobin Castle and remain there all night. He did so, and accompanied the Countess on the Monday morning when she went to "sit in the gate."

By and by, James Douglas came forward and told his story, dwelling on the hardship of his case, and requesting a decision as to how he was to be paid. The Countess then turned to the clergyman, and asked him to give his version of the matter. He evidently did not like the situation, particularly to state that she, as heritor, was by law bound to pay; but he was forced to reply, and gave a totally different account of the affair from what the plasterer had represented it to be.

The Countess then turned to Douglas and said, "Well, James, you have heard Mr. Mackenzie; what have you to say now?" For a moment James looked rather perplexed, and then he electrified the whole assembly; Countess and all, by the grimness of his answer—"Weel, my Lady, all I say is, there is one of us two telling a lie, and I know it's no me."

In 1843 the country was startled with the disruption of the Church of Scotland, when some 500 members of the Established Church threw up their livings. Out of thirteen parishes in Sutherlandshire, twelve abandoned their livings, and the people approved of and followed their clergymen.*

I happened to be staying with Mr. Gunn when he received Mr. Loch's instructions how the factors were to act. Mr. Gunn remarked to me how ungrateful these clergymen were to the Duke and Mr. Loch after all the kindness and favour so universally shown them.

I observed that this might be an ultimate advantage to the county; that as it was the duty of all ministers to preach morality and good conduct, they would have now twenty-four clergymen instead of twelve for this duty. The course for the Duke, in my opinion, would be to give

---

* All the ministers of the Church of Scotland must be well-educated men; but in propagating the doctrines of the gospel some adopt the literal meaning of the Scriptures, ignoring the new doctrine of evolution and non-existence of eternal punishment, as promulgated by Darwin, Canon Farrar, and others. Of course the Disruption caused much excitement, and also much talk throughout the country, and no doubt much pain and misery to the ministers who deprived themselves of their livings. It was said that one of these Sutherland ministers, in discussing the sacrifice they had made for conscience' sake, mentioned that no man had made greater sacrifices than he had, for besides the comfortable manse and glebe he had vacated he had to relinquish a snug farm requiring three pairs of horses, as well as the honour of a dinner twice a year with the Duke of Sutherland. He ended by asking, "What were the sacrifices the Apostle Peter made compared to these? A coble and a few nets!"

The same man, who is now a popular minister in his new parish, was solemnizing a marriage at which I was present. As far as I recollect, his address to the young couple was as follows :—

" The institution of marriage was established between two persons, because there were only two persons in the world when marriage was instituted. The angels were superior to man, and the beasts were inferior to man, and there was no companion for man; so God made a deep sleep to fall on Adam that he might feel no pain, and he took a rib out of his side, and out of that rib he made a woman, and gave her to Adam to be a helpmeet for him, and from that day a good wife was a gift from God."

facilities and encourage the party who effected most good
in the parish.

"No," said Mr. Gunn, "the recusants shall not have an
inch of land in the county to build either house or church;
and when they discover this they will soon find it convenient to leave the country." Meetings for worship were
consequently forbidden in any part of the Duke's territories.

What was the result? On the road-sides, and on the
sea beach between high and low water mark, the Free
Church clergy held worship and preached to the people.
The Established churches were empty, and the feelings of
the population in Sutherlandshire were hurt and indignant
by the tales of hardship and misery to which their
favourite clergymen and their families were exposed.

Then came the persecution of the schoolmasters (a school
being established by law in each parish in Scotland), most
of whom followed the clergymen and adhered to the Free
Church. The new Presbyteries called the schoolmasters
with Free Church proclivities to account, and summarily
dismissed them for their defection. Then the parents
would not send their children to the new schoolmasters,
and sites would not be conceded for a Free Church school,
so that for a considerable time most of the children in the
county were in a fair way of being left wholly uneducated.

A great sensation was created throughout the country by
these persecutions, and the subject was brought before the
Free Church General Assembly. The worthy Duke and
even Mr. Loch crouched under the eloquent invective of
Dr. Chalmers, and the result was that his Grace and Mr.
Loch were obliged to approach the leaders of the Free
Church and offer unconditionally sites and accommodation
for churches, manses, and schools in all the parishes
vacated in the county.

Many proprietors in other counties also refused sites
to the Free Church, and made themselves very unpopular. They were all ultimately compelled to yield, but
the secession in Sutherland was universal and marked, for
the remedy was in the hands of one man, and the proceedings are an evidence of the high-handed manner of
Mr. Loch's administration.

The feeling of proprietors at the time was that the disruption tended to shake one of the principles of our constitution, the union of Church and State.

I have no doubt the second Duke, who was a benevolent and good man, was much troubled at the unenviable notoriety he acquired by this untoward treatment of the clergy. Following so soon after the painful consequences of the clearances, it must have been to him a source of very unpleasant reflection.

A feeling of sympathy began early to spread in favour of the Highlanders, and disgust at the arbitrary acts of the Highland proprietors. The Duke felt, and the public perceived, that the policy of the clearances so suddenly and rigidly enforced was a grievous blunder. His Grace accordingly deemed it his duty to intimate to all the great sheep farmers on his estates that, at the termination of their leases, it was his intention to subdivide the farms and reduce their size to more reasonable dimensions ; * but he added that it was his wish, when the subdivision took place, that the present tenantry should have a preference of the reduced farms.†

I recollect Mr. Sellar (whom I met one day while travelling from Elgin) alluding to this new order. He told me that in replying to the Duke's letter he said that the lease of his farm extended over, I think, thirteen years from that time, and he expected by its termination that his Grace and he would both be in their graves ; so that it mattered little to him what new arrangements his Grace now proposed to make.

It was as he predicted : they were both dead before the termination of Mr. Sellar's lease. But I thought at the time it was not only in bad taste but an ungrateful answer, seeing how the family held by him when he was pro-

* Many of them were of vast extent, grazing some 12,000 and 20,000 sheep.

† This was never carried out. The Duke died before it could take effect, and I believe his successor found it would involve much expense in new steadings and buildings.

secuted, notwithstanding the odium which they acquired by the clearances. Yet Mr. Sellar was an intelligent and able man, and exemplary in his domestic relations, bringing up and highly educating a large family, many of whom have risen to distinction. He acquired by his talents in sheep farming a very considerable fortune.

Mr. Loch entered into the arrangements for the improvement of Sutherlandshire with certain theories which experience has proved erroneous. One was that, " owing to the moist and sharp air and exposure to the sea breezes," the country was unsuited to the rapid growth of timber, especially near to the sea coast. This was an unfortunate mistake, to which the magnificent timber on the sea-shore surrounding Dunrobin Castle ought to have given a practical contradiction.

Mr. Young told me that when he entered on the administration of the estates in 1811, he recommended that the Dornoch moors, a vast extent of barren heath extending for many miles in every direction, should be planted ; and if this had been done then, that part of the country would by this time have been covered with a great and valuable forest of timber. Subsequently this land was partially planted (some thirty years ago), and gives evidence of becoming of great value.

Indeed, Sutherlandshire presents in many places a most admirable field for extensive plantations. The climate is in many parts superior to Strathspey, a valley in the Highlands which has produced, and is now producing, as fine timber as any in the kingdom.

Another mistaken idea was that the valleys and mountain-sides of Sutherland were unsuited for arable culture. Mr. Loch states that " the air in the evenings among the mountains was very cold, piercing, and chilly, frequently accompanied with mildews and early frosts, which, sweeping down the courses of the burns and the glens, destroy every kind of crop and cultivated vegetable."

This view is not entertained at the present day, for the present Duke has entered on a very extensive scheme of reclaiming land at Lairg, and has cleared the valley of

Kildonan for arable cultivation in the centre of the county, and it is said with the intention of largely increasing in a similar manner reclamation in other districts.

The schemes of reclamation have attracted public attention and excited universal approval throughout the country.

A report has been made on these reclamations by the president, secretary, and a deputation of six directors from the Scottish Chamber of Agriculture. In July, 1878, they visited these works; first those at Lairg, which extend to 2000 acres and are divided into five farms. The party were much pleased with the appearance of the growing crops, and the admirable manner in which the whole arrangements had been laid in that quarter. From Lairg the visitors proceeded to Uppat, where they saw fine timber and excellent crops of all kinds, showing clearly that the climate of the county of Sutherland was not unfavourable to the growth of the best agricultural crops.

From thence they visited Kildonan, where the process of reclamation was somewhat different from that which had been followed at Lairg, arising from the improved implements now at work.

The Kildonan reclamations are being executed at considerably less cost than at Lairg, both on account of the improved implements and the experience acquired in working.

The cost of reclaiming in this quarter—in liming, fencing, road making, and buildings, including draining where necessary—was not expected to exceed £25 per acre; but the cost, it was said, of the Lairg improvements amounted in all to £130,000. From what the parties saw, and from the physical conformation of the country, all were satisfied "that there was nothing in the climate which prejudicially affected vegetable growth in this county."

It is fortunate that his Grace has entered upon these reclamations, because there cannot be a doubt that an increased quantity of arable land for winter feeding will enhance very materially the value of the Sutherland estates.

His Grace has a great predilection for mechanics, and has fortunately the means of applying mechanical science on a

large scale to the cultivation of the land ; but hitherto
these mechanical appliances have not tended to economy.
The deputation reported that his Grace had laid out in
these reclaiming implements and machinery no less than
£50,000. Hitherto reclamations in the Highlands on an
extensive scale, such as at Ardross, were carried out effectively by manual labour, and have not exceeded from £10
to £15 per acre. It is possible that the Sutherland improvements have been more perfectly done.

There is no doubt that experience has shown that a
certain portion of arable land is desirable for the carrying
out of sheep farming, and now throughout the whole Highlands sheep farmers look out for " wintering," as it is
called, for the maintenance of the weak and one-year-old
sheep of their flocks. These are sent down to cultivated
land in the low countries, where they are fed on turnips
and grass during the winter months, and are thus preserved.

If these arrangements were not carried out they would
die of cold or want of food on the mountains, the strong
sheep and sheep of maturer age only being able to with-
stand the hardships of wintering on their native ground.
Hence all sheep farmers whose possessions are in a high
and exposed locality find it profitable to search out a wintering, and in early winter time there is a general exodus
of young and weak sheep to the low country farms and
pastures.

George Granville, the second Duke of Sutherland, succeeded to the English estates on the death of his father in
1833, and to the Scotch honours and estates on the death
of his mother in 1839.

He married Lady Harriet Elizabeth Georgina, third
daughter of the sixth Earl of Carlisle. She was one
of the most beautiful women in England, a lady of tact,
great taste, and a distinguished ornament, for many years,
of the court of Queen Victoria. The Duke was very
handsome, and mild and kindly in disposition, but from
his infirmity of deafness he led a domesticated and
retired life, and did not take an active interest in public
affairs. He seems to have resigned to Mr. Loch, even more

directly than his father, the administration of his vast estates. He had great taste in architecture, and laid out large sums in rebuilding and ornamenting Trentham Hall in Stafford-shire, furnishing and decorating the palace of Stafford House in London, and altering and almost rebuilding the Castle of Dunrobin, besides other structures.

This latter noble structure is situated on the east coast of the county on a high wooded bank, overlooking the sea, commanding an extensive view of the opposite coast of the Moray Firth. It has a beautiful park, extending for many miles, of varied woodland, mountain, village, and farm.

On one occasion when in Sutherland, Mr. Loch, who resided at Uppat House, three miles from Dunrobin, in-vited me to dine with him to meet several gentlemen in the neighbourhood. Mr. Gunn, the factor, drove me to Uppat, and we called at the castle for the Duke's doctor, who was to be one of the party.

On my inquiring after the Duke's health, I said, "I was going to call upon him next day." He said, "He will be glad to see you; but do not stay long, for he is not very well." He said, "It is very hard; I prescribed a pill for him to be taken at night, and a draught in the morning. But his valet gave his Grace the draught at night, and the pill in the morning, and the Duke was of course worse instead of better." The doctor groaned in the spirit at the valet's irregularities.

I could not help reflecting that this was an instance of the disadvantage of being a great Duke, and having a doctor and some forty domestics to one's self. In humbler life such a mistake is not likely to occur.

CHAPTER XIII.

General Remarks on the Clearances in the Highlands.

THE clearances in Sutherlandshire came before the public prominently on account of the large number of people removed, the great extent of the country, and the sudden manner in which the evictions were carried out.

Unfortunately, before these changes and improvements in Sutherlandshire were projected, and during a considerable period while they were in progress, the noble proprietors were absentees. They had never seen the country except many years before, on a flying visit after their marriage, and apparently they were ignorant of the character, manners, and peculiarities of the people. Moreover, they moved in an aristocratic atmosphere, acquiescing naturally in great results, the general arrangements and details being left very much to the judgment and prudence of confidential agents.

The noble proprietors would be told that the only way permanently to improve the country was to remove the people. This was done elsewhere with much advantage to proprietors, and Mr. Loch would feel that as there was no Poor Law then in Scotland, it was unnecessary to deal more tenderly with the people of Sutherlandshire than other landholders in the Highlands who were similarly situated.

Moreover the agents entrusted with effecting these changes were active and energetic, not over sentimental, and rendered impatient by the passive resistance with which measures of improvement, so advantageous in their eyes, were viewed by the native population. The great object of the officials seemed to be to appropriate the land so as to increase the rental, without the slightest consideration for the feelings or the welfare of the people, and hard-hearted and cruel acts were done. To the disgrace of the clergy of that day they took the part of the oppressors.

There is no reason to doubt the benevolent intentions and desires of the noble proprietors, whose conduct in England displayed great consideration for their people. Besides, whatever necessity or imaginary necessity there was for harsh proceedings in other parts of the Highlands, no excuse of this sort could be pleaded in the county of Sutherland, for the fortunes of the Marquis and his lady were colossal, and increased money rents were, or should have been, to them a matter of little or no importance. Indeed, we may assume this from the vast sums they subsequently laid out on the works and improvements of the estates, without any apparent expectation of adequate return.

In a speech by Mr. Loch in the House of Commons, on June 31st, 1845, while defending his conduct in regard to these evictions, he pointed out the self-sacrifice displayed by his employers in benefiting the country. He stated that the whole rentals of these estates from 1811 to 1833, twenty-two years, besides £60,000 sent from England, were laid out on these improvements and changes.

The rental about this time was from £45,000 to £50,000 a year, and at £45,000 that outlay would amount to a capital sum of £1,050,000.

The friends of the people maintain that the expenditure of this large sum, along with some pains taken in the training of the younger portion of the population by the tacksmen and their natural superiors, whose guidance they would willingly have accepted, would have resulted in improvements as valuable; while a brave and industrious race might have been trained to civil habits, and preserved to the country with all their native fidelity and good qualities.

Unfortunately this view was not entertained or appreciated, and Sutherland has been changed and improved at the expense of much unnecessary suffering and misery to its aboriginal inhabitants.

A Highlander was assumed by the administrators of the Marquis and many others to be an ignorant and incorrigible idler, and was treated as such. Even Mrs. Grant, of Laggan, a friend of the Highlanders, says in her poetic style, " As well might you harness a deer to the plough as a Highlander to patient and regular employment." No doubt an aboriginal Highlander was an idler ; he had no inducement to be otherwise. He had been bred in idleness, and neither by example nor precept did he see any advantage in persistent hard work. But Mrs. Grant's remark may apply with equal force to any man even in a civilized community, particularly if he is of mature age and fixed habits.

I deny that a Highland peasant is not an industrious man, if the advantages of industry are made clear to him.

I have had fifty years' experience of Highlanders, in all parts of the country, and can testify to their fidelity and industry if properly treated. They are much superior to south country people of the same class in intelligence, and are of a grave, religious, and poetic temperament.

I have had under me some very able men, whose fidelity and talent were above all price. In domestic life there is no servant like a Highlander, once properly trained.

As to the upper classes, the chiefs of clans and proprietors, one cannot resist a feeling of admiration in witnessing the high spirit, the talent, the noble and disinterested traits of character, displayed by many of these gentlemen at the time of the Rebellions in 1715 and 1745. Afterwards also, when in command of the Highland regiments which they were induced to raise, and in the battles of their country in which they were engaged, they continued to maintain the same distinguished character for those high qualities.

Yet no sooner was law established, and communication throughout the country with the southern portion of the kingdom completed, than the nature and the conduct of these Highland proprietors seemed to have entirely changed.

From that time they seem to have felt their people to be an incumbrance, the old feudal and patriarchal feelings appear to have vanished, and their chief object seemed to be to increase their rentals irrespective of their duties as proprietors.

They appear to have been fascinated and enervated by the blandishments of southern society, and their inordinate pride (for pride is inherent in all Highlanders) led them to vie with southern proprietors of greater revenues and more valuable estates.

Some also had been trained and educated in England, and had no tastes like their ancestors for a residence in their native glens and among their own people.

They likewise required increased rents to gratify their newly acquired tastes for expenditure and luxury, and to maintain what they considered their high position as Highland chiefs and proprietors of extended territories.

Then came the bonds and deeds, which, until the roads were made, nobody would take, except in special cases on estates by the sea coast, and the increased rents from the sheep farms led too frequently to increased debts and obligations.*

Absolute power was assumed in dealing with their property, the people were held of no account, and the stern arm of the law maintained the proprietors' rights and sanctioned crofters' evictions. Sad were the evictions, for eviction from a Highland farm was a very different affair from the removal of a cottar in the south of Scotland, or in England. There either a small farm or work could be obtained without much difficulty. But a family removed in the Highlands from their remote glen or mountain-side knew not where to go. They were ignorant of any country beyond their own, and work or labour in the

* Along the Hebrides and the western shores of Scotland where kelp suddenly produced such increased rents, the sudden wealth led to the ruin of almost all the proprietors.

ordinary sense could only be obtained by removing to a vast distance, and that with great uncertainty.

Even if they did remove their families, their rude and scanty furniture was of no value except in the hut for which it was adapted.

Hence the greatest possible distress was experienced by families, particularly if they were encumbered, as they often were, with old or sick members and children.

Great numbers were removed bodily throughout the country, and the houses and crofts of such as were to remain were often changed for the convenience of sheep farmers to some remote and uncultivated corner of the estate.

Sad were the efforts of the people to stay in the old and much-loved locality, and the wonder is that, considering the thousands of able-bodied men and their families evicted, there was no loss of life from resistance or riot. As a matter of fact, however, there was no disturbance of any significance.

Some proprietors gave able-bodied men possession for seven or ten years of five or ten acres of bare moor at 1s. per acre a year, with perhaps timber to build a house.

If the man was industrious or fortunate in building a cottage, trenching, draining, and farming his croft, the agreement might be renewed at an increased rent of five shillings or ten shillings an acre ; but as, generally, several crofts were in proximity, the people got notice to quit at the end of their first tack. The crofts were then united into one farm, and let to a stranger for perhaps one pound an acre.

More frequently a poor fellow, after struggling with his croft, and cultivating more than half, abandoned it in despair, the proprietor reaping the benefit of all the labour expended on it perhaps for several years.

In very few cases were leases given. The poor people merely obtained possession from year to year at the pleasure of the laird, although, according to the custom of the country, leases were invariably given to the larger tenants.

I have alluded throughout this narrative to the hardships suffered by the Highlanders when they were evicted for the establishment of sheep farms.

The evictions are now chiefly for game and deer, the passion for sport having greatly enhanced the value of mountain property in the Highlands. When a deer forest is fixed on, such of the inhabitants as remain are unhesitatingly cleared away.

Indeed, many sheep farms are now converted into deer forests in all parts of the northern counties, so that instead of the bleating of sheep, and the solitary shepherd and his dog, we have now a large part of territory under game and deer, rendering the solitude of these regions still more oppressive, except to the enthusiastic sportsman and his few friends. This change is held to be more objectionable even than sheep farms, as diminishing the food-producing territory of the country.

As an evidence of how evictions are made on account of game, I may draw attention to a recent case in Ross-shire, stated in a letter in the " Inverness Advertiser."

" Mr. Tennant's evidence before the Game Law Committee appears most unfair.

" Both adjoining proprietors, according to the evidence, did not hesitate to remove tenants when it interfered with their favourite sports.

" Mr. Tennant was Lord Hill's agent when the Garton tenants were removed. They had lived on their farms for generations; they paid their rents regularly, and a more worthy, respectable tenantry did not exist in the country."

Another case came under my own notice years ago, while travelling through a valley in a large estate, on the west of Inverness-shire, purchased by a sportsman.

To extend his deer forest, he felt it convenient to remove a certain number of the people. Some went south, others found employment elsewhere; but one unfortunate fellow, with no means and a family, was in great perplexity where to go. In despair he took possession of a gravel-pit by the side of the public road.

I happened to pass, and saw some pretty little children

I

playing on the wayside, and in the gravel-pit adjoining there was a temporary tent of blankets, with various pieces of house furniture lying beside it. As superintendent of the roads and claiming authority over the gravel-pit, I asked the woman, who had a child in her arms, why they had planted themselves down there.

She said they had been removed from their croft and house by the laird. Her husband knew not where to go, so they took possession of the pit, where they had remained for the last three weeks during very cold weather. They had no alternative, for they were not allowed to remain longer on the estate, and her husband (whom I afterwards ascertained to be a respectable man) had nothing for it but to put his family here on the roadside, which it was supposed the laird could not claim, as it was assumed to be part of the road and public property.

Her husband was then, she said, "down the country," at a village some thirty miles away, to see whether he could get work, and a house to shelter his children.

I recollect, on one of my first journeys in Skye in 1825–26, travelling along the Drynoch road then in progress, and which extends between Sligachan and Dunvegan through an interesting and comparatively fertile valley.

A year or two before, it had been cleared of the tenantry, to the number of 1500 souls. They had emigrated, and the whole valley was converted into two great sheep farms.

The ruined cottages and green spots of the once cultivated crofts were to be seen scattered on the hill sides, indicating the sites of the abodes of the expatriated families; but all was then a solitude, and nothing was heard by the passing traveller but the bleating of sheep.

The laird in this case, instead of living among his people, resided in a distant part of the country, and spent large sums in futile parliamentary contests, which laid the foundation of the ultimate misfortunes of his ancient house. And thus gradually our gallant, religious, and faithful peasantry have been year by year cleared from the Highlands, until now labourers in many parts can scarcely be got to do the ordinary work necessary for the cultivation of land or the business of the country.*

Many years ago also I was witness to a sad scene at a place called Uig in Skye—the departure of emigrants for America.

When emigrants first sailed from the Highlands, many deaths and much misery arose from their being huddled together without the necessary room, and also from the inadequate supply of provisions provided on board the ships to meet the contingencies of an uncertain voyage.

A public outcry arose in regard to these defects, and afterwards no vessel was allowed to quit the country with emigrants until she was inspected by a Government officer, who had to certify as to the sufficiency of both her accommodation and provisions. The Government officer on this occasion was from the Customs at Inverness, and I happened accidentally to accompany him on his inspection.

As I have said, it was a sad scene. The day was beautiful, and the graceful vessel floated on the calm sea in the bay, unconscious of the agitated feelings of the poor people crowding on her decks.

There was a crowd on shore as well as on board. It consisted mainly of able-bodied people and their children who were to go, and the evidences of grief among the parties departing and those remaining were heartrending.

The old people and their neighbours sat on the shore with expressions of deep sorrow. Powerful men could be seen with the tears streaming down their cheeks, and the hysterical grief of the women as they embraced and bade adieu to each other was most painful.

The accommodation on board was very rough. The

---

* *November,* 1877.—This year, by continued rains, the crops in the Highlands, although most abundant, had not ripened till about this time. The farmers had only their ordinary staff for harvest work, and of course the produce of the year had to lie in the fields for weeks in some parts, under continued rain and snow, for want of extra people to gather it in.

Throughout the Highlands, wherever any extra work is to be done there is now the greatest difficulty to obtain labourers.

whole lower decks were cleared, and two rows of sleeping berths were erected on each side of the ship. The centre was piled with boxes, bags, chests, &c. Into this den—for it could not be called anything else—were huddled some 200 or 300 men, women, and children. Accommodation for emigration is much better now, but still there is much room for improvement.

I will allude to one other instance of eviction. I abstract it from the Memorials of Lord Cockburn, one of the Justiciary Lords of the Court of Session.

SEPTEMBER 27, 1849.

"This year" (he says), "except a most atrocious case of murder at Aberdeen, the most memorable thing was a case of rioting and deforcement, &c., at Inverness against four poor respectable men, who had been active in a Highland clearing in North Uist.

"The popular feeling is so strong against these (as I think necessary but odious) operations, that I was afraid of an acquittal, which would have been unjust and mischievous. On the other hand, even the law had no sympathy with the exercise of legal rights in a cruel way.

"The jury solved the difficulty by first convicting by a majority, and then adding this written, and therefore well-considered, recommendation :

"'The jury unanimously recommend the panels to the utmost leniency and mercy of the court, in consideration of the cruel, though it must be said legal, proceedings adopted in ejecting the whole people of Solas from their houses and crofts without the prospect of shelter, or the means of expatriating them to a foreign land.'

"That statement," says his lordship, "will ring all over the country. We shall not soon cease to hear of this calm and judicious censure of incredible, but proved, facts.

"For it was established—first, that warrants of ejectment had been issued against about sixty tenants, being the whole tenantry of this district of Solas, and comprehending probably about 300 people—warrants which the agents of the owners had certainly a right to demand, and the Sheriff was bound to grant.

"Secondly, that the people had sown and were entitled to reap their crops.

"Thirdly, that there were no houses provided for them to take shelter in, no poor-house, no ships. They had nothing but the bare ground, or rather the hard wet beach, to lie down upon.

"It was said, or rather insinuated, that arrangements had been made for them, and, in particular, that a ship was to have been on the coast. But in the meantime the hereditary roofs were to be pulled down, and the mother and her children had only the shore to sleep on.

Fireless, woodless, hopeless, resistance was surely not unnatural, and it was very slight.

"I am sorry for the owner whose name, he being the landlord, was used, but who personally was quite ignorant. He was in the hands of his creditors, and they of his factor.

"But the landlord will get all the abuse. The slightness of the punishment, four months' imprisonment" [not so slight] "will probably abate the public fury."

Lord Cockburn need not have been so reticent in regard to the name of the owner or landlord. Godfrey, (General) Lord Macdonald was the owner, an absentee, who, on his accession to his paternal estates, handed over the management to law agents.

The management has been twice or thrice changed since then, but is still in the hands of law agents, men of honour, no doubt; but what can an Edinburgh or Aberdeen lawyer do, who is an absentee himself, but enforce the collection of rents, and obtain as large a revenue as the lands will afford, or the people can be made to pay.

Since then North Uist has been sold to Sir John Orde, the rental in 1872 being £4975; and Kilmuir, on the mainland of Skye, to Mr. Fraser, the rental £6250. They were part of the Macdonald estates; but the rental in Skye is still recorded at £11,613, a revenue which might have spared the people such treatment as above described.

I have alluded to debts incurred by proprietors on the opening up of the country.

In the beginning of the century, as I have said, however much Highland proprietors were disposed to sell an estate, unless it were to a native who had returned from abroad with a fortune, nobody would buy, communication being so indifferent or so difficult as to afford little temptation—even to sportsmen. Moors were then of no monetary value. It was at first, as I have said, considered mean and below the dignity of a proprietor to take money for either snooting or fishing.

Still less was a Highland estate an object of interest as a land speculation.

Some gentlemen in Edinburgh, who had ventured im-

mediately after the roads were made in 1826–28 to purchase lands in Ross-shire as a speculation, were ruined by
their adventure; although, if kept till now, they would
have realized more than cent. per cent. upon the purchase
price.

No doubt, on the opening up of the country and other
changes, including the enlargement and improvement of
arable farms, and the adoption of sheep farms, a great impetus was given to general improvement throughout the
Highlands. The country was not so completely depopu-
lated as to retard very considerable material progress;
and there was a general advance in comfort and civilization.

But this was of little advantage to the proprietors. Their
debts continued to accumulate; and their increased revenues,
instead of going either to improve their lands or the condition of their people, were in most instances appropriated
to pay the interest on their bonds, or wasted on the gratifi-
cations of more luxurious living.

The depopulation of the country, the rapid increase of
rents and the consequent changes, have caused the ruin of
many of the proprietors; and when they removed the
people, they never expected that so many of themselves
would soon have to follow their tenants into exile.

I have seen nearly two-thirds of the estates in the Highlands in my time change proprietors. The properties of
families who for ages held a distinguished place in the
country, and brought up their children with credit and
honour, are now in the hands of strangers.

Even in Sutherlandshire most of the old proprietors are
gone. The country is improved and civilized in an eminent
degree; but the evictions are still remembered with heart-
burnings, and continue a fixed stain on the fair fame of
the otherwise benevolent lords of Sutherland.

The public works promoted by the Government, and
which were mainly designed to stop emigration and to
provide employment for the people deprived of their
holdings, had apparently a different effect.

Doubtless the Caledonian Canal afforded employment and
industrious training for a series of years to thousands of

Highland labourers, but curiously enough the construction of roads rather promoted the clearances than prevented them. For as peaceful possession and ready access were established in these remote localities by means of the roads, the store farmers in the south soon appreciated the advantages and profit of a sheep farm in the Highlands, and the people were for years without hesitation removed from the possessions they had held for centuries to make way for these new arrangements.

I have perhaps alluded more at large to the clearances of the Highlands than I might have done.

A great part of the country is now converted into large sheep farms or deer forests, and consequently the tenantry are almost wholly removed, and are yet being removed. Similar changes have gone on among the agricultural population in the southern counties of Scotland, arising from the altered system of agriculture called " high farming." There is now in these southern counties little or no gradation of tenantry as heretofore. There are now comparatively few of that unpretending class of well-to-do respectable people, peasant farmers, who with their families, or with some additional aid, worked their farms—persons who brought up their children to be people of character, often of education; and who, when they entered the outer world, earned for their country a distinguished name for sterling qualities wherever they were settled.

In no part of Great Britain has improved agriculture been carried out in so perfect a manner as in the Lothians, Berwickshire, and the neighbouring counties. There the country is laid out entirely in large farms. Every corner is in high culture.

There are now scarcely any gowany braes to be seen in that part of Scotland. Great capital has been invested by the farmers — the utmost appliances of chemical and mechanical skill have been brought to bear on the land— and farms in these counties have become vast manufactories of agricultural produce.

Under the above arrangement the inhabitants are sparse, certainly not happier or more contented. The rents are of course greatly increased, but the proprietors have become still more a separate class with not much communion of feeling, living apart from their tenants.

The tenants in these great farms are men of capital and education. Most of them keep hunters, but although they are very intelligent some are not over-refined, although of course there are many exceptions. The labourers are no better than serfs. They are called "hinds," and are doomed to labour for ever, without relaxation, and with no hope of advancement.

From what I have seen, the three classes have little in common. Each exacts as much as he can from the other, and the kind and affectionate feeling, and interest in the well-being of each which I have seen where farming is less perfect, is scarcely perceptible, if it exists at all, among the high-farming class of the population. In fact, "high farming" in these counties seems to have improved out of existence all but the capitalist and the labourer.

It is not my province to discuss an important political question. But it appears to me that the land tenure of Scotland is most unsatisfactory. Lord Cairns' Bill of last year has, however, advanced a great step in the right direction.

Scotland, in fact, does not belong to the people of Scotland. They are permitted to reside in it, and practise their callings, but they appear to be merely tenants at will. Beyond the feu of a house or villa, or the small space assigned as their last resting-place, few of the population can claim as property any part of their native soil.

Although our kingdom contains upwards of three and a half millions of inhabitants, who are supposed from their education to be the most enlightened and intelligent people in Europe, yet they possess no interest in the territory of Scotland. One-half of their country is owned by seventy proprietors, while nine-tenths belongs to seventeen hundred persons.

One proprietor owns 1,326,000 acres, besides 32,095 acres in England. A second has 431,000 acres; a third, 424,000; a fourth, 373,000; and a fifth, 306,000, &c.

Twelve proprietors own 4,339,422 acres, or nearly a quarter of the whole of Scotland.*

Then, again, these great Scotch estates seem unmanageable. With all the good qualities and talents of many of the proprietors, most of them appear helpless in regard to their pecuniary transactions.

They are almost all in straitened circumstances, and consequently cannot do justice to the improvements of the country or the land they possess. Notwithstanding their great revenues, they are mainly dependent on their lawyers for the administration of their affairs. This is greatly owing to the extent of their estates, the law of primogeniture, and the fetters of entail and settlement.

This state of affairs does not benefit the parties for whose advantage the laws have been made. While proprietors of entailed estates with large revenues are in pecuniary difficulties, their children, bred in their fathers' mansions in every luxury, are sent forth into the world to exist in a state of genteel beggary.

The junior branches of these families did good service formerly in the army, navy, and civil employment, and it is to be hoped will still continue to do so. Even this resource is partly closed to them, for they have now to compete for these employments with the aspiring and ambitious youths of the whole nation.

The injustice of leaving the whole of a great estate to the eldest son, to the great detriment of the junior members of the family, is now acknowledged throughout the greater part of Europe. It is to be hoped ere long some plan may be devised for a more equal and legal distribution of the territory of the country among the families of its legitimate owners. I have known very painful hardships suffered by younger sons of great proprietors, and serious loss to the public, from this state of things.

One feels, no doubt, a sentimental regret in witnessing the decay or extinction of old families ; but it is the doom of

* See Blue Book of 1872 containing the acres and rentals of all the landed estates in Scotland.

men, of cities, and countries to decay, and it is in vain to
struggle against what God has decreed.

The above was written in 1879. Since that time, Great
Britain has been visited with a succession of more bad harvests. Through this, with the overwhelming importations of
food from America, Australia, &c., the price of agricultural
produce has been lowered, and much distress has been felt
by the farming interests of the country. Many farms in
consequence have been thrown on the proprietors' hands
(there being no leases), and many generous, well-to-do
landlords have given from ten to twenty per cent. reduction of rent. But this cannot continue. Of course this
has created great alarm, and investigations and forecasts
have been made by parties well qualified to judge whether
the distress is temporary or permanent. If it is permanent, a change of agricultural arrangements will necessarily
follow, altering the system of farming with the view of
turning the land to more profitable account. Sheep hus-
bandry has also suffered from the importations of wool from
Australia and other foreign parts. Hitherto the sheep
farmer calculated that the wool paid his rent, and hence
sheep farming for many years has been a successful and
profitable occupation ; but of late great losses have been
sustained by sheep farmers, both in wool and sheep.

With regard to the crofters, an agitation has been got
up respecting their recent evictions. During the kelp
industry they gravitated towards the seashore, and gradually, in the Hebrides, their possessions and accommodation
became curtailed. This, with the increased population and
the failure of the fishing in many parts and raised rents,
has reduced them as a body to great poverty and distress ;
and the only remedy if the people are to remain in the
country is, from the depression in sheep farming, to increase their crofts to reasonable sizes, with the outrun for
cattle and sheep. In the early part of the century the
fisheries were unproductive, in consequence of the migra-
tory movements of the herring shoals and the difficulty of
access to market, which rendered the efforts of the High-

land Society of Scotland for promoting the employment of
the people comparatively useless. This society was headed
by the Duke of Argyll, the Earl of Breadalbane, and many
of the noblemen and gentlemen in the North, who, alarmed
at the emigration arising from the evictions of the people,
were anxious to find them employment, and a joint-stock
company was formed, which subscribed £150,000. They
obtained an Act of Parliament in 1780 "to erect towns,
villages, harbours, piers, and fishing stations, and appointed a governor and directors (who resided in London)
to administer the same." Stations were accordingly
erected at Tobermory, Ullapool, Oban, Stein in Skye,
and, I think, Stornoway. The Act states that "the people
being collected into fishing towns and villages would be
the means of forming a nursery of hardy seamen for His
Majesty's navy and the defence of the kingdom, and
the finding immediate employment at home for great
numbers of people would be the means of putting a
stop to the dangerous spirit of emigration now prevailing
and likely to prevail to a great degree, to the depopulation
of that part of His Majesty's dominions and loss to the
kingdom of many of His Majesty's useful subjects." Such
was the proposal of this society. This company carried
on a sickly existence, for although at that time many
shoals of fish appeared at intervals, salt and barrels were
not forthcoming, and the fishermen never ready. If a
shoal appeared at Loch Carron or Loch Broom there were
no stores of salt or barrels, by which they might be cured.
This effort in favour of the people turned out then a dead
letter. The stations were ultimately sold; Wick alone,
where the appearance of fish in the season has never failed,
is the only remnant of this ambitious society. The shoals
are still on the coast; at present they are in Loch Hourn,
where the fishermen this year are reaping a rich harvest;
but now steamers ply daily along the coast of the Hebrides,
and communication is by the telegraph very readily made
in regard to the movements of the fish.

Moreover, the fish merchants of the south have now become acquainted with the inexhaustible supply of fish of the

finest quality in these seas, so that crofters who are also fishers—and they are so along the whole coast of the North of Scotland—have now a new and certain industry to depend on. In my opinion, properly arranged crofts will be a much more profitable investment, and the industrious crofter, supplemented by the fishing, instead of the starving creature he has hitherto been, may be a well-to-do prosperous peasant; and the young men of the redundant population, now reckoned a burden to the country, may, as I have pointed out, find congenial and profitable employment in the service of the army and navy.

The crofters have hitherto been woefully neglected by the proprietors and their agents. Up to this time they have been allowed to herd among their cattle without control. It is to be hoped the present agitation will establish some means of obviating this very serious evil.

The distress and destitution of the peasantry in the Hebrides is not a new question—the whole subject was investigated and discussed in 1802-3. Soon after the clearances began, it was remitted, among other subjects for the improvement of the country, by the Government to the late Mr. Telford, to report how the wholesale emigration then threatened should be prevented; and he states (see his report in the first volume of the transactions of the Highland Roads and Bridges Commission of 1802-3) the inhumanity and impropriety of these clearances, and recommends to the Government a proposition, as a remedy—which was fully sanctioned by two Parliamentary Committees—to construct the Caledonian Canal, which ultimately cost £1,300,000, chiefly for the employment of the people, and also some £500,000 in opening up the country by means of roads. But these efforts were of little avail. Some thousands per annum of the evicted people were taught habits of industry during the progress of the works, and ultimately became absorbed in the general mass of the community. The construction of roads rather assisted the emigration; for the roads to these localities, as I have already stated, tended rather to promote it than otherwise. The fact of sheep farming being a third more profitable (although much less so now, from foreign importation) than the old system was too tempting to discontinue the evictions. I have no doubt the Royal Commission—which appears to be nobly doing its duty, headed by Lord Napier, with such admirable tact and judgment—will suggest a practical remedy. If in 1802 such large sums were contributed by the Government for this object, some assistance might be provided from the Exchequer; for it is to be feared that a great part of both proprietors and tenants will be unable, from their extreme poverty, to provide a remedy. From the evidence adduced, there is ample food and land for the people if judiciously distributed; the loan might be made without loss.*

Although there have been repeated clearances † year by year of the people for the last hundred years—some of them very cruel to my own knowledge—there are still a great number of the peasantry in the northern counties that may be deemed crofters and cottars.

They exist, as the Royal Commission can testify, in Caithness, Sutherland, Ross, Inverness, and Argyle. The forefathers of these men have borne the highest character in our armies for bravery, fidelity, and every good quality that a soldier or a citizen could display. Even at our last engagement at Tel-el-Kebir the Highlanders were first in the fray for victory, and the cavalry which took possession of Cairo were commanded by a Highlander, Sir Herbert Macpherson from Nairnshire, the youngest of a family of heroes. And who are now left as the guardians of order in Egypt but the Highland Brigade, under the command of Sir Archibald Alison, our gallant and distinguished countryman!

The depression of sheep farming, and particularly the rage for deer forests, bid fair to depopulate in a few years

---

* In an able lecture delivered in January, 1883, in Edinburgh, by Sheriff Nicolson (himself a Skye Highlander), he states that during the American and French wars Skye alone furnished to the army 100,000 privates, 100 pipers, 600 commissioned officers, 48 colonels, and 21 generals.

† See General Stewart's statements.

these counties of their peasantry, who have now gained the sympathies of the community.

Is the Government prepared to let this system either of starvation or of eviction go on for the sake of a few proprietors, many of them impecunious, and of the sportsmen, whose thirst for Highland solitude seems to have no bounds? Are they prepared to face the continued agitation of this question? No doubt, it is a critical political problem. The Government have taken the drink of these poor people, which from their poverty they cannot well afford, and have taxed it cent. per cent. for their physical and moral improvement. Are they prepared to impose a like tax on deer forests, and insist on their area being curtailed and the boundaries fenced; or are they prepared to countenance the wholesale expatriation of the people? That is a problem which will have to be faced sooner or later.

CHAPTER XIV.

The Right Hon. Edward Ellice, M.P.—His residence at Glenquoich—
His political connections—Purchases Glenquoich and Glengarry—
His hospitality.

WHILE adverting to the changes in the Highlands, I must
not omit a new proprietor, Mr. Ellice, M.P., distinguished
as a politician and statesman, who resided in the Highlands for many years in the autumn, enjoying its pleasures
and sports.

Mr. Ellice, at an early period, by his urbanity, kindness,
and hospitality, attracted to his residence a constant succession of visitors—politicians of eminence and persons of
rank and distinction in the fashionable world. His charming lodge at Glenquoich, the splendid deer forest, the sport
of fishing and shooting, boating on the lake for the ladies,
and driving through the beautiful scenery and clear mountain air of the glen, with the intellectual communings of
himself and his guests, rendered a sojourn at Glenquoich
in the season very agreeable and attractive. He was among
the first sportsmen who gave a tone and fashion to sport
in the Highlands, now so general and popular, which has
become one of the chief and most healthful enjoyments
of the aristocracy of this country.

Mr. Ellice was a native of Banffshire. His father was
Scotch, and a merchant in New York and Canada. The
son became a leading merchant in London, chiefly connected with the West Indies and the Hudson's Bay Company.
He married, in his twenty-sixth year, the Honourable
Hannah, sister of Earl Grey, and widow of Captain Butter-
worth, R.N.

In 1818 he was elected M.P. for Coventry, for which

borough he continued the popular member for many years. He was frank and kindly in manner, and esteemed a man of great talent and shrewdness, and very materially assisted his brother-in-law Earl Grey when Premier, during the difficult political period of the first Reform Bill.

His first wife dying, he afterwards married the Countess of Leicester, who prematurely died some months after her marriage. He was a distinguished politician, and in that capacity secured the friendship and regard of almost every eminent political man in Europe. He declined political honours.

In the midst of all his occupations he never seemed to forget the attractions of the Highlands and Highland sport. He first rented the deer forest of Invereshie, in Badenoch, belonging to Sir George Macpherson Grant; and when Glenquoich, the centre portion of the Glengarry estate, was for sale, he purchased it, and erected a shooting-lodge on the lake, which, as I have said, was for many years the attractive abode of much fashionable and intellectual society.

Mr. Ellice often invited me to Glenquoich, and in the autumn of 1850, I, with a friend, spent two days there with a large and fashionable company. In fact, with the exception of Mr. Ellice and his son and ourselves, every one bore a title.

We arrived at Glenquoich about three o'clock, anticipating dinner would be at six; but in order that the sportsmen might have as much daylight as possible the clocks of the establishment were put forward two hours, so that the breakfast hour was seven instead of nine, and the dinner hour four instead of six. We had consequently to make a hurried toilet.

The lodge was truly a shooting-lodge, furnished in the simplest manner with cane-bottomed chairs, and iron bedsteads. The bedrooms were small but numerous, and the whole system of living was simple and rational. Of course where there were Highland cattle and mountain sheep, and such abundance of the sports of the river, the sea, and the field, the fare was undoubted and abundant. But the peculiarity of the entertainment was that immediately after dinner, a large tray of toddy tumblers was brought in by the butler, and placed with special solemnity before Mrs. Ellice, the charming wife of Mr. Ellice, jun., who with practised art mixed up the grateful potation—our sole allowance.

The toddy was made very much in the terms of a rule laid down for a literary society at Inverness, of which, when a young man, I was a member. The drink of this society, by the rules, was limited to one stiff tumbler of toddy, and there was a note appended explaining that a stiff tumbler of toddy consisted of two full glasses of whisky with hot water and sugar in proportion.

Of course the gentlemen were early on the mountain side, while the ladies occupied themselves in boating, driving, walking, writing, sketching, and quiet gossip.

When the lower part of the Glengarry estate was sold, Mr. Ellice became the purchaser of the whole glen, a property for sport and natural beauty unsurpassed in any part of the Highlands.

Mr. Ellice died in September, 1863, at the age of eighty, a few days after he had presided at a banquet to the directors on the occasion of opening the Highland Railway.

His only son and heir, Mr. Edward Ellice, M.P., has built a handsome mansion on the banks of Loch Oich on the site of the old house of Glengarry, and there with every appliance and luxury dispenses on a more limited scale the liberal hospitality of his eminent father. Yet as I pass this beautiful residence, with the ruins of the old castle overhanging the lake, I cannot help feeling a pang of regret for the old chief of Glengarry and his old ways of living among his Highlanders and pipers, nor can I forget his personal kindness to myself.

In the country where the ancestors of Glengarry were distinguished men and resided for centuries, the sole possession the family retained when they parted with the estate was an acre on the loch side, on which the ruined castle stands (partially blown up during the rebellion of 1745), and the solitary mausoleum at the foot of Loch Lochy, where, after a fitful and restless life, repose the remains of the last chief of Glengarry.

K

CHAPTER XV.

The Great North Road through Sutherland and Caithness—Description
of the County of Caithness—Making of county roads—Improvements in this bleak region—Superiority of the peasantry of Caithness—Caithness in the olden times—The Dunbars—The Earldom of·
Caithness—Thurso Castle and the Sinclairs—The Sinclairs of Freswick—The Trails—Tragic story of the eleventh Earl of Caithness—
Mr. James Horne of Langwell—Islands of Orkney.

I HAVE already explained that, until the labours of the
Commissioners of the Highland Roads began, the whole
country beyond Inverness—to wit, Ross-shire, Sutherland,
and Caithness—was destitute of roads. The "Great North
Road" from Inverness to Wick and Thurso formed a very
important part of the Highland road works of the Board,
and was then a very formidable undertaking.

The large rivers of Beauly and Conon had to be spanned
by bridges of five arches of stone; and the Oykel at the
head of the Dornoch Firth was crossed at Bonar Bridge by
an iron arch of 150 feet wide, besides side-arches of stone.

At the river Fleet, an artificial mound was constructed
to dam out the sea (which rose here at high water ten feet).
This embankment was made with regulating sluices for the
discharge of the river, and of the land floods at low water.

Besides these, there were numerous bridges and arches,
some of a large size, equally important and necessary, along
the line.

From Bonar Bridge another road was made through
the interior of the country towards the north-west coast of
Sutherlandshire, by Lairg to Tongue House, the family

seat of Lord Reay, a distance of sixty miles. These two lines of road, one on the east coast and the other in the centre of Sutherlandshire, formed afterwards the basis of other county roads, which have opened up the country as effectually as could be desired. But beyond the Parliamentary road which crossed the Ord of Caithness (a precipitous mountain 1200 feet above the sea, standing at the threshold to the county), and which stretched northward to Wick along the east coast, and then across the county to Thurso, and which was only finished in 1817, there was no communication throughout Caithness except bridle-paths.

It is true that Sir John Sinclair—then M.P. for the county, a distinguished promoter of agricultural improvement—obtained an Act of Parliament in 1794 to open up the county of Caithness by means of roads, but the other heritors opposed it unanimously. One heritor writing to another ascribed this proposal to " personal vanity, because he (Sir John) as a rich man was able to keep a carriage, and wanted the public to make roads to show off his grandeur." The result was that the Act (33 Geo. III., cap. 120) became a dead letter.

County of Caithness.

The county of Caithness is peculiar. Its features differ from the other northern counties of Scotland. The southern boundary is defined by a range of high mountains running from near Helmsdale on the east coast to the western sea at Bighouse. The northern slopes of these mountains end in extensive plains, stretching in every direction to the sea shores, which are in a great measure rocky and precipitous, with sundry sandy creeks and bays. The general surface from the base of these mountains is flat, and with the exception of insulated patches of culture in the interior and round the sea shores, was in a great measure one vast level of moor and moss.

The soil is wet, and at two, three, or four feet from the surface rock is generally found ; but as the soil is moist and clayey it is easily cultivated, and with marl and the admirable manure of fish offal, which is abundant along the seashore, splendid crops of corn, turnips, and grass are reared. Indeed, much of the early improved land in the county has been brought under cultivation at a cost of from £5 to £10 per acre.

The climate, however, is so severe that no trees will grow to any height, and those planted round the houses of country gentlemen become stunted when they rise above the sheltering walls which surround them. Hence the general aspect of the country is bleak and sterile.

The Parliamentary road through this county in 1817 seemed to have acted like a fertilizing stream. On each side farms sprang up, houses and steadings were built, and in a few years the necessity and advantage of roads throughout the county became strikingly apparent.

In 1830 the heritors obtained an Act to open up the whole county by additional roads, and these on the whole have been judiciously laid out.

Mr. MacAdam, of European reputation, applied for the privilege of constructing these roads ; but, apparently, as the heritors knew me my services were preferred, and I agreed to undertake the making of thirty to thirty-five miles of road each year, the whole extent to be made throughout the county being 136 miles.

The first portion (thirty miles) I carried out, strengthening the foundation of the road to suit the moist and wet soil and climate of the county.

The experience of the first year satisfied me that the estimates framed by surveyors from Edinburgh were wholly inadequate, and I felt it my duty to report this to the heritors. As the funds were limited, each heritor in consequence was anxious to have his own road first made. The extent ordered was, therefore, beyond my power to undertake, and I resigned my charge, and Mr. MacConnell (MacAdam's nephew and partner) was appointed in my place. He reported that the sum provided was quite sufficient, which information was hailed with much satisfaction. Under him the roads were all made, and looked well in the first instance ; but as they were constructed with only a depth of three or three and a half inches of road metal on a wet soil (there being scarcely any gravel in the country), in frost and during winter the surface broke up with the traffic, and the proprietors soon found that my predictions were correct. This caused great disappointment after expending some £30,000.

Accordingly they requested the Commissioners for the Highland Roads to take charge of these roads, and thus indirectly to obtain my services in the management. This was agreed to on condition that some £8000 or £10,000 should be provided by the county for strengthening them, and accordingly an Act was obtained (1st and 2nd Vict., cap. 79) to raise the necessary funds for this purpose.

These roads were strengthened and maintained for twenty-two years under the Commissioners to the entire satisfaction of the public, and during all these years I had to traverse the wide and solitary expanse of this county two or three times annually.

The advantages of these works, the agricultural improvements which they were the means of promoting, and the enormous increase of fishings all round the coast combined, have suddenly brought a degree of wealth and prosperity to this otherwise bleak and sterile county, unequalled in any other part of Scotland.

Whether it is the race (which is evidently Scandinavian), the sharp climate, the good food, or all combined, with the parochial school education, I cannot say ; but I consider the peasantry of Caithness superior to any other in Scotland for intellect and physical development, and the comeliness of the women.

When I first visited Caithness in 1824–25, it was emerging from the pristine inert condition in which it had long lain during the eighteenth century.

The parliamentary roads had a few years before been made. The mail-coach was running, and direct communication by land was established with the outer world. The fisheries on the coast had made considerable progress, and their importance was being daily developed.

Still, many of the old habits existed. The great mass of the people were peasant farmers, a simple and kindly population, those on the coast combining fishing with agriculture.

I may say there was no middle-class, if we may except a few leading farmers, law agents, and the clergy of the Established Church, for there were no Dissenters. Almost all the proprietors lived on their own estates, and took great interest in farming, which they were not too elevated to practise, and which they found a profitable occupation.

Lord Duffus held a great property in the neighbourhood of Wick, which rapidly increased in value as the progress of the fisheries advanced. He had two sons, the Honourable George and the Honourable Robert Dunbar.*

Robert had a small estate on the coast, prettily situated, about twenty miles south of Wick, the rental of which was then some £500 or £600 a year. It is now the property of Major Stocks, the rental being increased to £1744.

I built a fishery harbour for Mr. Dunbar, and have often stayed a day or two with him at Latheronwheel, his residence. He was kind-hearted and hospitable.

George, the heir to the Caithness estates, fitted up and lived in the old tower of Ackergill, a desolate keep or peel tower on the seashore, some two miles from Wick.

Both the Dunbars were very handsome men in their youth. George was particularly so; and when seeing him on horseback, as I have frequently done, riding about Wick, he reminded me, from his graceful and manly bearing, and his solitary and desolate residence at Ackergill Tower, of the Master of Ravenswood in the romance of the "Bride of Lammermoor."

He succeeded his father, Lord Duffus, in May, 1843. He assumed the title of Baronet, and devoted himself exclusively to farming and the improvement of his estate, which, from the rapid progress of the county and his judicious outlays, he left free to his nephew, the rental being recorded at £11,044.

* They both resided on their lands in Caithness, and both died unmarried.

He lived much in solitude, and took no interest in the improvements of the county ; indeed his chief efforts were, in a great measure, to obstruct them.

County Families of Caithness.

Lord Caithness, the grandfather of the present Earl, resided in Edinburgh, and visited the county occasionally. His county residence was the picturesque castle of Barrogill, on the west side of the county, situated on the seashore, and commanding extensive views of the Pentland Firth, the projecting headlands of Hoy and Dunnet Head, and the Orkney Islands in the distance.

The external features of the castle, with its turrets, pepper-boxes, and embrasures, are striking ; but it must have been a rough residence for a nobleman, until his lordship, about the year 1830, laid out a sum of £6000 in modernizing, decorating, and improving the interior. He succeeded also in raising a shrubbery of timber of some fifteen to twenty feet in height, which very much added to its amenity as a residence.

Thurso Castle, close to the town of Thurso, was another of the old castles in the county. Its exterior was picturesque, but still less dignified and comfortable as a residence than Barrogill Castle. Yet here Sir John Sinclair, accustomed to all the amenities of a refined life in the south, resided with his large family. He was M.P. for the county for many years, an enlightened statesman, the friend of Pitt, and intimate with all the celebrities of his day.

He started the Highland and Agricultural Society of Scotland, a national institution which has done much for the agriculture of the world. He directed and carried out the first and second editions of the Statistical Account o Scotland, a most valuable index of the progress of society and the improvements throughout the kingdom, besides publishing many other valuable works.

He was dead before my time, but his son, Sir George Sinclair, succeeded him as M.P. for Caithness, and was reckoned a distinguished statesman and a man of refined literary tastes. The friend of Canning, Sir Robert Peel, &c., he was reckoned one of the leading orators of his time.

Sir George retired from Parliament after many years' service. He added to Thurso Castle, where he spent his latter years in acts of religion and charity.

Curiously enough, notwithstanding Sir George's reputation as a statesman and his readiness to regulate the affairs of the empire, and his highly-educated and refined mind, he could never be brought to look into his own affairs or estates, which were entrusted to agents; and soon after he took his permanent residence at Thurso Castle,* he resigned the management of his property to the present baronet, reserving for himself, it was reported, some £1600 a year, the present rental being upwards of £13,211.

No doubt Sir George was left with heavy burdens. Sir John, his father, had a large family, and was otherwise expensive in promoting his patriotic and literary pursuits.

Another considerable property in this county is Freswick. The proprietor was then Dr. Sinclair, a well-educated man, but eccentric.

Freswick possessed two residences, which were then in a state of dilapidation. One was Dunbeath Castle, about twenty miles south of Wick. It was a fine specimen of a feudal castle, some two hundred years old. It is built on a perpendicular cliff about 120 feet in height, overhanging the sea, to which there is a secret passage and winding-staircase, partly cut in the rock. Formerly, on the landward side of the castle, there must have been at the front entrance a moat and drawbridge, which thus rendered it a complete place of defence.

The castle looked very picturesque, both from land and sea. It was uninhabited, although habitable during the doctor's time. He lived in the town of Thurso.

The other residence is Freswick House, some eight miles

* Sir John Tollemache Sinclair, his successor, has since greatly enlarged Thurso Castle, and it is now a handsome baronial pile.

from John o' Gróat's, a large mansion, but with no external decoration except the coat-of-arms. The farmer had corn in the rooms when I saw it.

I recollect meeting the Laird of Freswick at the Honourable Robert Dunbar's, at Latheronwheel. We had a very jolly evening. Freswick had a cultivated mind, and we had a good deal of sarcastic wit. In the course of the evening he rose to drink our landlord's health, in a neat speech recounting his good qualities, kind heart, and amiable disposition, and ended by giving three hearty cheers, in which all the company joined—Freswick in his enthusiasm thereafter throwing his glass in the fire, an example followed by the other guests.

Mr. Dunbar was not to be behind Freswick, for soon after he proposed Freswick's health with equal enthusiasm, following up his speech by cheers and a like demolition of glasses in the fire.

After these were replaced, the servant came in and whispered to our landlord that it would be necessary to cease from any further sport with the glasses, as there was only another dozen in the house.

About twelve o'clock, instead of going to bed as we all moved to do, Freswick ordered his conveyance or country cart and set out for Wick, a distance of twenty miles in a very dark night. He insisted on going, and we all saw him off, rolled in blankets. This was his ordinary mode of locomotion through the county, and he generally travelled at night.

His daughter now possesses the estates, Mrs. Barbara Thompson Sinclair; rental £6207. She married Colonel Thomson, son of Thomson of Edinburgh, Burns' correspondent, who set his songs to music.

She has renovated Dunbeath Castle, which is now a comfortable residence; but in winter she will be rocked to sleep by the waves of the German Ocean, which wash incessantly the base of her solitary but picturesque abode.*

---

* This lady has since died, and her son is now the Laird of Freswick.

Sheriff Trail.

The most distinguished of the proprietors of Caithness at this time was Mr. James Trail of Ratter. He had been bred an advocate, and was Sheriff of the county. An enlightened and patriotic man, he took a lead for many years in all the improvements carried on in the county; and his career is a favourable instance of how an intelligent man may improve—indeed, acquire a fortune in so forbidding a locality, by residing on his own estate and perseveringly cultivating and improving it.

Sheriff Trail was the only son of Dr. Trail, the clergyman of the parish of Dunnet in the neighbourhood. The doctor succeeded to the estate of Hobbester, in Orkney, by the death of his elder brother, and he purchased at a judicial sale in 1789 the estate of Ratter, then belonging to the eleventh Earl of Caithness, for £8000.

Mr. Trail succeeded his father to these estates, which then had a very limited rental. By his continued improvements, however, during a long life, they have greatly increased in value, the rental being now recorded at Caithness £9694, Orkney £2861; in all, £12,555.

His son, Mr. George Trail, was a kindly, agreeable man, member for Caithness for many years, a great favourite. He left his estates to his nephew.

Mr. Sheriff Trail, besides his agricultural improvements, discovered valuable pavement quarries on his estate, which he opened up and worked.

As I was employed to repave the town of Inverness in 1827–28, and from my frequent professional visits into Caithness was acquainted with the value of this "flag pavement," which can be obtained of any thickness and any size, I stipulated that it should be used for the foot-pavements of the streets of Inverness. So well has it lasted, that it is only now, after fifty years' traffic, that the Town Commissioners have begun to replace it.

The fact of my having used the flags on so large a scale, and granting certificates of their quality, increased the demand so much throughout the country, that in addition to the works at Castlehill, other quarries have been opened up and successfully worked by steam-power in various parts of the county; so that now manufacturing flags in Caithness has become a staple and extensive trade, employing constantly several hundred men.

Mr. Trail's residence of Castlehill is a plain, comfortable mansion, situated on the seashore, and commanding extensive sea views. In a little valley and around the house he succeeded, as Lord Caithness had done, in rearing some plantations, which have contributed very much to the amenity of this residence.

The proprietors of this county in early days, having no internal communication, seem to have fixed their dwellings almost wholly along the sea coasts, naturally enough from the facilities of intercourse afforded by sea.

Mr. Trail married Lady Janet Sinclair, the sister of the eleventh Earl of Caithness, the former proprietor of Ratter.

He had a large family, and I had frequently the pleasure of visiting them, and enjoying their agreeable and cultivated society in this solitary and remote district.

Tragic Story of the Eleventh Earl of Caithness.

A sad history attaches to the eleventh Earl of Caithness.

It is well known that the Earls of Orkney and Caithness for many generations possessed extensive estates in both counties, and that they were the powerful chiefs of the clan Sinclair in the county of Caithness. George, the sixth Earl of Caithness, died childless in 1676, and being deeply indebted to Sir John Campbell of Glenorchy, alienated his estates and honours to that gentleman, who in consequence assumed the title of Earl of Caithness, and took possession of the Caithness estates.

But the clan Sinclair, indignant at his depriving their natural chiefs of their property and honours, by their turbulent acts made Campbell's residence in Caithness untenable, and he deemed it prudent to denude himself of the estates by sale, and relinquished the titles, he having managed to get created Earl of Breadalbane and Holland instead.

The consequence has been that the Earls of Caithness, although restored to their honours, have ceased to be great and influential landed proprietors in Orkney and Caithness as in former times. Their next-of-kin had small properties along the coast.

The earldom devolved on William, the Laird of Ratter, the tenth Earl, who was descended from Sir John Sinclair of Greenland, Master of Caithness, and grandson of George, fourth Earl.

His lordship died in 1779, and was succeeded by his son John, the eleventh Earl, proprietor of the estate of Ratter, his sole territorial possession. He had four brothers, who died unmarried. Of his two sisters, one died unmarried, and the other became Lady Janet Trail, the Sheriff's wife.

John, the eleventh Earl, was a captain in the army. In 1789 he visited London. He there mixed in society, and was distinguished, not only as the representative of a noble and ancient house, but as a peer of graceful bearing and manly beauty.

In the course of his sojourn in the great city he paid his addresses to, and won the affections of, a Miss Dehenny, the only daughter of a rich City merchant.

Her father, when consulted as to their union, although no doubt gratified at the prospect of his daughter's being elevated to the rank of a Countess, naturally enough considered it advisable to make inquiries as to the means of the noble Earl.

His lordship's explanations were, that although his estates in Caithness were not of much value, he possessed besides these a valuable property in the county of York.

Mr. Dehenny, with the prudence of a careful parent and man of business, thought he might as well make inquiries about the Yorkshire estate; and the answer was that although the Earl of Caithness had looked at this property on his way south, and talked of purchasing it, no purchase had been made.

The old gentleman was very indignant, and upbraided the Earl for his disingenuous statements and attempted deception.

The Earl, being a proud man, felt the truth of Mr. Dehenny's rebuke, and in a fit of insane remorse committed suicide. The young lady, his affianced bride, was thrown into the deepest distress by this sad event. Nothing would console her, and she ever after rejected other proffered suitors.

Mr. Dehenny, her father, in due time died, leaving his daughter his accumulated fortune. Miss Dehenny's affections were fixed; she never could be induced to forget her lost lord, but constantly mourned his sad fate.

In her distress and grief she wrote to Mr. Trail, the Earl's brother-in-law, begging she might be allowed to adopt one of his daughters, being a near relative of her affianced lord. She undertook to train up and educate the young lady in the best manner, and to bequeath her the fortune, which was then to her of little value.

Mr. Trail and his wife, Lady Janet, consented to this arrangement, and placed their eldest daughter under her care and training. In due time Miss Dehenny died, and Miss Trail, then an old maid, became the possessor of the Dehenny fortune.

The succession of the earldom of Caithness after the decease of the Earl devolved on Sir John Sinclair, Bart., of May and Barrogill, and the earldom has continued in regular descent to the present day, but devoid of the great estates formerly attached to it.

The present Earl enjoys the honours and dignities of this ancient house.

My friend, his father, had a great taste for mechanics and engineering. He cultivated my acquaintance, and he and his charming first wife used to pass days with me at Inverness on their way north. At one time he got a locomotive to run on the turnpike roads, and he and Lady Caithness intended to run with it from Inverness to Caithness. I did all I could to dissuade them from such an adventure, but both set out and reached their destination,

Lady Caithness saying that if Caithness blew up she was quite ready to accompany him.

Mr. James Horne of Langwell.

A man of very considerable mark in this county in my early days was Mr. James Horne, a native of Caithness, second son of a small proprietor, Mr. Horne of Stirkoke. He was bred a W.S. in Edinburgh, and bore the character of an astute lawyer.

He discovered in some of his researches that the settlements of the then Duke of Roxburgh were illegal.

It seems the Duke, irrespective of the original strict entail, of date 1648, had executed a deed of entail in 1804, settling the estates on various of his descendants and connections. This was found to be inoperative; and being determined to carry out his wishes in another form, he took advantage of a clause in the original entail of a power to feu. Hence he divided his estates into sixteen parts, and granted feus of the greater part, if not the whole estates, to the detriment and exclusion of Sir James Innes, who, Mr. Horne maintained, was the legal heir.

After long and tedious litigation—carried on, it was said, very much at Mr. Horne's risk and expense—this arrangement of the Duke's (although confirmed by the Court of Session) was set aside by the House of Lords in July, 1812, and the house decided that Sir James Innes was the legal heir to the dukedom and estates of Roxburgh.

Of course Mr. Horne reaped the natural reward of such an enterprising and important achievement, besides establishing his name as a successful and able law agent.

Mr. Horne purchased the estate of Langwell from Sir John Sinclair of Ulbster. Sir John had bought it for £8000 in 1790; but such was the rise in the value of land that Mr. Horne paid £34,000 for it in 1813. His nephew, who succeeded him, sold it in 1845 to the Duke of Portland for £94,000.

Langwell, where he resided for many years, is on the southern boundary of Caithness. The valleys of the estate are beautifully wooded.

He introduced on the farms a very superior breed of sheep, which brought the highest prices in the country. He purchased also the estate of Wester Watten, in the interior of the county; and he and his nephew (Mr. W. Horne, Sheriff of Midlothian) introduced there and at Stirkoke the modern system of agriculture practised in the Lothians, an example and pattern which many of the county people were not slow to follow, facilitating much the progress of agricultural improvement in Caithness.

Mr. Horne died in 1831, unmarried. He was always distinguished as a county gentleman for his public spirit, kindness, and hospitality.

Islands of Orkney.

As marking the progress of improvement in the far North, I may mention that in 1857 I was employed by the county of Orkney to survey and lay out roads in the mainland of these islands.

Before that period roads had been made in various parts (I presume by statute labour) very much along the old foot and bridle paths, which had been widened, with all their steep acclivities and sinuosities, and when I went there they were in a most deplorable state. A steamboat had shortly before then been established between Thurso and Stromness, and this constituted the main direct access to the county. The road from Stromness to Kirkwall was consequently hilly, and full of holes on the surface, almost impassable. I recommended the construction of an entirely new road between these two towns, almost level, which is now a very perfect communication.

Other roads were improved and repaired. I furnished Kirkwall with a plan of a low-water harbour, for which they obtained an Act of Parliament; but it was not carried out at the time, and an iron pier has been since erected. A steamer now plies between the various islands and Kirkwall.

The agricultural and other improvements in Orkney

display as great progress as in any parts of the northern Highlands.

In 1874 the Highland Railway being extended to Thurso, a powerful steamer was established, and runs daily between Scrabster Roads and Scappa, within two miles of Kirkwall, between which points there is a substantial road. There is besides a steamer trading weekly between Kirkwall and Aberdeen, so that the Islands of Orkney are now as well provided with communication as any other part of Scotland.

When I first went to Orkney in 1826, Kirkwall was very primitive. The only communication with the mainland was by boats and sailing vessels. Various of the country lairds had town houses in Kirkwall, where, with their families, they spent the winter, and they constituted an educated and agreeable society. Instead of carriages, they had their boats for conveying them between their islands and the capital, and for visiting.

I recollect once going with Mr. Trail of Woodwick to his Island of North Ronaldsay, to fix the site of one of the Highland churches. We started at four in the morning, and took twelve hours sailing within the islands.

North Ronaldsay is the furthest north island of the group; and being very flat, in thick and stormy weather it was not easily discernible, and numerous wrecks annually took place. There were sad evidences of this—the greater part of the houses were built of timber thus obtained; besides, here and there throughout the island were to be seen great logs of timber, capstans, anchors, and other parts of vessels which could not be moved.

The island is very fertile and the climate mild; wrecks and the droppings of cattle form the only fuel of the inhabitants. Fortunately a lighthouse was lately built, and there ought now to be few or no wrecks.

The chief feature of Kirkwall is the grand old cathedral of St. Magnus; it escaped the devastation of the Reformers, and is now used as the parish church. It is entire, of Norman architecture, 226 feet in length, and in breadth 56 feet. Beside it are the ruins of the palace of Patrick

Stuart, Earl of Orkney, built in 1600 ; and westward, but adjoining, are the ruins of the Bishop's palace, both displaying evidences of architectural taste shown nowhere else in the islands.

The chief proprietors are **David Balfour** of Balfour Castle, Island of Shapenshay, rental £7578 ; and the Earl of Zetland, rental £5617.

CHAPTER XVI.

The Chisholms of Chisholm—Funeral of the Chisholm in 1838—
Funeral of the Hon. Mrs. Fraser of Lovat—Vicissitudes of the
Chisholm family—Lady Ramsay and her matrimonial relations—
Visit of the writer to Dunrobin Castle—The first Duchess of Suther-
land.

Journal.

September 20, 1838.—This is the day of the funeral of the
poor Chisholm, our M.P. for Inverness-shire, only three
months since he was elected M.P. for the county.

He had disease of the heart, and died in Inverness on
the 7th—a sad fate to be cut off at the early age of twenty-
nine. Although not well known, he was the representative
of an ancient family and the chief of his clan. His sudden
death caused deep regret throughout the district, and
consequently there was a great gathering at his funeral.

I joined the *cortege*. The procession left Wilson's Hotel,
Inverness, at 11. The hearse was drawn by four horses
richly caparisoned, with white plumes, as indicating the
youth of the deceased.

The magistrates, with their officers bearing their halberts
draped in crape, conducted the funeral to the boundary of
the town, and the procession, which extended for more than
a mile, proceeded onward to Strathglass, the territory of
the chief.

The leading chiefs in the north attended—Lovat, The
Mackintosh, Glengarry, Macpherson, Grant, Cluny, Apple-
cross, Glenmorriston, Glenco (several in Highland costume).
There were upwards of one thousand people besides.

After crossing Beauly Bridge the road winds through a singularly romantic pass, close to the Falls of Kilmorack, and through the magnificent scenery of the Druim, extending for more than four miles.

The river Beauly rushes through a cleft of almost perpendicular rocks, 100 or 150 feet high; the road elevated nearly 80 or 100 feet, cut in the northern side almost parallel with the river. The hills on each side tower above, thickly clothed to the top by a profusion of natural wood, chiefly birch. Here and there, as the river winds its course, charming soft, green, daisied spots are seen by the water-side.

Through this beautiful pass, on which the sun shone with meridian splendour, the funeral *cortege* wended its slow way. It was a striking and mournful sight.

After passing the Druim the valley widens, and some miles up you approach Erchless Castle, the residence of The Chisholm, a fine old tower somewhat modernized. The procession was conducted along the avenue to it, the pipers playing a wailing lament, turning round to the place of interment, a beautiful wooded knoll above the castle. The burial service was read, and the young chief was laid in his grave.

Immediately thereafter the gentlemen sat down, according to country custom, to a sumptuous dinner, laid out in a large building adjoining the castle, and the country people were ranged out on the green in front of the castle, and entertained with bread, cheese, and whisky.

I left at five o'clock, and was home by 8.30. This funeral was conducted with great propriety. In previous times this could not be said of the funerals of Highland chiefs.

I remember, as a boy, seeing the funeral of the father of this chief. It consisted of even a greater gathering. A grand festival was held in Beauly, in the old priory of which he was buried. Some drunken brawls occurred, and a snowstorm having suddenly come on, several of the poor country people, no doubt with ample allowance of whisky, perished in the snow on their way home.

The last great Highland funeral I recollect was that of the Honourable Mrs. Fraser of Lovat, the widow of Colonel Archibald Fraser, son of Simon of 1745. She survived her husband for many years, and was in a measure forgotten, the estate having passed to a distant branch of the Frasers. At her death, however, public interest revived. She was buried in the Lovat vault at Kirkhill, seven miles from Inverness.

The Lovats have a handsome house called Wester Moniack, about a mile and a half from the place of interment. Here it was arranged the customary funeral dinner should be held, and the entertainment was somewhat prolonged.

At last notice was given for the funeral party to move; but when the procession had proceeded more than half a mile on the road, the undertaker came galloping up, calling, "Gentlemen, halt, for we have forgotten the hearse." Of course the procession waited, and the old lady was duly deposited in the Lovat mausoleum with all the solemnity due to her rank.

The vicissitudes of the Chisholm family have been striking.

The father of the deceased chief is reported to have been a person who had no proper conception of his rank or position, associating with the common country people. Not so his wife, who was a high-spirited dame, the sister of MacDonnell, the chief of Glengarry.

She had a daughter and two sons—the chief just buried, and the other an officer in the Guards. They were fine young men, and gave promise of distinction.

Unsatisfactory rumours arose early in the country side regarding the mother. In appearance she must have been an engaging and fascinating woman, and seems to have possessed the characteristic high spirit of the Glengarry family.

After her husband's death she lived in London, Bath, and elsewhere in England. She there became acquainted with Sir Alexander Ramsay, a general who had returned from India with a considerable fortune.

He got deeply in love and so fascinated with her, that he agreed if she married him to settle his whole fortune, not only on herself, but thereafter on her children by the Chisholm.

In a short time their tempers were found to be incompatible, and they agreed to separate; and as all his fortune had been thus settled on her, and for the behoof of her family, he had no means of living, and no alternative but to return to India and resume the command and income of his rank.

Of course he felt the bitter folly of denuding himself of his fortune; and considering the rumours so general regarding the reputation of the lady, he instructed his agents (lawyers in Edinburgh) to try to break his marriage settlements, and to institute an action of divorce.

The agent intimated his intention to the family lawyer of the Chisholms, Mr. William MacKenzie, W.S., and talked confidently of the proof he possessed.

The family lawyer was aware of these current rumours, which he apparently believed, although he repudiated them.

He recommended to the lady, for peace' sake, a prudent compromise in the interest of her family. Lady Ramsay spurned this advice, defied her accusers, employed another solicitor, the particularly astute and talented Mr. Hugh MacQueen, W.S. He brought the accusing party before the courts for defamation.

Meantime the husband, Sir Alexander Ramsay, died; and as his agent had no reason to follow up the case, he apologized on the score that he merely acted as agent. But she was not content with this evidence of his submission and her innocence; she insisted on his being brought before the Law Courts and a jury for defamation.

At the trial he made an ample apology. She produced witnesses on her part who gave evidence that they had never heard anything against her character; but as the accused did not resist, the witnesses were not cross-examined, nor was there any evidence brought against her. The jury gave a verdict in her favour, and assessed the delinquent in £200 damages, and so she considered her reputation cleared.

In order still further to prove her innocence, she published and distributed an elaborate account of the whole trial; which, considering the rumours current in the country side, did not improve her case.

Notwithstanding the bitter quarrels and separation, she retained the money settled on her and her family by Sir Alexander Ramsay.

She has now, with all her worldliness and high spirit, gone to rest; so have her two promising sons, without issue. The chieftainship and estates passed to a distant relative in the male line.

The rental of the estate is recorded at £8602. As there was no doubt about the next heir, little litigation was required to establish his title.

The heir was in Canada in a humble position, a clerk. He came, took possession of his estate, returned to Canada and married; but having no taste for mixing with his neighbouring chiefs, or residing as a landed gentleman in the Chisholm country, he occupies a mansion near Edinburgh, quietly enjoying the good fortune he has inherited. He is now a venerable and respectable man.

It is to be hoped that the young heir of the Chisholms, with his Canadian blood, will prove an honour and credit to this ancient clan, as well as a useful proprietor in the country.

Visit to Dunrobin.

On returning from the funeral of The Chisholm, I found Mr. Rose, the county clerk of Caithness, waiting for me. He came to arrange about the estimates for the new roads in Caithness, and on the 21st I set out with him for Sutherlandshire.

On September 22nd, 1838, had an interview with Mr. Loch.

Her Grace the Duchess of Sutherland invited us to dine. I accepted, but Mr. Rose declined, as he had to proceed on his journey northward.

Seven is the dinner-hour at Dunrobin; at six I went by appointment, having some business with Mr. Loch, who is one of the Commissioners of the Highland Roads.

I found him in a small library vaulted, approached by a turnpike stair. There were old pistols above the chimney-piece. It was a snug little place, well fitted for study, with an ancient writing-desk and old-fashioned easy-chairs.

We occupied an hour discussing various matters of business, and then went to the drawing-room, where we found the Duchess, Mrs. Loch, and one or two others, with Mr. William MacKenzie, her Grace's Edinburgh law agent. It was quite a quiet family party.

We had about three times the number of servants waiting that there were guests at table.

Her Grace was very affable and kind to me, complimented me on the excellent state of my roads, and said other pretty things.

Whether it was the compliments or being more alone, I had a better opportunity than before of admiring and noticing her sentiments as they were incidentally displayed in conversation.

Besides the urbanity of her manner, there was so much good feeling, such a sincere desire to do good, and to benefit in every way her people and the country, that I was quite charmed with her generous sentiments, and the prompt and business-like way in which she gave instructions and explained her views to her agents.

At half-past ten I took my departure; and next morning at six was on my way to Tongue, in Lord Reay's country.

The weather was glorious. In the comfortable inn at Aultnaharra, situated in the midst of a widely extended, dreary and desolate moor, I found Mr. Stewart, one of the Duchess's factors. We dined together; fresh trout from the loch, deers' tails, deers' tongues, and venison collops formed our repast.

This is Lord Francis Egerton's splendid deer forest, where he has a pretty and commodious shooting-lodge.

25th. Returned from Tongue, travelled to Ardgay, at the head of Dornoch Firth, sixty miles. The inns are all full of sportsmen, and as far as game, and every other creature comfort goes, the ordinary traveller has nothing to complain of.

26*th.* At Ardgay. Breakfasted in company with Mr. Dempster, of Skibo, who is here shooting. He is, I may say, the only large proprietor except the Duchess in the county of Sutherland. Curiously enough he is bitter against the Duchess's proceedings in Sutherlandshire, and is pledged to contest the Northern Burghs, a futile resolve with such a heavy opponent.

CHAPTER XVII.

Early efforts to obtain railway employment—Early surveys—Survey
of the Elgin and Lossiemouth Railway—The beginning of the
Scottish Central Railway—The winter's engagement and work—
Conduct of other engineers—Resignation of appointment.

The line of railway which was promoted in the sessions of
1837–38 between Edinburgh and Glasgow, encroached so
offensively on the property of the Earl of Hopetown, that
Mr. James Hope, W. S., his lordship's agent, employed me
to ascertain whether a more practicable and less offensive
line could not be obtained by the direct route by Bathgate.

I examined the country, took levels, and reported that a
very satisfactory line could be made in that direction with
gradients not steeper than one in two hundred ; but nothing
more came of this survey, which was made in March, 1838.
The bill for the existing line passed in July of that year.*

* *Edinburgh and Glasgow Railway.*—An attempt was made in 1831
to form a company for the construction of a railway between Edinburgh
and Glasgow, and Messrs. Granger and Millar, the eminent engineers,
made a survey of the line in the direction of Bathgate. The ground
was carefully gone over and the survey examined by George Stephenson, then almost the only great authority on railways.

He highly approved of the plan, and there is no doubt, with the
knowledge we now possess of railway construction and the powers of
the locomotive, it is out of sight the cheapest and best route. It was
shorter, being only forty-two miles (the line made is forty-six miles)
It had no tunnel, and the steepest gradient was 1 in 180. The opposition of the landed proprietors and canals was bitter and persistent,
and it was not till the autumn of 1835 that the project was resus-
citated and a new company formed.

That there might be no doubt about securing the best line, the promoters intimated that they resolved to employ two of the most eminent

In 1841 I noticed that the Government had instructed Mr. (afterwards Sir John) MacNeil to survey and lay out the main routes of railway through Ireland, and I thought a similar preliminary investigation would be a very valuable guide in Scotland.

My friend Provost Nicol, of Inverness, agreed with me in this view, and he got a memorial sent from the magistrates and Town Council of Inverness to the Treasury, suggesting that under the direction of the Commissioners of the Highland roads and bridges, whose employes were familiar with the country, a similar investigation should be made in Scotland.

Provost Nicol communicated with and induced other Town Councils to echo the wishes of Inverness ; but no result came from his movement.

railway engineers in England, gentlemen who had not hitherto been on the ground, to determine on the route. No sooner had this intimation been given, than Mr. Cunningham, W.S., issued a prospectus, stating that Messrs. Stephenson and Son, C.E., had for many months been engaged in surveying and selecting the best line, the details of which would forthwith be laid before the public. The promoters of the new company, alarmed at the prospect of an opposition company, offered the Messrs. Stephenson 1000 guineas for their plans, which Messrs. Stephenson at once accepted, as the engineering was not very elaborate, the sections being offsets from the levels of the Clyde and Forth and Union Canals.

The English engineers appointed by the company were Messrs. Rustrick and Locke, who followed very much the line traced out by the Messrs. Stephenson, as far as Linlithgow.

They reported that between two great cities such as Edinburgh and Glasgow the line should be as perfectly level as possible, and that the difference of level between the termini should be overcome at once by an inclined plane between Cowlairs, at the Glasgow end, and George Street, two miles of 1 in 40, with a tunnel, after the then manner of the Euston Square incline—a fatal error according to our present knowledge.

After a severe struggle in Parliament, the Act was obtained in July, 1838, and the railway was opened for traffic in 1842. Mr. John Millar was the engineer. Mr. Rustrick was appointed consulting engineer, and Mr. Locke put in a claim (through some of his Lancaster and Carlisle friends), and was appointed conjointly with Mr. Rustrick ; but Mr. Millar informed me that he did not require the extraneous help of either.

Survey of Elgin and Lossiemouth Railway.

Meantime railway works made considerable progress in the country, and it occurred to me that as the harbour of Lossiemouth, the port of Elgin, was six miles distant from the town, a line of railway from the sea would be a great boon to Elgin.

Accordingly I wrote to Mr. James Grant, solicitor in Elgin, afterwards Provost of the Burgh, suggesting that if he would undertake the duties of getting up a company, I would carry out the engineering of the works.

To this proposal he agreed, and I made an elaborate and complete survey, and obtained an offer for the construction of the railway from Mr. Forbes, a contractor of wealth and respectability. But although Mr. Grant held meetings, and made considerable efforts at the time, the public did not seem then to appreciate the advantages of the proposed scheme.

The Beginning of the Scottish Central Railway.

Sometime after, early in the winter of 1844, I met Lady Menzies of Castle Menzies in Edinburgh, from whom and from her husband, Sir Neil Menzies, I had, during my frequent professional visits in Perthshire, received much kindness and hospitality.

Her ladyship said she was anxious her younger son, Fletcher, should become an engineer. He was a clerk in the Foreign Office, which service he disliked, and she wished I would take and train him to my profession. I told her nothing would give me greater pleasure. Indeed, I said I had a great scheme in view, which would be important to me if we could carry it out, and which at the same time would very much facilitate the wishes of her son to acquire experience as a practical engineer. (Mr. Fletcher Menzies is now, and has been for many years, the very efficient secretary to the Highland and Agricultural Society of Scotland.)

This project was a line of railway between the Edinburgh and Glasgow Railway at Falkirk and the town of Perth. I had no doubt of its practicability. It would bring Perth and the whole north in direct railway communication with Edinburgh and Glasgow.

I stated that if she could induce the Marquis of Breadalbane, with whom she was on intimate terms, to be chairman of a preliminary committee, the scheme was certain to succeed. This her ladyship agreed to do, a matter of considerable difficulty at this time, for railways were then held in great disfavour by the aristocracy of the country.

Indeed, railways were opposed in every shape as disturbing innovations, and the cost for land and amenity for this railway is an instance of the outrageous extortion practised by proprietors during the early stages of railway construction.*

Her ladyship's family and that of the Marquis (according to the then aristocratic fashion in Scotland) were spending the winter in Edinburgh, and it required frequent interviews, and no small amount of diplomacy on her part, to induce the noble Marquis to entertain favourably the contemplated project.

At last I had a note from her to say he had agreed, and I was requested to call at his apartments in Holyrood Palace and explain to him what arrangements I thought necessary to carry out my views.

After our interview he directed me to communicate immediately with his agent, Mr. Reid of Perth. The Marquis thereafter, to inaugurate the scheme, called a public meeting in the Royal Hotel in Edinburgh.

---

* The land with severance was valued by respectable parties at fifty years' purchase of the annual value. This amounted to £66,000, but to meet contingencies £80,000 was put down as ample in the estimate. The quantity of land was 650 acres, and the cost to the company, including liabilities, amounted to upwards of £215,000, exclusive of £20,000 more to Road Trusts, who are the same parties as the landowners. The actual cost to the company was above one hundred and forty years' purchase of the annual value of the land. The aggregate claims amounted to little short of £300,000 for land, the annual rental of which was about £1500 a year.—*Report of Committee of Scottish Central Railway.*

The meeting was attended by the leading nobility and gentry in the counties of Perth and Stirling, as well as by many Edinburgh citizens.

Many patriotic speeches were made, and in the course of the discussion some gentleman incidentally asked whether the surveys and investigations of the proposed line would not involve them in very serious expenses?

Mr. Reid said no expense would be incurred on that score, as Mr. Mitchell, the engineer, was willing to undertake all the risks and expenses on account of the surveys; but in order to make sure of this, I was formally called upon by the chairman to confirm this statement.

I answered that I felt so confident of the success of the scheme and its remunerative character, that I undertook, without hesitation, the whole risk and expense of the Parliamentary surveys; but stated that, of course, if the Company was formed and succeeded, I expected to be employed as the engineer for constructing the works.

This was applauded, and thought very liberal on my part, and was at once agreed to; but that there might be no doubt on so important a point, and no risk to any of the members of the meeting, the clerk was instructed to record the arrangement in the minutes of the meeting, which I was asked to sign, and did sign.

The Provisional Committee consisted of the most influential nobility and gentry of the two counties, seventy-five in number. The Marquis of Breadalbane was chairman. The line was christened "The Scottish Central Railway," and the prospectuses were issued on the 30th of March, 1844.

Mr. Walker, the President of the Institution of Civil Engineers, being a Falkirk man, was, at my suggestion, asked in very flattering terms to be consulting engineer, and I was instructed as acting engineer to proceed with my survey without further delay.

The prospectus had not been published a week when more than double the capital was subscribed. The committee was much gratified at our success, and instructed their officials to carry out their respective duties with all due promptitude and diligence.

The line laid out is very much as it has been made, with the exception of two tunnels. One of these is at Dunblane, which Mr. Stirling of Kippendavie insisted on having made through the outskirts of his park. For permitting this, although it did not destroy the amenity of the park, he got £12,000, an expense quite unnecessary, as a better line could have been constructed on the opposite side of the river *in the open*, and not on his property at all.

The other tunnel was through Moncrieff Hill, close to Perth, upwards of a mile in length, which ridge I proposed crossing by an open cutting, descending to a point near the present station by a gradient of 1 in 160, the ruling gradient of the line being 1 in 75.

This survey was a source of great pleasure. I bent my whole mind to laying out the works in the best manner. A branch was surveyed to join the Edinburgh and Glasgow Railway at Castle Carey.

The pleasure of this employment did not last long. The Caledonian Railway was at this time projected, and was being surveyed by Messrs. Locke and Errington, the eminent engineers in London. Overtures were made to me to connect the Scottish Central with that scheme. This I declined. My great object was to form an alliance with the Edinburgh and Glasgow Railway, as that would suit whatever line southward might prove ultimately the best —then an open question.

The agents of the Caledonian Railway meanwhile got up an agitation in Stirlingshire in regard to the engineers.

They got the committee to ask that Mr. Locke should be conjoined with Mr. Walker as consulting engineer. To this Mr. Walker indignantly objected, and an angry correspondence ensued between Mr. Walker and Mr. Locke, which the former published and deposited in the Institution of Engineers.

It was clear from this correspondence that it was a deliberate intrigue of Mr. Locke through his friends to get employment as engineer and controller of the Scottish Central Railway.

Mr. Walker, from his high position, was indifferent about

the employment ; but he wished to maintain the principle, for the honour of the profession, that an engineer, once publicly announced as engineer of a particular work, should not be intruded on or superseded by another for no particular reason, except the mere whim of a committee or the intrigues of interested parties.

But Mr. Locke was not to be thwarted. The committee were in a dilemma. They suggested to Mr. Walker that Mr. Locke should be consulting engineer to Stirling, and that he should take the northern end to Perth.

This proposal Mr. Walker also declined, and the committee, notwithstanding the Marquis's flattering letters urging him to accept the employment, very coolly dismissed him. They at the same time appointed Messrs. Locke and Errington " sole engineers of the line," overlooking the arrangement they had made with me.

Thereafter Mr. Errington (Locke keeping in the background) came to me and said : " Notwithstanding the resolutions of the committee, we wish you to go on with your survey."

I answered that " of course I intended to do so ; the resolution did not affect me, as I was appointed engineer for carrying out the works, and that I presumed his firm were merely appointed in room of Mr. Walker as consulting engineers." He stated " that was a mistake, as they must have the sole control of any work they undertook, or to which they were appointed."

I said, " Then I suppose you mean that I should act as your assistant. This I decline."

Then came a wonderful degree of diplomatic plausibilities and kind and friendly expressions, for which Mr. Errington had a special talent (indeed his principal talent), which he exercised on me for several hours, but still maintaining his fixed purpose.

All this was very disturbing to me, for I knew Locke and Company had a resolute party in Stirlingshire in their favour.

I therefore took an early opportunity of going to Taymouth Castle, nearly fifty miles distant, to lay my grievances before the Marquis of Breadalbane, who, I must confess, acted very equivocally in the matter.

He stated that his impression was that Messrs. Locke and Errington were merely to act in room of Mr. Walker, and he begged that I would proceed with my survey, as my position was in no way affected by the change the committee had made.

He was very courteous, and asked me to dine with him and remain all night, which I declined. He then conducted me through the castle, a most princely and magnificent residence.

The Queen had been there a few years before, and Lord Breadalbane took me over the apartments Her Majesty occupied, which were preserved in the precise condition in which Her Majesty had left them.

My agreement with the committee was very unsatisfactory to Messrs. Locke and Errington, as without some understanding with me they could not rightly, or even legally, interfere with me; but they had acquired a habit, which I did not know then, of having little scruple on that score, and Mr. Locke (for Errington was powerless individually) did not hesitate to supersede any engineer, even his old master George Stephenson (to whom he owed everything), when it suited his purpose.

I happened to meet Mr. Walker in Edinburgh soon after. He earnestly recommended me, from the conduct of the Board, to throw up the employment.

I told him it was of no consequence to a man in his high position; but to me it was relinquishing the beginning of very important professional work.

After working for a week or two, however, I very foolishly adopted his advice, and so ended my ambitious hopes, so nearly accomplished, of constructing the Scottish Central Railway.

I was rewarded for my labours in getting up the Company and the survey (which was very nearly completed) with £1500; but my expenses were £1000.

Of course this was a great disappointment and annoyance; but perhaps, as it happened, it was fortunate, for if

I had continued engineer of the " Scottish Central Railway," I should in all probability have been drawn into the vortex of railway speculation which in that year (1845) was rife throughout the country, particularly in Perth, and by which about half the well-to-do people in that city were damaged and many ruined.

M

CHAPTER XVIII.

Railways continued—Excitement in 1845—Suggested construction of the Highland Railway—Appointment of a committee—Whole stock taken in a week—Objections of landed proprietors—Deputation to the Earl of Seafield—Labour and survey—Anecdote of a cattle-dealer—Parliament throws out the scheme—Publication of pamphlet in vindication.

THE construction of railways went on apace throughout the country, involving much speculation, causing ruin to many, and bringing fortunes to some.

In 1845, however, the mania for railway speculation reached its climax; no less than six hundred and twenty companies were registered, the united capital of which was £563,203,000. A newspaper described it as "A frenzy of speculation ! "

Of course it reached the North—and persons in Aberdeen had projected a railway from Aberdeen to Inverness. The northern public seemed thankful to have railway communication by this, apparently the most practicable, route ; but I, being familiar with the country, and having taken levels for shortening the road by the Highland route to Perth, felt satisfied of the practicability of a railway across the Grampians in that direction.

I immediately suggested to Inverness and the northern counties, that for the accommodation of the North of Scotland and its inhabitants that route, and not the line promoted by the Aberdeen party, was the railway which should command their consideration and support.

It was sixty-five miles shorter to the southern markets ;

and as a feeder I projected a base line from Inverness to Elgin, along the shores of the Moray Firth.

The main line in the direction of the Highland road being a herculean work, I recommended that we should bring the base line to Elgin in the first instance before the public.

A committee was accordingly formed in Inverness, and Mr. Peter Anderson, solicitor, and myself were authorized by them to proceed to Edinburgh, and there issue our prospectus, which was done on the 24th of March.

We calculated we would get the start of the Aberdeen project, which we did by a week, and so secured the capital we wanted.

The public responded to our prospectus in the most singular manner. The capital we required was £300,000, while we had applications to the amount of £2,000,000. Of course this great success brought the stock to a premium, and our Inverness committee were patronizingly dealing out the shares. The committee were so elated at our success, that Mr. Anderson and I were instructed to proceed at once to London, and there issue a prospectus for the great Highland line from Inverness to Perth.

We happened to have made preparation for this before, and had secured for the scheme the support of the leading noblemen and gentlemen in the North.

Reaching London, we put ourselves in communication with Messrs. Graham and Wemyss, the eminent parliamentary solicitors. It was deemed prudent to engage Mr. Locke as our consulting engineer. Messrs. Foster and Braithwaite were our brokers in the city.

The prospectus was issued on the 9th of April, 1845. 48,000 shares were required, and £2 10s. per share of deposit.

At this time the railway mania was at its height. The brokers assumed a dictatorial tone, and stipulated that they should have increased brokerage and have power to dispose of half the shares of the Company to such parties as they approved of; the other half might be reserved for subscribers in the northern counties.

The prospectus had not been out two days when Mr. Anderson reported that the stock sold like " wild-fire," and that the brokers begged they might be permitted to dispose of another fourth. My friend Anderson demurred to this, as in his opinion " it would destroy the local influence of the undertaking."

I told him by all means to let Messrs. Foster and Braithwaite have the other fourth as they asked, as our business was to secure the money in compliance with our instructions.

In the course of the week the whole stock was sold, no less a sum than £120,000 was deposited in the bank for the necessary preliminary investigations and parliamentary expenses, and Mr. Anderson and I returned immediately to the North.

A meeting was held of the provisional committee in Inverness, who issued instructions for the parliamentary surveys, and the necessary notices and information as to the traffic returns. Mr. Smith of Deanston, an eminent agriculturist, and largely employed at that time, was appointed land valuator.

Constant meetings of the provisional committee were held. Many proprietors through whose lands the lines would have to run objected to it, and no small difficulty arose, even for their consent to survey.

We were obliged to offer large sums in the name of amenity.

The Duke of Athole's agent positively objected at first even to the survey, as did also the then Earl of Seafield.

I recollect going to Cullen House, Banffshire, on a deputation to the last-named nobleman (the grandfather of the present Earl), with the view of securing his assent and approval to our line, which ran through some twenty miles of his Strathspey estate. The deputation consisted of Sir John Macpherson Grant, Bart., of Ballindalloch, Mr. Grant of Glenmoriston, and myself.

His lordship was out when we arrived, but we were graciously received by Lady Seafield, to whom we explained the purport of our visit. She very decidedly told us she "hated railways,"—they brought together such an objectionable variety of people. Posting, in her opinion, with four horses was the perfection of travelling.*

The dinner was served up in true Highland style, with piper and footmen in full Highland costume. There were present his lordship's chief factor and cashier, Mr. Fraser, and Mr. Cumming Bruce, M.P., a relative.

We discussed the whole subject, his lordship being reticent as to his views and decision; but from her ladyship's opinions, and Mr. Fraser's informing me in the course of conversation that a son of his was an apprentice to the engineer of our opponents, I confess my heart failed me, and I foresaw that our visit to Cullen House was a fruitless mission.†

My duty as the engineer was a very onerous one, as the main line and branches of our scheme extended over 183 miles of difficult country.

I employed from seventeen to twenty surveyors. Most of these I engaged at £2 2s. a day; but from the demand all over the country for surveyors, I had to increase some of them to £5 5s. per day.

What trials! What journeys to and fro to fix upon and secure the best ground and the easiest gradients at the lowest cost! for there were then in the North no ordnance surveys as a guide; but it was very enjoyable, and I must say my assistants worked most loyally. Our whole survey was thus finished by October.

Mr. Locke came and examined the ground, and approved of our work.

With difficulty the business of lithographing the plans

---

* This was the now Dowager-Countess Louise of Seafield.

† Such was the dislike to railways at the time, that Captain Grant, the factor for Lord Seafield in Strathspey, told me if the railway were made it would frighten away the grouse. Besides, he asked, what would become of his floaters, some forty men who were employed from time immemorial floating timber down the Spey, from the pine forests of Abernethy and Dulnan, to the sea at Garmouth. This was then the only mode of exporting timber from Lord Seafield's vast forests in the high grounds bordering Castle Grant.

was accomplished, and on November 30th they were deposited in terms of the standing orders of Parliament.

The railway mania raged through the whole year of 1845–46, and no engineer who was then actively employed will ever forget the labour and excitement of that period. Many died from over-fatigue and mental strain.

After November 30th came the preparation of the estimates, and checking the accuracy of our opponents' plans.

At length, on February 1st, we were summoned to London; but such was the pressure of work that session before Parliament, that it was quite uncertain when we should be called before either of the committees on standing orders or on the merits. All apartments in the vicinity of Westminster being engaged, we had to take rooms in the Colonnade Hotel, Haymarket (an establishment then much frequented by military men).

When our witnesses were up, and all assembled, we numbered about thirty—solicitors, engineers, assistants, traffic takers, land valuators, and cattle dealers. We were an idle and a jolly party.

One morning, when assembled at breakfast, Cruickshank, a herculean farmer and cattle dealer, who had never been in London before, said a strange incident had happened to him that morning. "I was just," he said, "lying in my bed, between sleeping and waking, when a man quietly opens my door, and very coolly carries off my clothes. I jumped up in my sark (shirt), and caught the fellow before he was half-way down the stair. I seized him by the collar, and said, You d——d scoundrel, nane of your London tricks wi' me. Come back wi' me claes. So I soon made him deposit them on the chair from which he had taken them, and an awfu' fright the fallow got. He was a starved-looking creature, and trembled when I threatened to kick him down the stair." This was the innocent "boots," who was carrying off the clothes to brush, according to the custom of the house; but Cruickshank, unused to such refinement, thought it was some London dodge to deprive him of his wardrobe, and perhaps his money.

We had a good laugh at this incident, bantered him about the fright he must have given the chambermaids, who were cleaning the stairs, appearing as he did in attenuated shirt and bare legs.

We were about two months idling in London in this unsatisfactory manner, waiting to pass the ordeal of standing orders before a committee of members, for there were then no official examiners.

One morning Mr. Reid, the Town Clerk of Perth, came to me, and said, ' Ye'll be gled to hear we have entered into a compromise with our opponents on standing orders ; neither party is to oppose the other." I expressed my great disappointment at this intelligence. I said, and he knew, the Great North of Scotland plans and book of reference were full of errors, the levels were wrong in many places—in one case to the extent of seven feet—and the line in approaching Inverness was laid down on the seashore for three miles, three feet below high-water mark.

This agreement was very provoking, for these errors were (then) sure to be fatal, and we should thus at once have got rid of our formidable opponents.

Mr. Reid expressed his astonishment at my remarks, for he said, " I am sure ye ken parliamentary solicitors never like to burke a bill on standing orders ; if bills yence pass standing orders, they are a drappin guse (goose) to them the whole session."

At last, on April 29th, 1846, the committee on the merits sat, and before it was a formidable array of forensic and engineering talent.

For the Great North of Scotland, there were—

Mr. Talbot ⎫
Mr. Wm. Austin ⎬ Barristers.

Mr. (afterwards Sir) Wm. Cubitt, Engineer.

Mr. Alex. Gibbs, Acting Engineer.

J. and Thos. Webster, Parliamentary Solicitors.

For the Perth, Inverness, and Elgin, we had—

Mr. Wrangham, Mr. Bellasis ⎫
Mr. Hope (afterwards Mr. Hope Scott) ⎬ Sergeants.
Mr. Gordon (afterwards Lord Gordon) ⎭

Mr. Locke
Mr. Errington
Mr. Hawkshaw   }Engineers.
Mr. Wood of the London and N. Western
Mr. Alfred Jee of the Man. and Sheffield
Mr. Mitchell, Acting Engineer.
Messrs. Graham and Wemyss, Parl. Solicitors.

The Committee intimated that they would proceed with
the inquiry regarding the Great North of Scotland scheme
in the first instance; and that *finished*, they would take
evidence and consider the engineering question of the
Perth, Inverness, and Elgin railways. We had very able
speeches from the leading counsel on both sides. Sergeant
Wrangham was leader for the Perth and Inverness; but
as he was engaged in some other committee, Mr. Hope
Scott was appointed to lead, it being the first case in which
that eminent counsel acted as leader before a parliamentary
committee.

Austin was very eloquent and very unscrupulous. He
ridiculed the whole of our scheme.

"Ascending such a summit as 1580 feet," he said, "was
very unprecedented. Mr. Mitchell, the engineer, was the
greatest mountain-climber he ever heard of; he beat
Napoleon outright, and quite eclipsed Hannibal. He read
a book the other day, of several hundred pages, describing
how Hannibal had crossed the Alps; but after this line will
have passed, he had no doubt quartos would be written
about Mr. Mitchell.

"Besides the decision of the committee in its favour,
there was only one other thing that would surprise him—
that was the making of the line."

The Duke of Richmond, Lord Lovat, and others were
put in as witnesses against us.

As our engineering only was in question, we produced
the first talent of the day. The inquiry occupied a fortnight, and at last the committee gave their decision,
"that the preamble of the Great North of Scotland Bill
was proved, and that the preamble of the Perth, Inverness,
and Elgin Bill was not proved."

The committee intimated that "they had come to this conclusion with reference to the proposed altitude and engineering character of the proposed Perth, Inverness, and Elgin Railway, as compared with those of any other line of railway now actually completed and in operation."

What dismay this decision created among the parties who seemed to feel they had in their pockets the large sums they stipulated for in the shape of amenity and for permitting the survey!

As may be supposed, I was much cast down and disheartened at such a termination to all our labours.

I took my faithful assistant Paterson (who had worked night and day at our plans) and my wife to Oxford and Gloucester, and so home.

I felt the decision of the committee was very unjust; and although my opinions were sustained by eminent engineers, the main blame of failure would fall on me as the original projector of the scheme.

With the purpose of vindicating my views, I published a statement of our case, giving an epitome of the engineering and traffic on which we calculated. This information being widely circulated, it germinated in the minds of the public, and greatly assisted in showing the accuracy of my calculations, and the importance to the northern counties of a railway through the central Highlands.

CHAPTER XIX.

Railway mania—Loss and misery through railway speculation—
Difficulties of the Great North of Scotland Railway— Harbour
surveys in 1847—Visit to London—Trip to Paris—Dr. O'Leary.

I HAVE already said that in 1845 the whole country was in
fever heat regarding railways. The frenzy continued in
1846. However absurd the scheme, the public rushed at
it, and every stock ran up to a premium ; in fact, there
was a mania which resembled the insanity of the South
Sea Bubble. Many thousands of people, who could pay a
deposit of £2 10s. expecting to get a premium and then
sell out, were involved in obligations for thousands of
pounds, and he was a fortunate speculator whose project
Parliament rejected and the Provisional Committee were
required to wind up.

Apart from speculators, for whom there may be less
sympathy, thousands of respectable people, believing railways an advantageous investment for their savings, were
ruined by the fluctuation in the value of their property,
mainly from the opposition lines and the uncertain actions
of the Legislature.*

* It must ever be a reflection on the Government of the time that
they did not take an enlarged and comprehensive view of the railway
question, and so control and regulate it for the benefit of the nation.
In 1860 I published a pamphlet showing the increase of traffic in
ten years and that it was progressive on the principal lines of railway
then at work, and very many of which were amalgamated. The
result since has proved my calculations correct, and with even the
tariffs now charged Government might have secured a revenue before

In 1847 came the railway crash, consequent on the wild schemes and speculation of former years, and which spread ruin and dismay throughout the country.

Directors who had their Bills passed entered on their works, and had to struggle through excessive difficulties. Some became involved in heavy responsibilities to the extent of their whole fortunes. Notable cases of this occurred in the Caledonian and Scottish Central, and other Northern lines.

Shareholders were prosecuted for calls to their absolute ruin. Stocks were unsaleable. Some railway companies suspended operations.

The Caledonian and Scottish Central contractors, Messrs. Brassey, Mackenzie, and Stephenson, who had upwards of 20,000 men engaged, could not get funds to pay their workmen for a time; and Mr. Stephenson, who had the

now of more than £20,000,000, and might have been able by this means to lessen taxes to that extent. Apart from this, they would have secured the control and regulation of the locomotion of the country.

From their remissness, want of foresight, and neglect, a great many unnecessary lines have been made, vast sums have been uselessly wasted in the exorbitant price paid for land and in legal contests, great numbers have either been ruined or pecuniarily damaged, and after all Government will still have to interfere in the interest of the public. The railway companies, to protect themselves, have so amal-gamated that they are now ten or twelve great monopolies which, if they chose to combine, could overcome any government. To control them, the Government, by their Commissioners and the Board of Trade, are now impotently struggling.

It is absurd to maintain that the Government could not manage this department of the administration of the country. We have evidence in the working of the Post-office and Telegraph that these departments, penetrating to the remotest recesses of the Empire, are administered most unobtrusively and efficiently.

Foreign governments, and especially the Belgian Government, have adopted a wiser course. They have secured moderate tariffs, a safe investment for their people's capital employed, and an immediate or ultimate advantage to the State by the working arrangements and agreements they have adopted. But it is to be feared the time has passed, the monopolies are too fixed and herculean, and it would now require Mr. Gladstone some twenty years younger to carry out such an advantageous project.

management of the works, in his distress and excitement, lost his reason and died.

The South Aberdeen Railway had to suspend operations, and our opponents, the Great North of Scotland Railway Company, who had got their Bill passed, were unable to proceed with their works.

When this company was formed, instead of issuing their stock to the public, the promoters distributed the greater part of it among themselves, calculating, as many did, that when they obtained their Bill the stock would run up to a premium, as was then common. Hence the law agents of the company had allotted to them 2130 shares, upon which they deposited £75,850. The secretary was liable for £25,000; the Edinburgh agents, £20,000; two other agents, £15,000; while eight directors subscribed for £170,000 of the stock.

The deposits had been apparently advanced by the banks, chiefly the North of Scotland Bank; but unfortunately the crash came before the calculations of the promoters were realized.

Then came a long period of monetary depression, so that not only had they no capital, as I have said, to carry on their works, but the banks got uneasy regarding the deposits they had advanced, and insisted on payment and security.

The unfortunate promoters of the Great North of Scotland Railway were thus involved in much pecuniary difficulty; some of the directors, it was said, were ruined. At last it was resolved before their power expired to go on with the works, but limit their efforts to the forty miles of line between Aberdeen and Huntly.

The works were contracted for, and, with the aid of contractors who took stock in part payment, they with great difficulty succeeded in completing that portion of the railway, thus giving little hope to the northern counties of obtaining railway communication even by Aberdeen.

After our defeat on the Highland Railway scheme, I resumed my ordinary duties for the remainder of the year on the Highland roads and harbours; also preparing for

Parliament plans for an extension of the Inverness Gas and Water Works, and for the improvement of the Inverness harbour.

Early in March, 1847, I was instructed to proceed along the west coasts of Argyleshire and the southern Hebrides, and to plan and survey with the view of constructing harbours along these coasts.

The immediate purpose of these harbours was to give employment to the people, who had been rendered destitute by the potato famine; but they were likewise intended to be permanently useful as fishery harbours. Her Majesty's steamer *Cuckoo*, Captain Parks, was placed at my disposal for this duty. The scenes on this mission have already been described.

∗   ∗   ∗   ∗   ∗

On the 17th May, 1847, I went with Mr. Falconer, the solicitor of the company, to London on the business of the Inverness Gas and Waterworks Bill; but when we reached the great city, we found the Bill would not come on for a fortnight, and as it then occupied eight days to go and return by coach to London, we resolved to take a run to Paris, and have another look at that gay capital.

In crossing to Havre we met some strange characters, including a young Irish doctor, O'Leary. He had been educated in Paris, and, after attending his sick father for three years, until the old man died, was on his way back to Paris to spend three months there, and to renew his acquaintance with the enjoyments of that city.

He took a fancy to our society, and accompanied us to the same hotel; and as he knew Paris intimately, we found him a most obliging and agreeable cicerone.

The early mornings were devoted to viewing the churches, at which time we generally found the funeral service being performed. The solemn music usual at that service was very impressive. Dr. O'Leary likewise conducted us to all the sights and objects of historical interest, and we dined and spent our evenings together. We parted on the promise that he was to visit us in the North, but he did not come.

Many years afterwards, at a conversazione, during the meeting of the British Association in Aberdeen, I noticed a little man with a black beard following me in the crowd and eyeing me very keenly. I began to button up my pockets, thinking some of the light-fingered gentry had taken a fancy to combine science with their ordinary vocations. At last he tapped me on the shoulder, and claimed my acquaintance as my Paris friend, Dr. O'Leary. He visited us at Inverness, and my friend Falconer, the solicitor, and I had a few agreeable days with him, talking over our Paris adventures.

Since we saw him, Dr. O'Leary had been a medical missionary in China, but was then Professor of Natural History in Queen's College, Cork.

After spending ten days in France, we returned to London on the 1st June, and having successfully carried our Gas and Water and Harbour Bills, we returned to Inverness on the 9th of the same month.

CHAPTER XX.

Floods in the River Ness—The flood of 1849—Part of town under water—Fall of the old bridge—Narrow escape of the wooden bridge—The breaking of the Canal bank—The works at the outlet of the Ness—The magistrates of Inverness and the Canal Commissioners—Proposed new bridge—Dispute as to kind of bridge—Costliness of suspension bridge erected by Mr. Rendal.

On the 25th of January, 1849, the inhabitants of Inverness were thrown into a state of great alarm by the flooded state of the river. Heavy rains continued to fall all over the upper country for three consecutive days, with violent squalls of wind, and the river rose to an unprecedented height, overflowing its banks and submerging about a third of the town on the west side of the river to the depth of two to three feet.

The poor people in that quarter were placed in great jeopardy, but by extraordinary efforts on the part of the inhabitants they were removed to the eastern side, and temporary means of subsistence were provided for them by the Town Council, who sat night and day during the floods, which continued from the 24th to the 27th.

I took an active part in assisting to alleviate the distress of the people. I visited Loch Ness, examined the outlets, and fixed gauges to ascertain the rise and fall of the lake, and stationed a person there to report at intervals its progressive rise or fall.

I found that there was a breach in the canal bank, above Dochgarroch Lock, 150 feet in width, through which the flood-waters poured, and which the canal engineer was vainly attempting to stem by trees, brushwood, and gravel. A little iron bridge at the Islands was swept away, and ultimately, about half-past six on the morning of the 26th, the venerable old bridge, built in 1681, succumbed to the power of the floods. The timber bridge on the lower part of the river was in great danger, the bed of the river having been scoured, and the supports of the structure bared of their holdings. I immediately ordered a quantity of quarried stones to be thrown round the piers, which preserved the bridge until it was further strengthened by additional piles when the flood had subsided.

The flood in the river was increased by a portion of the canal bank giving way, thus discharging suddenly into the river channel the whole water in the reach of the canal between Dochgarrroch Lock and Muirton Locks, a distance of about five miles. The canal was fourteen feet in depth, and on an average sixty feet in width.

This flooding and damage was supposed mainly to have arisen from certain extensive repairs and alterations which some years previously had been made on the works of the Caledonian Canal, particularly at the outlet of the river Ness from the lake.

Mr. Walker, the engineer, had been employed to carry out these works, and a sum of about £150,000 was spent in repairs and in rendering them more suited to the modern requirements of the navigation.

At the west end he erected a new lock, and enlarged the outlet of the river, to regulate the floods of Loch Lochy. At the east end, in order to deepen the channel through Loch Dochgarroch and secure a fixed depth of seventeen feet of water, he permanently raised the outlet weir, over which the river Ness flows, to a height of four and a half feet; and to provide for the extra flood-waters of winter, he constructed a waste weir at the end for upwards of one thousand feet. This, he calculated, would afford a safe escape into the river of the water from the additional winter floods of the lake, caused by these changes.

Mr. Walker did not perceive that the lower channel of

the river was wholly inadequate to contain and carry off this extra flood-water.

The consequence of the permanent heightening of the weir was, and has been since, that in the summer months a very scanty supply of water flows down the Ness; but in winter, from the water running over the waste weir, the river is swollen to a great height, and runs through its short course to the sea in rapid and majestic volume.

Beyond this change in the condition of the river in summer and winter, no disadvantage arises from ordinary floods; but this was an extreme flood, and arose from three days of heavy rain over the whole drainage area (some seven hundred square miles), together with a rapid thaw of snow, which had lain heavily at the time on the adjacent mountains. These confined and accumulated waters had to be discharged through the river channel.

When such a conjunction of circumstances arises, a like flood must necessarily occur, and a similar flood, though of less intensity, did happen a few years since, again submerging the lower part of the town.

The authorities of Inverness attributed their sufferings and loss on the occasion to the alterations on the canal works, and they requested my professional assistance to report on the whole question, authorizing me to select another engineer to advise and act in conjunction with me. I fixed on Mr. James Leslie, of Edinburgh.

We proceeded forthwith with our investigations, which were very elaborate. It was a very interesting engineering question. We came to the conclusion that the floods in Inverness arose from the imperfect condition of the canal, the raising of the weir, and damming up Loch Ness four and a half feet, and other alterations of the canal works which had recently been constructed. Mr. Leslie and I, during our investigations, obtained a steam-tug to convey us to inspect the middle reach of the canal between Loch Oich and Loch Ness.

The magistrates of Inverness immediately represented their case to the Government, and Sir John Burgoyne, the eminent military engineer, was requested to report. He

N

recommended a settlement, but unfortunately estimated the restoration of the bridge at £8000. In the meantime I was instructed to erect a temporary timber foot-bridge, and to prepare plans for a permanent stone structure in room of the old bridge.

Thereafter, the provost, town clerk, and myself were sent to London as a deputation to lay our case and our plans for a new stone bridge, estimated at £13,000, before Sir Charles Wood, the then Chancellor of the Exchequer.

Sir Charles demurred to the expense and offered the Corporation half Sir John Burgoyne's estimate (£4000). This was represented as totally inadequate, and I suggested that he should send Mr. Rendal, or any other eminent engineer he might fix on, to report on the plan and the cost.

Mr. Rendal visited Inverness. I had known him, when a lad with Mr. Telford. He dined with me, and I furnished him with the prices, and all the other local information. I was requested to impress upon him, in the name of the Town Council, that whatever he recommended he should not propose a suspension bridge.

Mr. Rendal sent in his report, and notwithstanding our friendly intercourse, and the information given, he ignored my existence and that of my plan, and sent a design of his own for a box girder bridge—a plan of bridge then newly introduced for spanning great widths.*

---

* Being a local or country engineer, in some of the important works which I had to do, it was desirable to have my plans and recommendations confirmed by men of acknowledged experience and name. I am sorry to say, in almost every case, those consulted attempted to usurp the employment.

Mr. MacAdam hoped to secure the Highlands roads for his nephew, Mr. Macconnell. Messrs. Locke and Errington pounced upon the Scottish Central Railway ; and Mr. Rendal seized the Inverness bridge ; his services at which, as above related, did not elevate his professional reputation, for in this case the public got an ungraceful bridge at an extra cost of £22,000.

No doubt local engineers in general are not assumed to have the experience and knowledge of metropolitan engineers who have acquired a name : but I felt, from my training under Mr. Telford, and from my

He gave sundry scientific reasons for its being unsafe to erect piers in a river like the Ness, exposed to such heavy floods.

The county, through the convener, Mr. Tytler, took up the question, and decidedly objected to a "box girder bridge," which was in fact a horizontal iron wall of some fourteen feet high on each side of the roadway, and which would have effectually excluded the view of our beautiful river. Mr. Rendal, therefore, altered his plan to the design of the present suspension bridge now erected, and which he estimated at £15,000.

To this plan the county also objected; but the Chancellor of the Exchequer curtly intimated that if they did not accept Mr. Rendal's plan they would get nothing.

They had, therefore, no alternative, and Mr. Rendal proceeded to construct the bridge.

He had great difficulty with the foundations, owing to the erection in the first instance of an imperfect coffer-dam. He had to alter his plans, and the work, besides ruining the contractor (who lost £5000 by his bargain), took five years to complete, at a cost to the Government of £30,000 in all. To defray the extra expense, an application for additional funds had to be made to Parliament.

Some years after, when the railway was made into Ross-shire, I constructed the present very handsome stone bridge, of five arches of 75 feet span, half a mile down the river, for £13,500.

large experience, as competent to carry out whatever works I under-took as any metropolitan engineer.

But during all my professional life, it required no small tact to stave off such usurpations; and I was pretty successful in keeping in hand my own professional preserves in the northern counties of Scotland.

CHAPTER XXI.

Become tacksman of a Highland farm—Its interesting situation—
The difficulties of farming—Quit the Farm.

THE scenery of the Highlands, through which I had so frequently to travel, constituted one of the greatest enjoyments of my wandering life.

The graceful mountain outline, the wooded hills, the expanding glens, and the innumerable pure and limpid streams, as they pour down the hillsides, or murmur through the rocky, wooded, or cultivated valleys, were all scenes which afforded me intense pleasure.

It is said the love of scenery is an acquired taste, that our ancestors did not appreciate it; but from my earliest youth our beautiful mountain landscape has been to me at all times a source of great enjoyment.

At this time, 1852–53, I began to despair of railway employment. The various efforts I had made had failed. Still I had good reason to be thankful for much professional work and prosperity. I was very happy in my family, and, besides my house at View Hill, I indulged in the poetic vision of a cottage in the country, which would be a change for my children, and in the summer months a rural retreat for myself and my friends.

Clunebeg, in Glen Urquhart, fifteen miles from Inverness, I found just the sort of place I fancied.

It was a small farm on a hillside, with woods and water-falls, about 300 acres of hill and wood, and 50 acres arable, and a cottage sweetly situated, commanding an extensive view of Glen Urquhart, one of the most charming of Highland valleys. It was close to, and opposite Lord Seafield's residence of Balmacaan, and I had the privilege of enjoying his woods and walks.

The cottage had to be enlarged and embellished at a cost of some £600.

My intention was not to vegetate idly here, but to make the land profitable.

For information, while in England, as to farming I visited Mechi's farm in Essex; but was astonished to find, notwithstanding his letters in *The Times*, and his assumed authority in agriculture, that all the farms adjoining his were better cultivated and the crops richer. I was satisfied that there were shams even in the profession of farming.

However, I thought, by improving, liming, and introducing artificial and liquid manures, I ought to make a profitable investment, or, at any rate, an investment without loss, in this charming locality.

I was advised also to lease the sheep farm in conjunction, which the former tenant had held. This consisted of a range of some five miles of wood along Loch Ness side, and some 4000 acres of hill and mountain grazing for 1200 sheep.

The beauty of this farm was also a great attraction; it had a cottage on the lake side, charmingly situated in the midst of woods, beside a fishing stream, and with some five acres of arable land around it.

Nothing could exceed the rural beauty of these two places, and for several years it was a very enjoyable retreat for my wife and children; but, clever as I thought I was, the farm was a source of continued little vexations.

I learned, like many others, that unless I gave hourly inspection, or employed some person to superintend (which the extent of the farm could not afford), all sorts of irregularities occurred.

The crop was not laid down in time, the harvesting was too late, men could not be got when wanted, cows were allowed to choke on turnips, work which should be done at a fixed period was not done.

The result was that, although I had laid out £500 or £600 on land improvements, &c., I was very glad to sublet the land, retaining the cottage and garden, after having incurred a loss in working of about £120 per annum for six years.

As to my sheep farm, the first two years were devoted to perfecting the stock, and it bade fair to be profitable; but when my stock was complete, and I calculated on a profitable return, Lord Seafield coveted it to add to his deer forest. He had purchased the lease of an adjoining farm on very profitable terms for the tenant, and to perfect the forest my sheep farm was thought to be absolutely necessary.

Unfortunately I was heard to say, that if his lordship wanted my farm after the expense I had incurred he would have to pay for it as he did the other. I had a lease of twenty-six years, and his chief gamekeeper incidentally was heard to express an opinion that "Mr. Mitchell, he had no doubt, would soon sicken of his sheep farming." I had made an agreement with his lordship's gamekeeper *per se* to keep an eye over my farming interests. I don't mean to say that the gamekeeper had a hand in it, but the first year after, I lost sixty sheep, said to have perished in a snowstorm. The second year one hundred and fifty were missing, and there was no accounting for them— they were gone.

The Procurator Fiscal of the county instituted inquiries; but no trace of the lost sheep could be discovered, so I thought it was best to make overtures to my friend the gamekeeper that I was willing to relinquish my lease on reasonable terms. In ordinary hands it would have been a profitable adventure.

Apart from these disagreeables, I confess, except for a few days, this Arcadian life was dull, and now and then I felt restless.

I had been too much accustomed to active employment for farming to be a source of continued and quiet contentment. Besides, this rural life was very soon upset, after it was formed, by a movement for the resuscitation of the railway schemes in which I had been formerly engaged, and to which my exclusive thoughts were now directed.

CHAPTER XXII.

Renewed efforts to promote Highland Railway—Effect of pamphlet on public mind—Effort to resuscitate scheme—Interview with the North-Western directors and Mr. Brassey—Construction of line to Nairn—Progress of railway eastwards—Negotiations with the Great North Company—Extension to Keith—Unfortunate accident.

I HAVE explained how in 1846 our efforts to establish railway communication in the Highlands had been defeated, and that by way of explaining the objects and acts of the promoters I published and circulated a pamphlet narrating the proceedings before the Parliamentary Committee, and criticising their decision, which I felt was not justified by the evidence laid before them. I also gave some calculations of the profit, and pointed out the advantages that might have been derived from the proposed railway.

This pamphlet had, as I have said, the effect of instructing the public mind in regard to the importance of this scheme, and as the Great North of Scotland Railway directors had at last intimated (1851) that it was not their intention, owing to pecuniary difficulties, to carry their line beyond Huntly, it was quite clear that unless those interested in the North of Scotland made some effort, the northern counties might be deprived of railway communication for an indefinite time.

Accordingly, in 1851–52 a committee was formed, and some £300 or £400 subscribed in the North to defray the expense of a deputation to London and elsewhere to urge

the Southern railway companies to assist in another effort
to promote the Highland Railway scheme.

Mr. Mackintosh of Raigmore, Mr. Peter Anderson, and I
were appointed the deputation for this purpose.

We communicated with all the great proprietors con-
nected with the North, whom we found most favourable.
We proceeded to London, where we had a meeting with the
London and North-Western Railway directors, and with
Mr. Locke the engineer and Mr. Brassey the contractor.

These latter gentlemen were then constructing the
Lancaster and Carlisle and Caledonian Railways, and,
knowing the importance of the line as a feeder to them and
the London and North-Western Railway, they urged us to
get the proprietors along the line to show practical evidence
of their willingness to give the land required on advantageous terms.

The money market, they stated, was not then favourable
for the project. When the time came, however, Mr. Locke
considered that the traffic to be brought on the London and
North Western Railway would warrant the directors taking
a third of the stock. Mr. Brassey, as the contractor, might
take another third, to which he agreed, and the remaining
third should be contributed by the Northern public. In
this way, he said, the capital for the works might easily be
raised.

I explained that I had got full details of the cost of the
works and of the traffic from our investigations in 1846;
but suggested that Mr. Brassey should satisfy himself as to
the estimates, and if he sent down an agent in whom he
had confidence, I would go over the ground with him, and
I suggested Mr. James Falshaw, then in Perth, for this
purpose.

This was agreed to, and further consideration of the
project was postponed until Mr. Brassey was enabled to
make a formal tender and estimate for the works.

On the return of the deputation a public meeting was
held in Inverness in April, 1853, to report the result of
their proceedings.

At this meeting an elaborate report was given, and I

made a statement, pointing out that lines in the Highlands, to be successful, must not follow the example in the South of expending £30,000 to £35,000 per mile on their works. They must construct their lines as in America, at a cost suited to the requirements and the limited traffic in the country.

I said that in the parliamentary contest of 1846, I had estimated a single line at £8817 per mile, and I had no doubt if the works were constructed on that moderate scale, the project would be amply remunerative. Singularly enough the line was completed and executed for £8850 per mile, including land and all expenses.*

The meeting thanked Mr. Anderson and me for our efforts, and appointed an influential committee to carry out the project, instructing us to revise our estimates and traffic returns, preparatory to resuscitating the company and issuing a new prospectus.

Mr. Falshaw, as representing Mr. Brassey, came to Inverness to go over the ground ; but was obliged then to abandon his examination on account of the inclement state of the weather.

Seeing that from the state of the money market there was little prospect of our great project being carried out, and considering that the powers of the Great North of Scotland Company had lapsed for the compulsory pur-chase of land, I addressed a letter to the Railway Committee dated 15th Sept., 1853, from which the following is an extract.

" You are aware that the great contest in 1846 between the promoters of the Aberdeen Railway and their opponents in the North was for the possession of the ground between Elgin and Inverness. By possessing this latter portion of the line, the Great North of Scotland Company calcu-lated to divert the entire northern traffic to the Aberdeen route.

" They have now abandoned this project, solely because they do not possess the means of constructing their line so

* See my paper " Description of Highland Railway Works," read before the British Association at Dundee.

far north, and for which they had obtained renewed parliamentary powers.

"It appears to me therefore that the present time is favourable for those interested in promoting the direct Highland Railway taking possession of this ground, which in fact forms the key to the North, and the possession of which will secure to the proprietors of the northern counties the means of constructing the through short line whenever the favourable opportunity arises.

"I would therefore propose that we should forthwith form a company for making the railway between Nairn and Inverness as part of the great scheme of communication.

"The easiness with which the line can be constructed, and the local traffic, will make it undoubtedly profitable, and it may be accomplished by subscriptions within the locality.

"Of course guarantees should be taken that whenever the means are forthcoming for the construction of the through line, it should on a proper equivalent be merged into and form a part of the great scheme.

"By this arrangement the committee will be making a step in progress, they become a tangible body by possessing these works, and will have the means of more readily pushing forward and carrying out their original project.

"The line to Nairn should be no obstruction or objection to the Aberdeen company. The more traffic passing to and from Morayshire on the line would always increase their traffic, and they would be entitled to facilities and arrangements.

"I am decidedly of opinion, therefore, that as the first step in the great scheme, we should proceed to Parliament for power to construct the portion of the main line, between Inverness and Nairn, the parliamentary plans and documents being almost all prepared."

The committee happily approved of this suggestion, and resolved to go to Parliament that session for the line to Nairn.

The plans were laid before Mr. Falshaw, at Perth, on

the 9th November. I obtained an offer from Messrs. Brassey and Falshaw for the works at £85,000, the contractors taking £20,000 in the shares of the company

The prospectus was published in 1853.

The inhabitants of Inverness and Nairn came forward handsomely with subscriptions. It was a great triumph, after being so thoroughly defeated in 1846, for the Inverness people themselves to be able to construct the line to Nairn.

Lady Seafield was good enough to cut the first turf on the 21st September, 1854.

We had a procession of the magistrates and notabilities of the town on the occasion, and a dinner in the town hall, where the railway future of the North was eloquently prognosticated.

The works, being of a simple character, were soon constructed, and on November 5th, 1855, the Nairn line was opened for public traffic.

Further Progress of the Railway to Keith.

The directors, having got to Nairn, were determined to carry out their original scheme to Elgin, and I was ordered in the spring of 1855 to prepare plans of the line, with the view of going to Parliament in the next session.

The Nairn railway was promoted chiefly by citizens of Inverness ; but the movement for extending the railway to Elgin induced the two great potentates and political rivals in the counties of Moray and Banff (the Earls of Seafield and Fife) to come forward and join, each subscribing £30,000 ; and they very properly thereafter, from their rank and interest in the country, took a leading part in carrying out the undertaking. Their object, naturally, was to complete the railway communication through their extensive territories to Aberdeen.

The directors of the Great North of Scotland Company, who, as explained, obtained parliamentary power in 1846 to make the whole line from Aberdeen to Inverness, and who at this time (1855) intimated that it was not their intention to extend their line beyond Morayshire, objected to the Northern Company terminating their line at Elgin, and thus leaving to them, as they said, the heavy works of crossing the Spey, and the construction of the line through the difficult country from that river to Keith, the works, according to their plans, being of a very formidable and expensive character.

Ultimately it was arranged that both companies should join in the centre of the Spey viaduct, each contributing their moiety of the cost of that work, and that in the event of the Northern Company being unable to raise the capital for this addition, in time for that parliamentary session (1855), the agreement should hold good for the succeeding session of 1855–56.

The application to Parliament was accordingly delayed till the session of 1855–56, by which means I obtained time to examine the country more carefully, with a view to lessening the expense of these formidable works.

I found that by altering the gradient of the line for two and a half miles east of the Spey from 1 in 100 to 1 in 60, and thus lowering the height of the viaduct and works some thirty feet, a saving could be effected of about £50,000.

The Aberdeen Company, on this, proposed that the Highland Company, instead of joining them at the Spey, should extend their line to Keith station, in which event they would contribute £40,000 to the cost of the work. To this the Highland directors agreed.

The Bill was accordingly passed in July, 1856, for the whole line from Nairn to Keith, which was named "The Inverness and Aberdeen Junction Railway."

Thus, singularly enough, notwithstanding the bitter contentions of the Aberdeen Company before Parliament in 1846, for the short line between Inverness and Nairn (fifteen miles), the Highland Company ultimately became the possessors of one-half of the railway between Inverness and Aberdeen, fifty-five miles. By this means they secured a more extended base along the shores of the Moray Firth for their great plan of the direct railway through the central Highlands.

When the Bill passed, the working drawings were prepared, and contracts were entered into at once, for the eastern end to Keith with Messrs. Mitchell, Dean, and Co., and for the portion from Nairn to Elgin with Messrs. Brassey and Falshaw.

The works were heavy and formidable, and were constructed for a double line, a single line of rails being laid down in the meantime.

Three great rivers had to be crossed, besides the Lossie and minor streams, and for the foundations of the large bridges rock had to be reached through the deep channel of the rivers, and through a bed of solid gravel varying six, eight, and ten feet in depth.

The Nairn is crossed by a stone bridge of five arches. The Findhorn by a bridge with stone piers, having three openings spanned by iron girders, each 150 feet. The Spey viaduct is seventy feet in height, and the river is crossed by an iron girder, 230 feet long, with six side arches of stone for the passage of the flood-waters. This was a formidable and difficult work, costing in all £34,482.

The works were finished and the line opened to Keith on the 18th August, 1858. It was amalgamated with the Nairn line, and both became one concern.

The superintending and constructing of these works was to me an unalloyed pleasure, although I had no small difficulty in keeping the contractors to their specifications.

Mr. Falshaw, the partner of Brassey, who managed this contract, displayed a talent for great organization in carrying on his works. But he never forgave me for compelling him to execute the works in terms of his contracts.

Difficulties on the Opening of the Line.

The works were carried on with great rapidity; but the directors, particularly the deputy-chairman, who took an active part in the business of the company, could not be restrained, in more than one instance, from insisting on opening the line prematurely.

Twice did they bring the Government inspectors on the ground without my sanction, and twice were the works rejected as incomplete.

The Board of Trade would not sanction the opening of the line for carrying the traffic over the scaffolding erected for the construction of the Spey Bridge. The directors, however, determined to take their own way notwithstanding, and they opened the line and carried on the traffic on the timber scaffolding.

I did all I could to prevent this, and finding at last that the weight of the iron girders, as they were being fixed, together with the vibrations of the locomotive and trains passing, was forcing the scaffolding to sink, and diminishing the camber of the bridge, I officially intimated that I would not be in any way responsible for the safety of the bridge, or any accident which might consequently occur.

The directors were in a dilemma. They were unwilling to exhibit vacillation in their actings by stopping the traffic they had so prematurely begun, and they instructed that platforms should be constructed at either end of the viaduct, and passengers were asked to walk over the suspension bridge adjoining. The empty train then without the locomotive passed slowly over the staging, when passengers got in again at the east platform, then the train with another engine had to start to Keith at the foot of the incline of 1 in 60.

This arrangement, although awkward, answered so far; but on one occasion, 4th September, 1858, in their effort to start, the break van got off the rails, and all their efforts could not then replace it.

The driver, in order to keep his time, and to forward his passengers to Aberdeen, detached the van, and proceeded to Keith with the remainder of the train, intimating that he would return immediately for the van left at the bridge, requesting the men there to have it on the rails by his return.

The station of Mulben is situated two and a half miles at the top of the incline, and to prevent any loose carriages from accidentally getting on the incline, and so descending by their own gravitation, the incline was locked, and any carriages that might accidentally escape from the station were thereby thrown on a level siding, which terminated on a perpendicular gravel bank.

The driver having delivered his train and passengers at Keith as arranged, rushed back to the Spey for the van left, taking with him the stoker, a porter, a pointsman, and three cleaners, William Mackay, John Hughes, and John Williams.

The engineman on reaching Mulben station did not recollect, or was unaware, that the incline was locked, it being Saturday night. His engine accordingly, instead of descending the incline, rushed on the siding, when it suddenly dashed against the gravel bank, crushing the three cleaners standing on the engine between the tender and furnace. There they were hopelessly transfixed, for there was no means of moving the engine or relieving the unhappy men, caught and held in the front of the furnace.

The engineman and the three others escaped with comparatively little injury ; but the three unfortunate cleaners fixed on the engine expired in about two hours after the accident, being in a measure burnt alive.

The manager and I were telegraphed for, and we reached Mulben about nine a.m. Some assistance had been got from Keith in the meantime, and the bodies of the unfortunate men were removed to the station ; but it was a sad sight.

The poor engineman was arrested, and at the assizes in Inverness got six months imprisonment ; but, as Sydney Smith said that dangers on railways would never be averted until a bishop was burnt, so justice would have been more fairly dealt out, if the parties who authorized the traffic to be carried on while the line was incomplete, in defiance of the Board of Trade and the warning of their own engineer, had been brought to account for this melancholy catastrophe.

CHAPTER XXIII.

Extension of Railway to Invergordon—The Highland Railway—Visit
to the Duke of Athole—Construction of Line—Banquet at Inverness.

WHILE the works of the Inverness and Aberdeen junction
were in progress, I was ordered to make a preliminary
survey and estimate of the line northwards to Dingwall.

In October, after the junction line was opened, Messrs.
Inglis and Leslie, writers to the signet, our Edinbugh
agents, were in communication with me as to the extension of the railway into Ross-shire, and I furnished them
with such information as my local knowlege and surveys
afforded.

In January, 1859, meetings of the country gentlemen
were held at Inverness, and a provisional committee
was appointed to carry out the undertaking through
Ross-shire. I was instructed to prepare a parliamentary
survey, and on the 3rd July, 1860, the bill was passed for
the line extending from Inverness to Invergordon.

The works on this line passing through a picturesque
country were not very heavy, except the bridges, which were
formidable, and the construction of some very effective
mason-work was interesting.

The Ness, a deep and rapid river, is crossed by a handsome stone bridge of five arches of 75 feet span, with four
land arches of 20 feet, and two cast-iron openings of
27 and 35 feet span for roads; the length being 669 feet;
the cost was £13,500. The successful construction of this
bridge across the Ness for so small a sum was to me a
source of pride and satisfaction.

The Caledonian Canal is crossed by a wrought-iron swing-bridge, 126 feet in length, 78 feet of which spans the canal on a skew of 65 degrees.

But crossing the river Conon I considered a great triumph of bridge engineering. The structure is 45 feet in height, 540 feet in length, and consists of five arches of 75 feet span, built on a skew of 45 degrees with the river : that is, the north abutment is built 304 feet lower down the stream than the south abutment, and the skew is effected by a series of right-angled stone ribs spanning from pier to pier. The whole was so perfectly fitted together that when the centres were removed no joint in the whole building showed any indication of setting. The cost of this bridge was £11,391.

Several other bridges of considerable size were also built on this line, and the railway was opened for traffic to Dingwall, in June, 1862, and to Invergordon on May 23rd, 1863.

Preliminary Arrangements and Construction of Inverness and Perth Railways.

The line being open to Keith in 1858, through communication was established from Inverness to Aberdeen. Unfortunately there was a break at the latter city of about a mile and a half.

The directors of the Great North and those of the South Aberdeen railways did not work harmoniously, consequently a considerable portion of the goods reaching Aberdeen from the North was detained there and sent by sea. Moreover, passengers from the North, by the then traffic arrangements, were generally compelled to spend a night in Aberdeen.

Meeting after meeting of directors was held with a view to completing the through communication, and so removing this serious detention at Aberdeen, but it was to no purpose. The Northern traffic was purposely retarded, and to a certain extent diverted.

Again the Aberdeen directors attended the meetings in Inverness in right of their subscription, and were very

o

obstructive. They claimed a right to interfere from their holding £40,000 of the Junction Company's stock.

Mr. Matheson, the chairman at a meeting, January 5th, 1860, said that, seeing they were so frequently antagonistic, he would relieve them of their stock of £40,000 if they wished; and to our surprise the Aberdonians assented to this proposal. The transaction was agreed to, and we had no more obstruction at the meetings from the directors of the Great North of Scotland Company. Still the obstructions in the traffic continued, and there appeared no hope of filling up the gap in the line at Aberdeen.

The directors of the Northern lines, therefore, saw no alternative but to resuscitate the former project of the direct railway by Strathspey and Athole. This was the more pressing as our opponents were surveying a line up Spey side to Grantown ; and at the south end a railway was being surveyed to extend from Dunkeld to Pitlochrie. It was clear, therefore, immediate action was necessary, as evidently these schemes were intended to block up and obstruct the direct and short line of communication to the South.

A committee was therefore at once appointed, consisting of Sir Alexander Cumming, Bart., Mr. Mackintosh of Raigmore, Colonel Fraser Tytler, the law agents, and myself, to confer with the proprietors along the Highland line, especially the Duke of Athole, through whose estate the railway had to pass for twenty-four miles.

They met at Dunkeld on June 9th, and had an interview with his Grace.

The duke stated that he objected to all railways in the Highlands. He was opposed to the scheme of 1846, but he objected still more to the branch to Pitlochrie, now proposed by the chairman of the South Aberdeen Company.

If he consented to a railway at all, it would be a through line as now proposed, as such would be most beneficial to the general public; but he would give no opinion on the subject until the line was pointed out to him, and until he was satisfied that it was not detrimental either to himself or his tenants.

The deputation agreed that his propositions and requirements were reasonable, and I was instructed to wait upon
his Grace at any time he should fix, in order that he
might understand fully the direction and bearings of the
railway.

His Grace was very courteous, entertained the deputation
at lunch, and as Sir Alexander Cumming and he had been
Eton boys, they discussed their early adventures while
resident at that distinguished school.

Visit to the Duke of Athole.

In terms of the arrangement with the duke, I went to
Blair in September to explain to his Grace the direction
and bearings of the railway, and he politely requested I
should be his guest at the castle during my sojourn.

At this time the duke was a keen sportsman, ready to
endure any amount of fatigue, brave and active, fond of
agriculture and a promoter of it.

In my subsequent interviews with his Grace, I had ample
opportunities of knowing him. He was manly, kindhearted,
and upright, proud of his dignity, of his magnificent estates,
and people. He was no politician, and whatever wayward
and impulsive eccentricities he displayed arose very much
from imperfect education and training.

As to the duchess, she was the very beau-ideal of a
Scotch lady of high rank—charitable, considerate, with
tact, good sense, and kindliness, and withal gracefully
bearing the dignity of her position. It is no wonder she
has been the favourite companion and lady-in-waiting for
many years to the Queen.

On reaching Blair Inn, at 2 p.m., I asked the landlord
at what hour they dined at the castle. He said, eight
o'clock is the fixed hour; but I would advise you to lunch,
for it may be much later. Which advice I followed, and
then proceeded to look after my survey.

The servant said dinner would be about nine; but he
would give me due notice.

Having dressed for dinner, I sat down with my book to

while away the time; but when nine o'clock struck, and there was no notice of dinner, it occurred to me that the servant had forgotten my existence; so I found my way up the grand staircase to the drawing-room, which was lighted up; but there was neither duke, duchess, nor guest, and I had nothing for it but solitarily to revert to the newspapers on the table. At ten precisely, the duke, duchess, and Miss Macgregor appeared, the duke in full Highland costume. After the usual salutations we walked into dinner, at which we had three stalwart Highlanders waiting in full Highland dress.*

---

* The duke, as I have said, was somewhat eccentric, and although the demesnes of Blair Athole and Dunkeld, with their beautiful woods and walks, perhaps the finest in Great Britain, were open at all times to strangers, he got into bad odour with the public by obstructing with his gillies, tourists and botanists from passing from Braemar, through Glen Tilt, which he held to be his private property, and he objected to its being used as a public thoroughfare, on account of disturbing his deer.

The newspapers took up this question of obstruction, and Leech, in *Punch*, caricatured the noble obstructionist and his deer-stalking propensities.

For several years Leech spent his holidays at the beautiful inn at Birnam, near Dunkeld; and the duke told me, after the appearance of one of his severe caricatures, he wrote to him to say he was misrepresented and misunderstood, but if he (Leech) would do him the honour of spending a week at Blair, he would show him what real deer-stalking was, and he would meet some jolly sportsmen. Leech accepted the invitation.

He spent a happy week with the duke, and made them some very pretty sketches of deer-stalking and stalkers in the Athole forest. The duke said he and Leech were good friends ever after.

In Duke John's time they tell a story of Sheridan, who was a guest at Blair and invited to shoot in the forest. There was then no road except a stony bridle-path through Glen Tilt. Sheridan was unaccustomed to such excursions on a Highland pony, and went up to the forest in fear and trembling.

After spending some hours there, they were regaled with lunch and a liberal allowance of Athole Brose (Athole Brose consisting of a mixture of four-fifths whisky and one-fifth water, with a good allowance of honey). Sheridan felt elevated with these mountain refreshments and rode back with confidence and pleasure. On his return to the castle, he reported with great glee that there was nothing that improved and smoothed a mountain road like "Athole Brose."

In the course of conversation, I remarked that it was thirty-six years since I first breakfasted in that room, and I then recounted my first interview with his Grace's grandfather.

"Ah! how odd," the duke remarked, "your father built the Tilt bridge and made the new road below the castle, and now you are come to make the railway." And the duchess said, "The young lady who brought you to breakfast is now Lady Oakley."

It was arranged that next day at eleven we should proceed to examine the line. In the carriage I laid out my plans. The duke said I had better explain to the duchess, she understood plans better than he did. Fortunately I had ordered the line to be staked out for several miles, indicating the direction by little white flags, which very much pleased his Grace, and I gained his confidence by explaining that by the line passing through a certain bank two or three fine oak trees would have to come down. He said he would not submit to that, he was determined; but the duchess, with admirable tact, threw oil upon the waters, and explained that in a wooded country some sacrifices must be made, and that his Grace, she was sure, had no want of fine trees, and could very easily spare a few for so important a purpose. He was, however, much pleased at what he called my honesty in explaining this.

His Grace had made a handsome new approach through his park of some two miles in length to the north of the castle, and as we could not carry our gradient of 1 in 70 without crossing the north end of it and cutting a little corner off the park, he was very decided in his objections. It would destroy his beautiful approach, which had cost him so much. I assured him it would not be seen, as we would go over it or under it; and besides, the company, I was sure, would give him a handsome lodge, so that the railway would be an ornament rather than an eyesore at the north entrance of his demesne. I drew a rough sketch of the lodge which might be made, and with which the duchess was much pleased.

His Grace accepted the railway over the approach.

Another difficulty was crossing the river Garry at Struan, four miles from Blair, where there were waterfalls and plantations, through which there were pleasure walks to view the falls. This interesting spot he objected to have touched, and I got over this difficulty by spanning road and river obliquely at the narrow point by a three arch bridge, thus not interfering with either his plantations or walks. The railway bridge was, in fact, an ornament to the falls, and he was much pleased with what he considered the ingenuity of the arrangement.

In fact, from that time, for nearly two years during the progress of the works, I seemed to have secured his goodwill and confidence, and he insisted on my being his guest whenever my duties brought me to Athole.

As to the valuation of his land, he would not allow a law agent to interfere. He would leave all to Mr. Elliot, a gentleman extensively employed by railway companies on land valuations, an honest and upright arbitrator.

He took great interest in the works, which seemed to give him a new pleasure, and had he lived, from his desire to do right and the interest he began to take in public matters since the railway began, he would have proved a valuable man of business; but alas! it was not to be. He was seized with cancer in the throat, from which he suffered great agony. He bore his fate with a manly and intrepid spirit.

Although very ill, he insisted on travelling on the line. And on the eve of its being opened a truck was fitted up for him, and, accompanied by the duchess and myself, we travelled between the County March and Pitlochrie, and he seemed to enjoy the rapid motion in descending from the County March at the rate of fifty miles an hour—rather a dangerous speed on a new-made line.

A few months before his death, at an entertainment given to his Athole Highlanders at Blair, he came in after dinner with wonderful coolness to express his regard and gratitude for their attention and discipline. He felt he would never meet them again, and he was there that day to bid them a kind and affectionate farewell.* He died on January 16th, 1864.

During his illness, which was long and painful, no lady of whatever rank could have displayed towards her husband more devoted tenderness and attention than did the admirable duchess.

Construction of Railway Works.

The chief of the Mackintoshes and the Laird of Glentruim in Badenoch, in their enthusiasm for the railway, offered their lands gratis. Their offer, of course, was not accepted, as all the other proprietors claimed compensation.

I had great difficulty at Castle Grant. We could not get a line without encroaching on the park. I took levels in every direction, but it was of no avail; and I had to tell Lord Seafield that there was no alternative but to go through the park, that I would depress the line and make it as little objectionable as possible, and for injuring the amenity of the park he would obtain compensation. This he handsomely repudiated and declined. For his liberality the company built him a pretty lodge as the line entered the park at one of the gateways of the castle.

The notices were given, and the parliamentary plans were duly lodged before November 30th, 1860. The directors met to authorize the Bill to proceed; but Mr. Bruce, Lord Seafield's agent, who was supposed to be flirting with the Great North of Scotland Company, was absent, and they declined to enter upon so serious an undertaking without the assent of either Lord Seafield or his commissioner, his lordship being so deeply interested in the undertaking. I told the Board if they prorogued their meeting till next day (which they did) I would go to Glen Urquhart and endeavour to

---

* Duke John, the grandfather, raised a regiment, like other chiefs of the time, "The Athole Highlanders," or "71st Regiment." And the Duke in 1839 called out a body-guard of Athole men for the Eglinton tournament. Afterwards, in 1842, during the Queen's first visit to Scotland, they were augmented and called out. In the year 1844–45 they were formed into a Royal Guard at Blair Castle during the Queen's residence there. Her Majesty presented them with colours.

They consist of four companies of forty men each, exclusive of officers. They now assemble annually during the "Athole games."

induce Lord Seafield to attend. His lordship was ill, but at great inconvenience he came down, and along with the other directors sanctioned our going to Parliament that session, which I considered a great feat.

The Bill passed July 22nd, 1861, all opposition being withdrawn. The directors met immediately after to elect a chairman and officials. Mr. Matheson had conducted the business of the junction railway so satisfactorily that both the directors and the public looked upon him as a matter of course as the future chairman for the Highland Company; but at this meeting, to the surprise of every one, Major Cumming Bruce, father-in-law of Lord Elgin, got up, and after a short allusion to the Hon. Thomas Bruce's qualifications, proposed him as chairman. Sir Alexander Cumming seconded the motion, and Raigmore and Lord Seafield approved of it, and the election was accomplished, the Hon. Thomas Bruce taking the chair. The other directors and officials were not only astonished but disappointed at this arrangement; but Mr. Matheson was too astute not to overcome this difficulty, and the next thing we heard of some weeks after was that Mr. Bruce had retired from the chairmanship, Mr. Matheson becoming chairman, and Mr. Bruce being appointed managing director at a salary of £500 a year during the progress of the works, subsequently reduced when the works were finished to £250, so that Mr. Bruce has always been a leading adviser in the administration of the railway. Mr. Bruce is an able man and devotes about ten days per annum of his time to the service of the company.

With the view of promptly completing the works I divided the whole distance between Forres and Dunkeld (104 miles) into nine contracts, besides the Aberfeldy branch. They were undertaken £15,705 below my estimate, and completed twelve per cent. over it, the total cost, £919,204, or £8860 per mile, including all the great bridges, land, engineering, and parliamentary expenses.*

* At a preliminary meeting held at Inverness, December 16th, 1852, I stated the cost of the line would be £8117, so that the ultimate cost of the line came pretty nearly to the sum originally calculated in the estimates of 1846.

The directors resolved in beginning so important a work, in which the Northern public were so deeply interested, to have a public demonstration on the occasion of cutting the first turf.

Accordingly, on the 17th October, 1861, a great meeting of gentry and general public assembled from north, east, and south at Forres to witness the ceremony.

Lady Seafield was kind enough to perform this duty, for the line passed through a large extent of the Seafield property, and Lord Seafield had most liberally and substantially subscribed for the work.

Bands of music were in attendance, and the Seafield Highlanders, headed by General Sir Patrick Grant, K.C.B., were there with their pipers.

Her ladyship performed her duty with a grace and dignity that drew forth the admiration of the assembled people. It was indeed a day of rejoicing for the whole Highlands, for the line shortened their communication by railway with the South some sixty miles.

The Divie viaduct and the Dunkeld tunnel had been commenced shortly before; but the whole works of the line (104 miles) were completed in the period from cutting the first turf (17th October, 1861) to the passing of the line by the Government inspector, 9th September, 1863, being one year and eleven months.

Considering the difficulty of the country, and the necessity of collecting men and materials from distant parts, no work of a like magnitude that I know of has been carried out in so short a time. The line was opened no doubt prematurely by some weeks, and caused the officials much anxiety during the winter. It was much against my will; but the directors naturally wished to catch the tourist traffic of that season.

On the 9th of September the directors commenced the traffic—an adventurous proceeding, for no preliminary trains had been run through to test the line and the working of the engines; and the drivers were new men, unacquainted with the line and the gradients.

At 10.18 a.m. a long train started from Inverness,

having on the several carriages, " York, Euston Square, King's Cross," &c., and a young lady in the carriage in which I travelled said to me with innocent delight, " We shall be in London to-morrow morning." I had not the cruelty to dispel her pleasing delusion.

Another train was to start from Perth for the North in the middle of the night. The clerks at the different stations could not work, or worked very imperfectly, the telegraph, and at Dumphail station, where I stopped, we had no trains and no communication the first day.

The engineman from Perth arrived at Struan, where from some cause or other the engine refused to ascend the incline, and there he was, he and his passengers, in a mountainous country, unknown, in the dark, within hearing of the adjoining Falls of the Garry.

These irregularities were overcome in a few days, and there was much reason for thankfulness that no accident occurred beyond the detention of the innocent and unhappy passengers who ventured to travel the first two or three days on the Highland line.

We had to keep a large body of men working (but half idle on account of frosts), watching the new permanent way and unfinished water-courses on the hill during the whole winter, which in 1863–64 was fortunately more open and free from snow than any winter since. But to me, who knew the dangers to which the trains were exposed, this state of things was a matter of intense anxiety.

No accident happily occurred, and the public were well pleased with the convenience and facilities afforded by the new route. I mention the circumstance, however, as a warning to directors not to interfere, as Mr. Bruce did, obstinately, in matters so purely professional as the opening of a new line.

In order to testify their sense of the great advantage of railway communication in the Highlands, and particularly the construction of the Highland lines, the noblemen and gentlemen in the Northern counties entertained the directors to a splendid banquet on the 10th September, 1863.

The dinner was held in the Northern Meeting Rooms.

That distinguished statesman, the late Right Hon. Edward Ellice, M.P., was in the chair. About three hundred and fifty gentlemen were present, including all the leading proprietors in the North. Indeed, I never recollect in Inverness so distinguished a gathering. Among the strangers were the Right Hon. Robert Lowe, Shirley Brooks, &c.

"Mr. Ellice, in giving the health of the chairman and directors of the two railways, spoke in high terms of the readiness with which the aristocracy and gentry of the country had assisted in contributing to these railways. They had given their land moderately, and subscribed liberally, particularly the Duke of Athole, the Duke of Sutherland, the Earl of Seafield, the Earl of Fife, and Mr. Matheson, M.P.

"The gratitude of the district was due also to Mr. Mitchell, the engineer ; for their lines had been made with great prudence. Their cost had not exceeded one-third of most of the railways in the South.

"Mr. Mackintosh of Raigmore proposed the health of Mr. Mitchell, the engineer of the line, and his staff.

"He would say nothing of Mr. Mitchell's position in his profession generally ; but he believed he spoke within bounds in saying that for the immediate purpose of this railway, for carrying an iron road through the Highlands, no engineer in Britain was so well qualified, and no other person had such a knowledge of the country or such a staff of well-qualified assistants for carrying out this undertaking. Not a sportsman or poacher in the country knew every corry and glen in the Highlands so well as Mr. Mitchell and Mr. Paterson.

"It had been the good fortune of the company to find among the officials of the company not only good servants, but men who could work for them with a will, and of no one could this be said with greater truth than of Mr. Mitchell, who had unhappily, but he trusted temporarily, injured himself in this service.

"Mr. Mitchell returning thanks, said 'he still recollected that on the eventful occasion when the first turf of the railway was cut so gracefully by Lady Seafield, he viewed the ceremony with mingled feelings; first of great satisfaction that a long-cherished scheme had been so favourably begun, and then of anxiety lest he should fail to carry out effectually those great works which the kindness and good opinion of the directors had put under his charge.

" ' The work was now accomplished, he hoped, effectually, and it remained only for him to express his acknowledgments for the support and consideration he had received under the many difficulties they had to encounter, and also his thanks to his staff of engineers for their earnest and energetic labours to complete the work, without which it could not have been accomplished in the time.' "

The most important engineering works were, first, the viaduct across the Tay, six miles from Dunkeld, being two iron trellis girders, one 210 ft. span, and the other 141 ft., on stone abutments and piers; the total length 515 ft., the cost £20,395.

Two iron trellis bridges, one being also a viaduct across the Tay at Logierait, of two spans of 137 ft. each, and two side spans of 41 ft.; length 419 ft., cost £11,156. And also a bridge at Ballinluig across the Tummel of two spans of 122 ft. each, and two side spans of 35 ft.; length 350 ft., cost £13,772. These girders were supported by cast-iron cylinders sunk 27 ft. deep into the bed of the river, with interior masonry in Portland cement.

Killiecrankie viaduct of stone, ten arches of 35 ft.; total length 508 ft., cost £10,000.

Viaduct over the Divie near Forres, seven arches of 45 ft.; total length 477 ft., height 106 ft. above the bed of the river; cost £10,231.

There are two tunnels, each some 300 yards long, near Dunkeld and at the pass of Killiecrankie, which were made in order to preserve the amenity of these beautiful localities.

The line has now been in full working order for twenty years without an accident having taken place from any defect in its construction; and, although the works are not on a magnificent scale, I may claim credit for ascending the highest summit level—1588 feet—from the valley of the Tay to the valley of the Spey, and from the valley of

the Spey to that of the Findhorn, which are separated by
a mountain range 1046 feet above sea level. This was
accomplished with gradients not exceeding 1 in 70, and
without tunnels. I have also in my prosessional life
crossed every great river in Scotland, with the exceptions
of the Tweed, the Clyde, and the Forth, with good substantial bridges ; the only temporary bridges erected being
over the River Beauly and at Newtonmore, which, in consequence of deficient capital, were built of timber, but they
are now being replaced by iron or stone bridges.

On the Central Railway from Dunkeld to Forres, 104
miles, being a single line, there are eight viaducts, 126
bridges over streams, 119 trellis and accommodation-road
bridges, 8100 yards of covered drains, varying in size from
18 to 36 inches square.

There are 1650 lineal yards of breastwalls, 304,700 cubic
yards of rock-cutting, and 3,416,000 cubic yards of earth-
work, being rock and earth at the rate of 35,776 cubic yards
to the mile. The largest embankment was at Rafford, near
Forres, which contained 308,000 cubic yards.

The permanent way consists of larch and natural grown
Scotch fir sleepers of the usual size 3 ft. apart; the rails
are 22 lbs. in weight; the ribs weigh 75 lbs. to the lineal
yard, are in lengths of 24 ft., and are fished at the joints.

The total cost of. the works, including all extra and
accommodation works, amounted for the 104 miles to
£798,311. The land, including severance, to £70,000,
and the preliminary parliamentary, engineering, and law
expenses to £50,893, making the cost of this portion of the
company's lines £919,204, or £8860 per mile.

In tracing out the line there was no small research and
difficulty in finding good working gradients at the least possible cost, also in passing through a country so rugged and
liable to the floods of these great rivers and innumerable
minor streams.

As the Highland Company had by this time got possession of one-half of the line between Inverness and Aberdeen,
I had to alter the original starting-point of the main line
southwards from Kildrummie and Nairn to the town of

Forres, so as to make the through line available not only for the northern counties, but for the fertile and populous country along the shores of the Moray Firth.

The passing of the Bills and the construction of those railways constituted the busiest part of my life. Not but that I was always busy, but there was during this period an extra mental strain, having in so short a space of time to plan and carry out so many difficult and important works.

Mr. Bruce, our managing director, was very urgent for progress. I was always willing, but I recollect writing to beg he would not press too much the willing horse. The strain was too much; I was seized with paralysis on the 4th May, 1862, and lost the use of my left side. My head was clear, but my left arm and leg were powerless. Here, then, was apparently an end to my busy life and useful work.

To the surprise of myself and my doctors I was able to walk across the room in a month, and was ordered in July to proceed to London, and afterwards to Norwood and Brighton for a change. I suffered much from sciatica and exhaustion after even a short walk.

I returned to Inverness in the end of September very much better, but with little power of walking beyond about half a mile, and that very slowly. The directors of the railway and my other employers showed great sympathy.

Fortunately all the railway works had been planned and contracted for, and placed under the superintendence of qualified resident engineers and inspectors. Mr. Bruce, our managing director, took an active interest in the works for two or three months. This led to some complications afterwards.

I was, however, enabled to resume my duties, although imperfectly, by the end of the year 1862. Considering the importance of the works in hand, and the projects with which I was more or less connected, I felt it was necessary, if I continued my professional work at all, to have more recognized assistance, and I engaged as partners, Mr. William and Mr. Murdoch Paterson. The former had been in my service twenty-two years, the latter had been eighteen years, and had been trained by me from his youth.   Both were most efficient in their respective departments, and were intimately acquainted with all my plans and arrangements.

CHAPTER XXIV.

Abolition of the Commission for Highland Roads and Bridges—
Construction of Railway to Bonar—The Sutherland Railways—The
Duke of Sutherland—The Sutherland and Caithness Railway.

It is said that misfortunes seldom come singly. Besides
the serious illness which had deprived me for a time of the
power of locomotion, I got notice in June following from
the secretary, Sir Thomas Erskine May, that the grant of
£5000, paid in aid of the maintenance of the roads and
bridges in the Highlands, had been withdrawn by Parliament, and that the commission had virtually ceased, and
would have to be wound up.

This notice was a break-up of agreeable professional
service, of duties which had become second nature after
nearly forty years ; and that with my ill-health created a
pang of painful regret. I felt at the time it was like a
notice that the end was drawing near. My duties for years
under the Highland Road Commission went on pleasantly.
My intercourse with the proprietors was agreeable and
friendly. Occasionally some of the heritors expressed discontent on the old ground of having no voice in the management. They felt that the Commissioners and secretary were
high officers of state, chiefly residing in London, and
although they were aware of my consultations with the
convener of the counties, I, as general inspector, appeared
to have absolute control of the works and repairs.

I happened about 1842 to excite the enmity of two or
three parties in the country, particularly a solicitor who
acted as agent at the county meetings for several heritors

in Inverness-shire. He was a man of astute and powerful intellect. At a county meeting in that year he made very unscrupulous statements in regard to the administration and the heavy expenses of the roads, which the county had to bear, and which, he said, he would prove if he were granted a committee of investigation.

The meeting, with an air of injured innocence, could say nothing but that they knew nothing, which was true, for they had never inquired. I happened to be present, and stated that I was the officer of the Commissioners and not the servant of the county, that I attended their meeting as a matter of courtesy, to give whatever explanations might be required. They knew the detailed accounts were published, and that the convener was cognisant of all the contracts and proceedings. That as there was nothing to conceal, I would, with the authority of my employers, afford ample explanations and lay before the committee every document and paper which they might require.

I urged the Commissioners to authorize the investigation, which they did, and in their report to Parliament in March, 1843, they allude to the committee in the following terms :—

"In the month of February, 1842, a committee was appointed by the county of Inverness for the purpose of investigating the management and cost of the roads under the charge of the Commissioners, against which complaints had been raised by individual heritors.

"The Commissioners, in the belief that their system would bear the closest investigation, directed every facility to be given to the inquiry by the production of all necessary documents, and the personal examination of their officers, of which the committee availed themselves to the fullest extent.

"The charges alleged were : (1st) the exorbitant expense of repairs, and in particular for materials used ; (2nd) the practical exclusion of competition for the repair contracts by want of publicity, undue preference, and vexatious enforcement of conditions ; (3rd) excessive cost of management and inspection. The committee entered into a

P

minute and searching analysis of the whole items of expenditure, on the four most expensive lines, viz.: Beauly, Fort George, Moy, and Badenoch roads; other lines were subjected to a similar examination; and to afford the means of comparison, statements of the expense of roads in various other parts of the kingdom, obtained by Mr. Mitchell from the most authentic sources, were laid before the committee.

" The investigation by the committee into the several points above enumerated occupied nearly ten months, necessarily involving much sacrifice of time and convenience to the principal inspector during that period; but the result has been too gratifying to him and to the Commissioners to permit of regret."

The report of the committee, 2nd November, 1842, after giving a general sketch of their proceedings, concluded with the following paragraph.

" The committee having given their best attention to all the evidence produced before them, and having spared no pains to arrive at the truth, are of opinion that the parliamentary and military roads, under the charge of the Honourable Board of Commissioners, are maintained in a very perfect state of repair, and at less cost than any other roads of a similar description. This they conceive to be the best proof that could be obtained of the high approach to perfection attained in the system of management."

This investigation, as the Commissioners stated, extended over ten months, and as the law agent, who was my chief accuser at each meeting, was being constantly baffled, he did not hesitate to call for every document in my office for the ten or twelve years previous, which he thought might turn out a subject of inculpation.

However this report was a great triumph after all the annoyance to which I had been subjected.

The Inverness committee might well report as they did, for during all our transactions (over thirty-nine years) I am not aware of any act done by myself or my assistants that was not in the interest of the counties and for the public benefit.

The old inspectors employed by the Commissioners a few years after my appointment in 1825 had died off, several in great poverty from inadequate pay ; and Lord Colchester, on my representation, obtained an increase in their allowances of £200 per annum among the six. I had to select others from time to time among the intelligent masons with whom I came in contact throughout the country, and it is gratifying for me to record how faithfully and ably those men performed their onerous duties.

When I received the notice that the Commission was to be wound up, I wrote to Sir Thomas E. May that "I had procured maps of the several counties, and laid down on these maps the position and names of the various roads in each county to be handed over by the Board, also schedules of the names, distance, and cost per annum of the repair of each road, showing the extent of current obligations attached to each from the 31st December last. These maps and schedules were presented to the counties at their annual meeting on the 30th September last. I also caused a careful inspection by a qualified assistant (being unable myself to do this from ill-health), of all the roads, including every bridge, under the charge of the Commissioners, and such repairs as were thought necessary have been executed, so that I have the satisfaction of reporting that the works under the charge of the Commissioners are now handed over in complete and perfect order.

" The several counties, I understand, on learning the proposed termination of the Commission, have appointed committees to determine their future proceedings, and it is to be hoped that they may make such arrangements as will secure the works being maintained in the same good repair as they have hitherto been under the charge of the Board."

And so ended the Highland Road and Bridge Commission. As already explained, it began its duties in 1803–4, and terminated in 1863.

During eighteen years of that period my father had constructed the whole of the roads planned and laid down

by Telford, so that the works were under his and my
charge for the long period of fifty-eight years.

When it was ascertained in 1822 that the Government
would contribute no further sums for the construction of
additional roads, the several counties, having appreciated
the importance and advantage of the new roads made by
the Commissioners, obtained Acts of Parliament to construct district roads throughout each county; and there is
now no part of Scotland better served than the Highlands
with the means of road communication, their satisfactory
construction being very much facilitated by the superintendents and workmen, who were trained on the parliamentary
roads.

The little superannuation fund which Mr. Rickman in his
kindness had formed during a series of years, chiefly
deducted from their scanty pay, and deducted wholly from
my salary, was a misfortune, for it was like a superannuation, and yet it was our own money, and of course was
readily handed over to us.

The Commissioners in their final report remark that
" the removal of the officers of the Board without adequate
notice has been to them a matter of deep concern.

" Mr. Mitchell, their general inspector, has filled that
office for a period of forty years with eminent zeal and
ability; the other inspectors have also performed their
various duties with skill and ability, and some have served
for many years, and represent that they have a claim for
compensation for loss of office. The Commissioners state
that they have neither authority to determine nor means to
satisfy these claims; but they have submitted them to the
Lords Commissioners of Her Majesty's Treasury."

Still I made representations to the Treasury. My own
claims, although nothing could be more just, were of less
consequence, as I had been permitted to supplement my
income by such professional work as did not interfere with
my public duties, and which ultimately became very considerable in so wide a field; but my superintendents had
no such advantage. The only satisfaction we got was a
letter from my Lords " regretting that compensation to the

officers of the Board had not been included in the Act transferring the roads and bridges from the charge of the Commissioners to that of the several Highland counties."

" The Commissioners further state that in resigning the trust which they had the honour of executing for sixty years, they cannot look back upon the result of their labours but with satisfaction.

" They have watched with the deepest interest the improvement of the country, which it was the beneficent design of Parliament to civilize and enrich; they found it barren and uncultivated, inhabited by heritors without capital or enterprise, and by a poor and ill-employed peasantry, and destitute of trade, shipping, and manufactures.

" They leave it full of wealthy proprietors, a profitable agriculture, a thriving population and active industry.

" The value of the land has been incalculably increased, and the condition of every class of people improved.

" Nor have the contributions of the State in aid of local expenditure been without ample return in other forms. By such results as these has the wise foresight of the Legislature been confirmed, and its liberality been rendered fruitful."

Such is the peroration of the final report of the Commissioners, yet the instruments through whose labour and skill these beneficent works were carried out for a period of sixty years, and whose remuneration, from the early period at which their allowances were fixed, was on the most limited scale, were dismissed by " my Lords " of the Treasury on three months' notice, in advanced years, and without compensation.

Construction of Railways from Invergordon to the Boundary of Sutherlandshire.

The directors of the railway, notwithstanding my ill health, instructed me to survey the Ross-shire extension from Invergordon to Ardgay.

The plans were lodged and an Act obtained in 1863. The whole works were finished and the line opened to

Ardgay in October, 1864, thus bringing railway communication to the borders of Sutherlandshire.

This line from Invergordon to Ardgay is 26½ miles in length, is comparatively level; but several parts skirt and run through the sea, where the works had to be protected at a considerable cost.

The cuttings amount to 550,000 cubic yards, of which 20,000 are rock. There are 27 bridges over streams from 40 ft. to 50 ft. span, 26 public and accommodation-road bridges.

The rails were 70 lbs. to the yard, fished. There are ten stations with permanent dwelling-houses for the agents and porters. The works on this line are of the most substantial character and quality; the cost £5180 per mile, or, including land and all expenses, £5888 per mile.

I instance this line, considering the time and the works, as a specimen of very economical railway construction.

Survey and Construction of the Skye Railway.

Mr. Hope Scott, the eminent parliamentary barrister, had purchased a Highland estate on Loch Shiel, near Fort William; and having advocated many a wild railway scheme in Parliament, he did not hesitate to suggest and countenance a line from Kingussie, along Loch Laggan side, and thence to Fort William, a distance of forty-five miles. He thought that this line, while convenient for himself, might become a valuable communication to the west coast of Inverness-shire and the Hebrides; and my friend Mr. Bouch, C.E., was induced to make a flying survey, and held several meetings at Kingussie and Fort William, with the view of promoting the scheme.

Knowing the country intimately for many years, I could not resist stating in a letter in the *Inverness Courier* how delusive and visionary was Mr. Bouch's proposal, from its pastoral character, and from the utter desolation of the country as far as regards population.

I indicated the proper route to Skye and the Hebrides was a line from Dingwall to Kyleakin Ferry. This line would be the most direct and nearest route south from the

west coast of the counties of Inverness and Ross, as well
as Skye and the other islands of the Hebrides, and I had
no doubt that a line in this direction would ultimately
be made. Thereafter we heard no more of the Kingussie
and Fort William railway.

My letter, however, seemed to have had some influence
with the gentlemen of the west coast of Ross-shire and the
Hebrides, for in 1864 they formed themselves into a committee for promoting the Skye project, and, accordingly,
in the summer of that year, I received instructions from
them to survey and lay out the line.

Although the population was sparse, the district to be
served was vast, the resources of the country were wholly
undeveloped; particularly the fisheries, which were inexhaustible, and as the scenery along this route was unsurpassed in Scotland for beauty, variety, and grandeur, it
was thought that a cheap line in this direction would be
fairly remunerative.

Mr. Matheson, the chairman of the Highland railway,
possessed the large property of Lochalsh, and property elsewhere in this locality, and he became an active promoter.
The other Highland lairds, and those in the Hebrides,
fully appreciated the advantage of the line, but they were
generally too poor to contribute liberal subscriptions.

Through Mr. Matheson's exertions, however, we were
enabled to go to Parliament in November, 1864, and the
Bill passed in July, 1865, after a vigorous opposition from
Sir William Mackenzie of Coul.

The line extending from Dingwall to Kyleakin Ferry
was sixty-seven miles. Kyleakin Ferry, half a mile wide,
opposite Skye, being the point where Hutcheson's steamers
daily passed to and from Glasgow to the Hebrides. The
railway, however, hung fire for want of funds, although
the company had obtained their Bill.

There was great anxiety afterwards with the parties interested to have the line made; and Mr. Fowler, C.E.,
who had acquired a large property at Lochbroom, recommended a narrow gauge of 3 ft. 6 in.; but as the traffic
would necessarily be cattle, sheep, fish, and other heavy

commodities, a break of gauge was rejected by the directors, as the saving with inferior works on full investigation amounted to only £50,000.

Other alterations were suggested.

First, a change in the direction of the line, avoiding Strathpeffer spa and the village of Contin, connecting Strathconon, and passing the beautiful falls of Rogie.

The second alteration was fixing the western terminus at Strome Ferry instead of Kyleakin Ferry, the original terminus.

The alteration of stopping at Strome saved fourteen miles of very expensive railway making; but it was an unfortunate necessity, for the Hutcheson steamers passing to and from Glasgow daily at this point, passengers taking the railway here would thus reach Glasgow and Edinburgh in fifteen hours, instead of occupying two days in sailing in the steamers by Oban and the Clyde.

My calculation in making Kyleakin the terminus was that the railway could have advantageously competed with Hutcheson's steamers for goods and cattle—particularly for fish.

This latter plan, however advantageous, had to be abandoned. The first alteration, however, avoiding Strathpeffer, was a serious mistake. It saved of capital no doubt £15,000 to £18,000, the cost of the works; but Strathpeffer is the Harrogate of the North, rapidly increasing. The coaches yielded a traffic of £3000 or £4000 per annum before the railways were made.

This traffic, I have no doubt—had the railway passed by the original route—would by this time have amounted to £8000 per annum.

Mr. Fowler, being a director, was consulted, and, in his ignorance of the country, approved of this alteration, and his opinion was held omnipotent.

The result of these changes has been that the Skye Railway has hitherto been unremunerative. The directors, having failed to come to an understanding with Messrs. Hutcheson and Co., have been obliged to establish steamers of their own to Skye and the Lews, and these running in opposition to those of that company have hitherto been an annoyance and unprofitable expense, an expenditure in fact which would have constructed the line to Kyleakin.

A Bill was obtained by the company to authorize these changes in 1868, and as my partnership with Mr. Murdoch Paterson had then expired, and as I had from failing health arranged to retire from my profession, the directors secured Mr. Paterson's services, and the works of this important railway have been successfully carried out and completed by him, and, with the exception above alluded to, in accordance with the plans of J. Mitchell and Co. The line was opened for public traffic in August, 1870.

There is, as I have said, a vast district to be served. The scenery along the whole line and in Skye is unsurpassed in beauty and grandeur, and is already attracting thousands of tourists, who are annually increasing.

Besides, the fisheries on the coast and round the Hebrides are inexhaustible ; and as the railway is the shortest route to the southern markets, several steamers are now bringing cargoes of fish to the railway. When this traffic is developed, even this article alone will prove a considerable source of revenue.

Survey of the Sutherland and Caithness Railway.

As the traffic on the railways opened in the Highlands was proving satisfactory, the noblemen and gentlemen interested in Sutherlandshire and Caithness were anxious that the benefit of railway communication should be extended northward through these counties, and in 1864 I was requested by the Duke of Sutherland and the heritors of Caithness to make a preliminary survey of a line through these counties to the towns of Wick and Thurso.

The fixing and laying out of this railway was an intricate problem.

In Sutherlandshire the line was intersected by two arms of the sea along the east coast, and along the northern boundary of the county was a ridge of high mountains, extending from Helmsdale on the eastern to Bighouse on the western sea.

The main route in and through Caithness to which the people were accustomed was the then existing parliamentary road through land much cultivated, and along which a numerous part of the inhabitants resided. The ground was of a most precipitous, rocky, and irregular character; but the people were accustomed to it, had no conception of the engineering difficulties, and knew no other, and hence their persistent cry for a coast line.

The survey of the county involved much patient labour and investigation, and the difficulties may be judged by the fact that the fixing upon the best line for the Northern seventy-seven miles through Sutherland and Caithness involved the surveying and levelling of upwards of two hundred and four miles.

My report was printed and circulated, and as the line through Sutherland as far as Brora (thirty-two miles) was approved of, the parliamentary survey was made for this portion of the line, and the Bill authorizing it was passed in the summer of 1865, and the works for twenty-seven miles, to Golspie, were ordered to be proceeded with at once.

Some of the works on this part were of considerable magnitude.

A stone bridge of three arches crosses the Carron—two arches of fifty-five feet span each. The bridge crossing the Oykel consisting of an iron girder opening of two hundred and twenty feet span, with five stone side arches, and fifty-five feet in height above ordinary spring tides. There were other heavy rock-cuttings, breastwalls, and embankments.

The route through the demesne of Dunrobin Castle was left for further consideration. We were a good deal perplexed about passing through the park.

The duke wished the line to be carried along the seaside; but this direction was opposed by all his Grace's friends, for it was close to the gardens, and immediately below the castle, and would form an unpleasant barrier, and destroy the privacy of the charming plateau between the castle grounds and the sea-shore.

The line I proposed was above the turnpike road, which runs through the park, in a cutting where it could not be seen, and fully half a mile above the castle. We had a multitude of opinions, and by some eminent engineers, but ultimately my line was adopted.

The Duke of Sutherland and Dunrobin Castle.

The survey and works through Sutherlandshire brought me much in contact with the duke and his officials, and by his Grace's kindness I was a frequent guest at Dunrobin.

The duke was then (1864) in his thirty-sixth year, and had been in possession of his estates for three years.

He had married at the age of twenty-one Anne Mackenzie, the heiress of the Cromartie estates, young and beautiful, bred quietly in the country, and unaccustomed to the gaieties of London life, in which she was afterwards destined to take a prominent part.

How changed was Dunrobin since I first recollected it in 1824–30. Then the Marquis of Stafford and his intellectual and charming wife, the good duchess-countess, presided over this vast territory. After them came the present duke's father and his beautiful mother, with their refined and elevated tastes.

Mr. Loch, senior, and Mr. Gunn, the genial factor and my kind friend, and most of those I used to meet in the country in kind and friendly intercourse, were gone. The people were not more changed than the demesne of Dunrobin.

The late duke, no mean architect, had transformed the old castle into the present magnificent palace, and the late duchess, with intuitive taste, arranged the interior with all the elegance and amenities of educated and refined life.

The young duke seemed indifferent to those refinements. He indicated force of character and manly activity, and his first development was yachting—rather a rough occupation in our northern seas.

In 1864 he had been in full possession of his estates, as I have said, for three years, and looked earnestly into the details of their administration.

Mr. George Loch had succeeded his father as commissioner, but he had a different master, and the servant had less command. Mr. Loch was a barrister and an excellent man of business.

All the old factors were gone except Mr. Maciver, of Scourie, so also most of the old tacksmen—grand fellows of fixed character and mark, and very hospitable.

To what a splendid inheritance the duke succeeded! perhaps a position unequalled in the world, possessing the highest rank in the State, and widespread family and political connections. He was handsome and in the prime of life. His landed territory was of greater extent than that of any other nobleman in Great Britain.

He was the lord of thirteen hundred thousand acres in Scotland, thirty-two thousand acres in England, with valuable mines, and the possessor of three palaces, Stafford House, Trentham, and Dunrobin, besides five other territorial residences in England and Scotland.

His revenues are calculated at some £200,000, £142,000 of which arise from land. These worldly advantages (which the laws of this country put under his undivided control) placed his Grace, as far as regards personal enjoyment and freedom of action, in a more enviable position than even the occupier of the throne ; for he has no State duties to which his personal attention must be daily devoted.

His high rank and great wealth secure him with little effort the most distinguished society. In art, science, and literature he has the most enlightened in the land ready to communicate with and consult; and, such is the silent influence of hereditary nobility, that the most eminent are pleased and flattered to give him the benefit of their varied knowledge and experience.

Even if he had not studied any particular subject, the oral instruction of these enlightened men is generally at his command. The duke has a great fancy for mechanical engineering, and cultivates the society of eminent engineers of that class.

I recollect on one occasion going through locomotive workshops with his Grace, and there hearing a full and graphic explanation of the structure and functions of every part of the locomotive engine, so that a man of less intelligence than the duke would retire from the prelection with no mean knowledge of the locomotive.

The duke is no politician, but as the editor of *The Times*, Mr. Delane, was a frequent guest at Dunrobin, he had an opportunity of obtaining an enlightened view even of important political questions.

To the parties he ordinarily comes in contact with his Grace is courteous and kindly, and very liberal in his hospitalities, not restricting them to lords and ladies, as do many of our aristocracy. He has secured great popular favour from his frank manner, and the festivities he dispenses on the occasion of the volunteers assembling annually at Dunrobin (some four hundred strong) for the purpose of drill and inspection.

In his younger days he was noted for extinguishing fires. He has waged war before the public against the overcharges of West End tradesmen and their perquisites to servants. He prohibits all gratuities to his domestics on pain of dismissal.

Notwithstanding his immense possessions, he is rigidly economical, and has disturbing suspicions that his interests are not sufficiently guarded. A most unjust inference—at any rate in the North, for I have known all the agents and factors on his Scotch estates for the last fifty years, and whatever may be their shortcomings otherwise, never were men more devoted to the interests of the Sutherland family than they have uniformly been as far as I could notice.

I have often thought that a man possessing such great power and high position with all its advantages is not to be envied. With the best intentions he is bewildered. If he takes his own way he lacks experience, and is sure to get into difficulty. How little real knowledge can he have of the intricacies of agriculture, of mining, and of railways. Then the difficulty of exercising his patronage. If he asks extraneous advice it may not be, and often is not, the wisest or best. He is apt to listen to the person who has tact to advise that which he feels will be most agreeable and acceptable although not the wisest. His Grace's active mind naturally seeks advice regarding his multifarious concerns, which I have no doubt he has found sometimes more plausible than judicious.

A Mr. Murray, a Ross-shire local bank agent, proprietor, and farmer, became a great favourite for some years. His views on most subjects—and he professed to have knowledge on all subjects—his Grace seemed to prefer to the opinions of his legitimate employés. Poor Murray died lately, and that influence is gone; but it was paramount while it lasted, not always for harmony in Sutherlandshire.

In accordance with his Grace's habit he consulted, with my approval, an eminent English engineer; for I was anxious he should have every advice as to the best mode of passing through Dunrobin Park. His Grace naturally asked the engineer's opinion of the railway works then progressing in Sutherland.

This gentleman professed to be a friend of mine, and I believe he is. He explained to his Grace a self-evident fact, that railways in the North and in Sutherland to answer, must be made economically with plain work and less perfect gradients and curves.

He was pleased to talk of his friend Mitchell in laudatory terms; but said that he was unfortunately addicted to extravagance, that his bridges on the Highland line were unnecessarily ornate, and that a railway through Sutherlandshire should be of the plainest description, and should not exceed £7000 per mile. It did not amount even with the heavy works to that sum.

I wrote of this to Mr. Fowler, complaining of this :—

ENGINEERS CHAMBERS, INVERNESS,
October 2, 1865.

MY DEAR FOWLER,—I sent the other day plans and papers of the line through Dunrobin policies and the result of our conference; making the lower line £46,992, or to £10,070 per mile, and the upper line £45,340, or to £9542 per mile.

I daresay the duke will take some time to consider the subject. I am afraid you have unwittingly done me mischief with the duke.

He has got a notion that I am very extravagant in my construction, and said at a meeting of the Highland Board this was the opinion of English engineers.

He has ordered that everything should be done on his line on the cheapest scale, and I have had difficulty in assuring him that everything is so done consistently with good workmanship. For as we run on the surface, and follow the course of the valleys, you would see, if you looked at the plans, he cannot have steeper gradients or quicker curves than the ground will admit of.

We have let these contracts 24⅔ miles for £142,393, or £5773 per mile exclusive of land; and when you consider that £22,336 of this is for two viaducts across the Oykel and Carron, it leaves for the 24⅔ miles £120,057, or to £4867 per mile; and if you take £1873 per mile for permanent way off this sum, there is £2,994 for works.

You must observe, also, that although our trains in general will be light, we shall have often very heavy cattle and sheep trains.

I am, &c.,

(*Signed*) JOSEPH MITCHELL.

Mr. Fowler replied that the duke had misunderstood his remarks. He offered, on the duke's return to London, to put this difference of opinion all right. This, in the multiplicity of his engagements, he either forgot or failed to accomplish. I regretted this much, as I had received considerable kindness from the duke, and I was very unwilling to lose his Grace's good opinion.

His Grace, with his economical proclivities, got alarmed at the unfavourable opinion of a metropolitan engineer, and at a meeting of the Highland Board at Inverness publicly accused me of extravagance in my works.

Feeling how earnestly and anxiously I laboured to construct the Sutherland Railway, and indeed all my works, not only with efficiency but with strict economy, I indignantly repelled the accusation; but the mischief was done. The duke got alarmed, and his favourite, Mr. Murray, was instructed to watch our progress, and to check any appearance of extravagance of outlay.

As a land valuator of the company, Mr. Murray had to approve of the accommodation works (that is, the private roads, bridges, and accommodation for tenants) which are provided in the contracts, and which, in Ross-shire, he insisted on largely increasing to please the lairds and tenants ; but in the case of Sutherlandshire he, in accordance with the duke's economical views, as largely diminished. To this it was not my province to object. But when Mr. Murray interfered with the dimensions of the bridges and watercourses, and other works affecting the stability of the railway, and of which he was entirely ignorant, I treated his interference with the contempt it deserved, conscious I was doing the best for the duke's interests.

Railway Surveys North of Dunrobin and through Caithness.

In the autumn of 1865, while the works in Sutherlandshire were actively going on as far as Golspie, the report and plans which I had made the previous year for the further extension of the line to Wick and Thurso were under consideration. An agent of Mr. Brassey's, the great contractor, a Mr. Nettan Giles, brought me a letter from Mr. Loch. In that letter I was asked to show him the plans through Sutherland and Caithness which I had made, and give such other information as he might require in regard to the railways through that country. This I did ; and I introduced him to Lord Caithness, who was then at Barrogill Castle, and to others.

Mr. Giles had been for years Mr. Brassey's agent in negotiating with foreign governments and parties for the construction of railways abroad. That service had nearly ceased, and although he held out to me that his visit to Scotland was a tour of pleasure, it was clear he meant business, and, in compliance with Mr. Loch's wishes, I afforded him every facility ; but felt the country was too poor for Mr. Brassey's mode of working.

Mr. Giles remained in Sutherlandshire and Caithness some six weeks, and obtained from Mr. Falshaw, Mr. Brassey's partner, an estimated cost of the proposed lines to the North.

The duke, Mr. Loch, and Lord Caithness, and some of

our Highland directors were anxious to secure the services of so eminent a contractor as Mr. Brassey. They were under the delusion that he possessed some secret mode of making railways cheap. Mr. Brassey was invited to Dunrobin, and came with Mr. Falshaw to Inverness, and there tendered for the works, stipulating to take £100,000 of the price in railway shares, of course under the conviction that the rest of the capital would be subscribed by the promoters.

In prospect of this agreement being carried out, I was asked to undertake the parliamentary survey within a short time, and at an inclement period of the year. Mr. Loch's proposal was unique, viz., "That I should make the whole plans and surveys at my own risk and cost, and if the county of Caithness subscribed £100,000 "—which I knew they would not do—" and if they went to Parliament and got their bill, I should be paid *on the completion of the railway two-thirds* of my *actual outlays* in cash, and the balance of my professional services in Caithness Railway shares."

Of course I declined this offer. While this negotiation was in abeyance my friend, Lord Caithness, called on me and begged that I would agree to the proposal made, and finish the great works I had hitherto so successfully carried out ; for if not, he understood Mr. Giles was prepared to telegraph for English engineers, who would undertake the works on the terms offered.

I stated that it was evidently not meant that I should agree to this proposal, and as the whole matter was in the duke's hands, I wrote him a letter which Lord Caithness delivered at Dunrobin on his way north, offering to make the survey and carry the Bill through Parliament on being paid the usual professional charges—the promoters thereafter being free, if they thought fit, to employ any other engineer they might select for the construction of the works.

The duke declined this offer, and Mr. Giles telegraphed for other engineers. These were Messrs. Maclean and Stileman, engineers employed by Mr. Brassey abroad, Mr. Maclean being then President of the Institution of Engineers.

Q

Lord Caithness was very anxious to promote any project which would bring railway communication to his county.

Mr. Giles was hospitably entertained and taken into his confidence, and the people of Caithness displayed great enthusiasm for the railway up to the point of subscribing for the stock.

The English engineers were unable to make the survey of the whole line within the limited time, and their efforts were confined to the local line between Wick and Thurso, twenty-one miles, for which they got the sanction of Parliament, the duke declining to have anything to do with this short line.

Next summer, 1866, Messrs. Maclean and Stileman surveyed the through line, and the Caithness people were rejoiced, as they were sure their favourite coast route, or some line better than mine, would be selected.

The local papers congratulated Caithness that they had gone to " head-quarters " for engineers. The " headquarters " spent three or four months in investigating the country, but were very reticent as to their proceedings.

At last their report was presented, and a meeting of the railway shareholders and others was held at Wick on the 2nd October, 1866. " They approved of the survey, and called for the co-operation and support of all the noblemen and gentlemen interested in Caithness and Orkney to support an undertaking so eminently calculated to promote the well-being of all classes."

At the same meeting " the special support and co-operation of the Duke of Sutherland was earnestly asked." But neither the duke nor the public responded to their solicitations, and their Bill was consequently withdrawn.

As these proceedings tended to lower my professional character in my own locality, and the conduct of Messrs. Maclean and Stileman was very unprofessional, I could not resist drawing public attention to these transactions in a letter in the *Inverness Courier*, dated 28th November, 1866. I there maintained and showed that Messrs. Maclean and Stileman, after three or four months of investigation, were obliged absolutely to adopt the line I had selected and laid down. That the short deviations they made in Caithness had been surveyed by me and rejected ; that their line did not communicate with the harbours of Wick and Scrabster, and so did not accommodate the traffic of Orkney and Shetland. That of the population of Orkney and Caithness amounting to 105,000, 79,700 of these would suffer a détour for themselves and their traffic of nine miles in travelling south by their line ; that as the rivers of Wick and Thurso were crossed at their mouths at these towns where they were wide, the waterways being 183 feet and 156 feet respectively, expensive bridges would be required, whereas by my line some miles up the country, small bridges with cheap approaches and waterways of 120 feet and 130 feet were only necessary. Hence, when they did not adopt my line, the extra railway making and bridges would cost an additional and unnecessary outlay of £45,000.

Then, again, the estimate of the line laid down by me was calculated, including every expense, at £5000 per mile. Mr. Brassey's tender, adding the outlay for land and amenity, was £6500 per mile, making a difference of cost in the whole distance of £127,000 more than my calculation. But Mr. Brassey agreed to take £100,000 of the stock of the company in shares, and well he might, as if he made the line at my estimate, which he could and for less, he would not only have that £100,000 of stock, but £27,000 of profit besides.

My letter recording these proceedings dispelled two delusions. First, " That the eminent engineers from 'headquarters' could not and did not improve the line as laid down by me. They made it clear that however useless were their professional services to the county of Caithness, they did not mean to give them for nothing; and as the Caithness Railway shares were not forthcoming, their bill, amounting to £4000 for the surveys, was presented and had to be paid, I believe, very much by Lord Caithness and Mr. Brassey. Second, " That employing Mr. Brassey as a contractor was clearly not the way to have the Caithness and Sutherland Railway economically made."

His Grace the duke, with his love of economy, seemed to apprehend this, for he very early repudiated the acts of Lord Caithness and the promoters, and contributed nothing to the survey of Messrs. Maclean and Stileman, although he was the means of engaging them; and notwithstanding the blandishments of Dunrobin so liberally offered, he did not accept Mr. Brassey's tender. S) the whole extension to Caithness stood in abeyance, and I concluded my letter by predicting "that the route now being fixed, the Caithness Railway will at no distant period be made; but it will not likely be undertaken as a contractor's line."

Sequel of Proceeding in constructing the Sutherland and Caithness Railway.

In November, 1866, although my health had greatly improved, I was advised to go to Italy for six months. During my sojourn there I enjoyed much the wonders of art and nature in that favoured land.

I returned to Scotland in May, 1867, and found the works of the Sutherland Railway, which were in progress when I left under my partner, Mr. M. Paterson, now nearly completed. During my absence my partner felt so much the annoyance of Mr. Murray's interference, and which the duke upheld, that I deemed it my duty to tender my resignation—which his Grace accepted.

Mr. Murray and the superintendent I left finishing what required to be done for opening the line.

When I presented my professional bills charged at the same rate as I had been paid for similar work done elsewhere, and which were reported on by the auditor of the Court of Session as moderate, the duke refused to settle. They amounted to £5500. The duke offered £4000 in full. I objected to any such deduction. My claim could have been readily established at law, for they were the usual charges, and the authority for the work was not denied; but my doctors would not permit me to enter into the excitement of a lawsuit, and I had nothing for it but to lie out of my £4000, acknowledged to be due to me, for an indefinite period.

My friend, Mr. Carter, the solicitor for the Midland, obtained from Mr. Loch an advance on the duke's offer, which his Grace repudiated, and I had no alternative but to submit.

As a sequel to these proceedings, I may mention that the extension of the Sutherland and Caithness Railway remained in abeyance till October, 1870.

The duke had extended his railway along the level coast to Helmsdale (17 miles) ; but he found the traffic of a sparse population, in a pastoral country which had been cleared, wholly unremunerative, and the only hope of obtaining a return for the outlay for the railway works that had been made, was to extend the line through Sutherland and Caithness to Wick and Thurso.

The duke got a subscription of £50,000 from the Highland Company, and other small contributions in Caithness and elsewhere, and resolved to extend the line to Wick and Thurso, as a feeder to his lines in Sutherlandshire.

My late partner, Mr. Murdoch Paterson, had just completed the Skye line and was then disengaged. His Grace secured his services. The Parliamentary surveys were made according to the line laid down by J. Mitchell and Company ; that line has been creditably and satisfactorily completed by Mr. Paterson. Not at Mr. Brassey's estimate of £6,500 per mile, but was opened for £5,077 per mile.

It would have been even under my estimate of £5000 a mile, as Mr. Paterson writes, had not the price of rails risen in the interval from £8 to £13 per ton.

So ended my professional career, which extended over a period of forty-five years. In course of it there were many anxieties, which, however, were counterbalanced by many pleasures. I look to the past with satisfaction in the hope that my efforts have in some fashion contributed to the improvement of the country, and the welfare of the people.

I have a grateful remembrance of the kindness and consideration which I almost invariably received from those with whom I came in contact. I am now in the eightieth year of my age; but my affection for the Highlands and their people is as warm as ever, and I am thankful that I am still able to take the deepest interest in everything which contributes to their welfare and prosperity.

APPENDIX.

APPENDIX.

—⋆—

I.

Mr. George Hudson, M.P.

IT may be interesting to give a short notice of my intercourse with Mr. George Hudson, with whom, though unconnected with the Highlands, I came in contact accidentally from being a holder of railway stock in the lines under his administration, and although, in no degree palliating his faults, his wonderful and chequered career cannot be read without interest and commiseration.

A relative of mine whom I frequently visited in Yorkshire recommended me to invest some of my professional savings in the stock of the Midland Railway. The line, he said, formed part of the great central route of communication between London and the north. It passed through a country rich in minerals, and connected great manufacturing towns. The works were of the most substantial character, for they had the personal superintendence of the father of railways, Mr. George Stephenson. I consequently purchased at various times some of the stock during the progress of the works.

When the line opened in 1840 the traffic was very disappointing, the works at Normanton had not been paid for, and the directors to meet this and other outlays had to issue new stock at a discount of £47 in the £100, which I took up.

The staff of the line, which then extended from Derby to Leeds, seventy-two miles, was reported to be on an extravagant scale, and it was maintained that the traffic was not being properly developed.* Hence there was increased discontent among the shareholders, and they had many meetings at Sheffield, presided over by a Dr. Carr. I noticed from the newspaper reports that the chairman and shareholders at these meetings appeared to know little about the administration of railways; indeed very few did at that time. Their whole working and management were new, and all parties connected with them were apparently groping in the dark.

Interested as a shareholder, and knowing from my profession a little on the subject, I put myself in communication with Dr. Carr and his committee, for I was loath without a struggle tamely to lose upwards of £2000 of my hard-earned savings, and I took a good deal of trouble in collecting and furnishing them with what they considered valuable practical information.

The Sheffield committee were very indignant at the directors for their supposed mismanagement and extravagant appointments. They found the directors were at war, and in bitter competition, with their neighbours the Midland Counties, and the line between Birmingham and Derby; and it was clear that if the Midland was to be made profitable this contest must cease at any rate. With new blood added to the board it was still hoped that economical and more efficient administration would be established.

The committee circulated a statement to the shareholders of their views, and asked support by proxy or by personal attendance at the next meeting. When the meeting took place with the directors, Dr. Carr stated that the committee held proxies which would enable them to dismiss the entire board if they saw fit; but they were unwilling to do this

---

* It was the belief of the committee and public that the traffic, now so overwhelming, was not sufficient to warrant a staff on such an expensive scale.

provided one half of the directors voluntarily retired to make room for new directors—to be appointed by the shareholders. This was agreed to; one half of the board resigned, and the committee proceeded to select directors to fill the vacant seats. Dr. Carr wrote to me to say that the committee had after much anxiety selected such men as they considered efficient to occupy the places of the retiring directors. One seat was still unfilled, and on account of the assistance I had given them, they desired to place that seat at my disposal. Some of the committee, he said, wished to appoint instead a Mr. Hudson of York; but it was thought "he would be too much York for them," and they hoped I would agree to undertake the duties of director at the new board. As I had fixed professional duties, and lived at such a distance, this proposition was out of the question, and while thanking Dr. Carr and the committee for their good opinion, I told him I must decline. I stated, however, that I had incidentally heard that Mr. Hudson was very eligible, that he was a man of great energy and force of character, was chairman of the York and North Midland Railway (then only twenty-four miles in length), and consequently must have some experience in railways, and, in my opinion, they could not do better than appoint him; he was accordingly elected. And thus was inaugurated the stirring railway career of Mr. George Hudson.

It was not long before he displayed his administrative talents. He was appointed chairman of the new board, and his first move was to amalgamate the three companies which centred in Derby and then in fierce conflict. By some magical power he seemed to overcome all prejudices, great local influences, and the vested rights of officials,* and suddenly converted these contending companies into one harmonious and profitable undertaking. The traffic was facilitated and rapidly increased, and instead of the shareholders receiving no dividend as under the former manage-

---

* This was no ordinary affair; for besides other difficulties, the enginemen struck, and an accident happening at the time, the board got all the blame.

ment, the dividends gradually rose, and Mr. Hudson was soon able to pay 7 per cent. on the ordinary stock of the company.*

The success of the Midland stimulated other projects throughout the north, and to counteract opposition a direct line from London to York was being surveyed. Mr. Hudson promoted lines across the country to Peterborough and Lincoln, and afterwards the Ear Wash Valley line, and a railway to Bradford and Colne, and others. As chairman of the York and North Midland Mr. Hudson projected the line to Scarborough as a profitable feeder, and to Hull and other towns adjacent. By his great influence on the lines of which he was chairman, he purchased the Great North of England Railway from York to Darlington.† He pro-

---

* As an evidence of the improved condition of the Midland I may mention that on the prospect of its improvement under the new board I increased my holdings in the united company to £5000. Immediately after Mr. Hudson carried out the amalgamation, the traffic of the united companies rapidly increased, the shares quoted in 1842 at 41½ discount rapidly rose in 1845 to a premium 95 per 100. The dividend was 7 per cent. I looked on this increase with complacent satisfaction. It was gratifying to feel that without the hard labour it cost me to earn my first £5000, I should be the possessor of £10,000. I began to think, however, it would be well in case of accidents to invest the money in some less fluctuating, and more permanent security; and as I happened to have a meeting with Mr. George Stephenson, the engineer of the line, I thought I might obtain his opinion. He said, " Well, my shares in the company I sold some time since, but then I wanted the money; I think when they reach £200 per share you may sell." I took his advice; they never reached the £200, they receded from the 95 premium and went back and back until in April, 1849, they sold as low as 31-34 the 100, and so vanished my golden visions of fortune for the time. With all its varied dividends and quotations I have held my stock till this day and increased it. It is now 127 per 100. My several purchases averaged £70. I have little reason to complain of Mr. Hudson, or the present administrators of the Midland Railway.

† The purchase of this railway is an evidence of Mr. Hudson's courage and accurate estimate of its value, in which I in the far north was a fortunate participator. I held shares in the extension to Newcastle, then in progress, and concluded that when the line opened to that city, the York and Darlington, then at a discount of 20 per cent., would reach par, when I would sell and so secure a moderate

jected the lines to Newcastle and Berwick with their various branches. Almost all of these projects and lines ran up to high premiums, and their success was very much attributed to the untiring energy and genius of Mr. Hudson. By these strokes of policy and enterprise his advice was courted on all hands. He became the greatest authority on railway enterprise throughout the country. He was thrice Lord Mayor of York, and was elected M.P. for Sunderland, which he represented for thirteen years.

He was courted by the highest aristocracy in the land.* He and George Stephenson visited Sir Robert Peel at Drayton Manor, and his practical opinions were listened to with much interest by that distinguished statesman. In Parliament his opinions and views on railways were received with respect and attention. At the several meetings of the shareholders his recommendations were passed with acclamation; naturally enough, because thousands were enriched by the sound projects which he promoted.

From 1842 to 1847 he was perhaps the most popular man in England. He was christened the "Railway King."

profit. Accordingly I invested £1000 in Darlingtons, and took up the £40, £30, and £15 shares which the Directors afterwards issued. Soon after this purchase the stock ran rapidly up to 100, 120, 150 per £100. At last it was announced that a purchase had been provisionally made by Mr. Hudson in June, 1845, of the railway at the price of £250 for each £100 shares, the other shares increasing in proportion. I must confess the rise looked fabulous; but the fact of Parliament confirming the bargain in July, 1846, left no doubt on the subject : Mr. Hudson did not then hold a single share of the Darlington, nor did he reap any advantage from this transaction. My investment of some £2000 was thus increased to £5000.

* In a book, published by Lord William Lennox, entitled " Celebrities that I have known," his lordship in a very patronizing manner alludes to a dinner given by his brother, the Duke of Richmond, at which Mr. and Mrs. Hudson were guests, and he records the malapropos remarks of the " Railway Queen," whom he took in to dinner. According to him she interlarded her conversation with French phrases misapplied. I do not credit this specimen of her conversation. Whatever Yorkshire blunders she may have made in her mother tongue, I think she was innocent of venturing on French. As to Hudson himself, he was bluff and straightforward in his manner, but perfectly intelligent. He might be proud of the society into which he was

He was assumed to be rich. He purchased landed estates, had his country house at Newbry Park, near York, and established his town residence at Albert Gate, now the abode of the French Embassy.

His speeches at the numerous railway meetings displayed great tact and talent, were frank, and indicated perfect confidence in the ultimate success of all his undertakings. The shareholders readily acquiesced in all his proposals, which were on a herculean and gigantic scale, for he was chairman of the whole of the Midlands, the whole of the York and North Midland, the whole of the York, Newcastle, and Berwick, with numerous branches—his sway extending from Gloucester, Birmingham, and Rugby in the south to the town of Berwick in the north. This extensive authority produced in him the conviction that he might do what he liked, for his recommendations were so uniformly successful that shareholders readily confirmed very extensive actings carried out in his individual capacity. This sudden elevation to a place of vast authority, wealth, and social position seemed to have upset his sounder judgment, and brought on a catastrophe which with all his farsightedness he never seems to have anticipated.

The success of railways from 1842 brought railway projects by 1845–46 to a climax. At that time the whole country was in a ferment of wild railway speculation. Railways were surveyed in every possible direction. Parliament was overwhelmed with Bills. In 1846 no less than 272 Acts were passed for 4790 miles of new railway, at an estimated cost of £121,500,000. The public of every

---

admitted. Lord William says: "When coffee was announced the 'Railway King' remarked, 'Three live dukes; well I never before sat down with three live dukes.' They were the Dukes of Newcastle, Buckingham, and Richmond. He talked of the good things he put his friends up to, and directors who pocketed £400 and £500 a year." The tone of Lord William's remarks is that he was associating with vulgar people beneath him, and he exhibits their vulgarisms in an unkind and patronizing way, yet he says previous to leaving England, "I saw a good deal of Mr. Hudson, and after a time the slight acquaintance ripened into a warm friendship." Well might Hudson say, "Save me from my friends"—particularly my aristocratic friends.

rank rushed to take shares, many subscribed a deposit, sold out, and secured large sums of money. But a greater number who were able to pay a deposit were ruined by further calls. The lines that had been opened, or were in course of construction, had been run up to fabulous premiums, stimulating still further speculation and the thirst for gain.

In 1848–49, however, came a rapid reaction; railway property fell more rapidly than it had risen, and shares in the best lines became depressed and almost unsaleable for several years.* Of course Mr. Hudson's projects suffered with the rest, and the belief began to be entertained that he was going too fast, and criticisms were rife as to the prudence and propriety of his acts. I recollect going from Scotland to York with others purposely to oppose two projects he at that time promoted: we got the Bills made permissive, and they were afterwards withdrawn.†

At that meeting, January 20th, 1849, two members of the Stock Exchange, a Mr. Prance and a Mr. Love, publicly complained that large quantities of Great North of England Stock had been thrown on the market by parties connected with the company. This they denounced in strong terms, as it upset the calculation of dealers in the

---

* In December, 1849, the £50 shares of the York and North Midland were selling at £16, the £100 Midland shares sold for £45–46; the Caledonian, £50 for £11½; Edinburgh and Glasgow, £50 for £28–30; Lancashire and Yorkshire, £100 for £54; and Berwick, £25 for £16.

† We had bargained for the Newcastle and Carlisle line to pay 6 per cent. for three and a half years, and 7 per cent. after in perpetuity on a capital of £1,550,000. The new directors a few years after did not improve this bargain, for they purchased the line at 7 per cent. on a capital of two and a half millions.

We had also agreed to lease the North British Railway, being then the line from Edinburgh to Berwick, and the Hawick branch at 8 per cent. Lucky had it been for the shareholders and public if that agreement had been carried out, for during the last thirty years the North British has been a ruinous concern, paying sometimes nothing, sometimes 1 or 2 per cent., ruined by bad management by its branches, and speculative projects. But Hudson in these transaction s was before his time.

stock, and was unfair to the public, and they demanded to know who it was that sold these shares. Mr. Hudson at once acknowledged that it was he that sold them; whereupon they obtained the appointment of a committee of shareholders to investigate the matter.

This committee reported that Mr. Hudson, the chairman of the company, had sold shares to the amount of £131,397 for the benefit of the company; but by which transaction he had secured, as they maintained illegally, for himself an additional price of £8418. The publication of this report, the depression of railway property throughout the country, and the floating rumours of jobbery, created so strong a prejudice against Mr. Hudson, that before the meeting assembled to consider the report, he resigned his chairmanship.

When the shareholders met on the 4th of May, 1849, to receive this report, somewhat excited, they appointed another committee with full power to investigate the whole affairs of the company, as doubts had been thrown on various actings of both Mr. Hudson and the board. Public confidence was also shaken throughout the north of England, and committees of investigation were likewise appointed by the shareholders of the Midland, and York and North Midland, over which Mr. Hudson presided, and which committees issued reports. The investigations of the committee appointed by the York, Newcastle, and Berwick were most important. They were microscopic in detail, displaying remarkable and creditable pains and labour in their minute and protracted inquiries.

This committee, among other items of inquiry, report that Mr. Hudson had subscribed, in the plentitude of his authority on the part of the railway company, £75,000 to the Sunderland Docks, he being member for the borough. This, in the usual way, had been readily agreed to by the shareholders; and subsequently he subscribed for 2045 additional shares, equivalent to £51,071, in the docks, which was paid by the directors. But as the transaction had not been minuted, nor had the shareholders confirmed this further sum, the committee considered the company should not sustain it, and Mr. Hudson was called on to repay it with interest.

The committee complain also of the transactions connected with the Brandling Junction Railway, which Mr. Hudson purchased on his own authority for £550,000. 22,000 shares were issued; 20,000 to pay the purchase price, and 2000 were placed by the shareholders at the disposal of the directors, who placed them at the disposal of the chairman. Mr. Hudson distributed 700 of these among the directors and officials, retaining the remainder to himself, and as they ran to a premium of £21 per share, the committee remark that it was equivalent to a bonus of £27,000 to Mr. Hudson. Perhaps this reward might have been made in a more delicate and regular manner; but it was well earned, for the purchase was acknowledged to be worth double the value of the price paid by the company.

The committee also report that Mr. Hudson, the chairman of the company, had in January, 1845, before the Bill for making the Newcastle and Berwick Railway was brought into Parliament, possessed himself by purchase from Thomson, Fireman and Co. of 10,000 tons of iron rails at £6 10s. per ton, and thereafter sold 7000 tons to the Newcastle and Berwick line besides, and 3000 to the York and North Midland, at £12 per ton, the then market price, thereby securing to himself a large sum, which, they pointed out, was illegal, he being chairman of the company.*

The committee omit to notice that another person of distinction and name supplied the company by contract

---

* Mr. Allport, the distinguished manager of the Midland, told me that he was present with Mr. Hudson in the office of Mr. Crawshay, the great iron master, when Mr. Crawshay said, "Now, Mr. Hudson, I hear you have purchased 10,000 tons of new rails. I will give you £60,000 for your bargain," and began to write out a cheque for the same. "No," said Mr. Hudson; "I must have £65,000;" on which Mr. Crawshay tore up the cheque, and threw it in the fire. Had Mr. Hudson accepted the offer, he would have secured this profit without any reflection being cast on his character in regard to this transaction.

R

with the whole coke required for the engines (coke being then exclusively used), and thus the profit from it should have been repaid also; but it was not.

They also state that he had got shares in the allotment of the York, Newcastle, and Berwick lines and others, beyond the number of shares to which he was entitled as a shareholder, and for which he had no authority either from shareholders or directors, realizing thereby large premiums on these shares.

That he was in the habit of obtaining cheques from the directors for large sums of money to meet claims for land and work pending his negotiations with the parties, which sums were placed in his private bank account,* and which the committee considered should be restored to the company with interest, which was done.

The whole tone of the report of the committee is condemnatory of Hudson, and the conduct of Hudson alone. Yet the other directors, men of position, who, as trustees and guardians, were as much bound to protect the interest of the shareholders as Hudson, were not implicated. If they had done *their* duty these irregularities could not have taken place, and the committee notice them only with a passing censure. The auditors also of the different companies, during the several years in which these irregularities took place, pass them over with no sign of discontent or disapproval.

The only evidence of a remonstrance in all these transactions is from one official, Mr. Allport, the traffic manager. Close, the secretary, writes to him, February 3rd, 1849, in contemplation of a general meeting: " *In order to make things pleasant,* Mr. Hudson wishes you to add your traffic, amounting to £7269 4s. 7d., to the mer-

---

* I can well understand his taking the land settlements into his own hand, not that he should put the money into his own bank account. I recollect being authorized by a relative, a large proprietor on this line between Scarborough and Hull, to negotiate with Mr. Hudson as to the land through four miles of his estate. Hudson said, " I think you had better leave it to me; I think I can satisfy your friend without a lawyer." And this was done in a fair and liberal spirit.

chandise traffic beyond what had been earned that year."
The manager answers that he has "complied with Mr.
Hudson's instructions, but the account added will have to
be deducted from the present quarter's account, and you
must not complain when the March account is sent in, as
I have no alternative but to deduct the sum to make our
books balance."

The committee in dealing with this question should not
have omitted to consider the great services which Mr.
Hudson had conferred both on the public and the several
companies of which he was chairman during his career.
He did good service on the Midland by amalgamating the
companies, to the great advantage of the shareholders and
the public. He was the original chairman of the York and
North Midland Railways, and carried out all its extensions
and branches.

As the chairman of the Midland, the York and North
Midland, and the York, Newcastle, and Berwick, he purchased, as has been said, the Great North of England Railway as part of the main line, and by his own influence
and authority he ultimately secured it for the York, Newcastle, and Berwick Railway. Mr. George Stephenson and
he purchased together the Durham Junction Railway for
£80,500, and on his own authority he bought the Brandling Junction for £550,000, being at nearly half their
value, and forming part of the main line. These railways they afterwards presented to the York and Newcastle
Company.

Mr. Hudson fought with energetic persistence the great
battle of the Atmospheric, with Lord Howick, a plan
which, if carried, would have ruined the through communication to Scotland. He examined the country by the
Carter Fell with his engineers, and fixed on the coast
as the route to Edinburgh by Berwick.* He erected the

---

* I recollect breakfasting with him in Edinburgh by invitation.
On this occasion he was then at the climax of his authority, and was
accompanied by a staff of engineers and some of his directors. His
two sons, lads of twelve or fourteen, were treated with marked
distinction by the gentlemen in attendance.

magnificent viaducts at Newcastle and Berwick, constructed the Scarborough and Hull lines; and indeed almost every extension and improvement over the whole eastern district, that the succeeding directors afterwards carried out and amalgamated under the name of the "North Eastern Railway."

All these works Mr. Hudson projected and arranged, and now when wholly united as a great company, they have, during these later years, notwithstanding the drawbacks at the beginning, paid 9 and 10 per cent on the capital, and even this last half-year (1878), with all the depression of trade, they yield to the shareholders 7 per cent. on their investments.

While one cannot palliate the irregularities that first took place in the hurry and excitement of the projects, and when it was difficult to distinguish between capital and revenue (and some Boards even now have a difficulty in doing this), it was no small merit for Mr. Hudson to conceive and carry out so satisfactorily these great undertakings.

How many of the shares he appropriated went to conciliate parties, overcome obstacles, and secure the important purchases and the amalgamations he effected, we cannot now know with certainty; but this incidentally crops up, for we find the directors of the Midland Counties accepting 500 shares each of £100 in the amalgamation transaction. Other directors and parties accepted shares. A Northumberland squire (disposed to approve of Lord Howick's project) told me how liberally the company had paid him for his land, besides the shares he had obtained.

The depression of railway property in 1850–51, still further depressed by the reports of the committees of investigation, brought down below their real value all railway investments, and as Mr. Hudson's fortune consisted in these, the sums he was required to pay at their depressed value very much embarrassed him.

The new directors of the North Eastern entered into litigation with him in a spirit of bitterness not very com-

mendable in a great company. At last, in 1859, after a
tedious legal controversy, a settlement was agreed on, and
it was provided that if Mr. Hudson on a certain day paid
the sum required, the company would grant him a full
discharge. Unfortunately Mr. Hudson was ten days behind time with the required payment, and the directors
repudiated the agreement.

Thereafter Mr. Hudson was a ruined man, both in
character and fortune. His properties were sequestrated,
and he, of all the supposed numerous railway delinquents,
had to bear the brunt and odium of this speculative time.
One cannot help wondering, with all Mr. Hudson's great
talent, his readiness as a public speaker, his administrative qualifications, the power and influence he possessed
over others, that he should have become so utterly ruined.
It was an evidence how completely he became deluded by
the power placed in his hands. Had he kept by his side
an astute lawyer instead of his old shopman, Close, to have
recorded in minutes the whole of the transactions of the
companies and their directors, these personal acts so repudiated would have been authorized or condoned by his
shareholders, as well as the profitable purchases and amalgamations they so readily agreed to and adopted; and with
his influence and knowledge of railway affairs he might
have secured for himself legally and with credit an ample
fortune.

For many years Mr. Hudson wandered about on the
continent, dwelling sometimes in Paris, sometimes in
Berlin, sometimes in Boulogne, meeting occasionally his
old friends, who used to look up to him in his days of
prosperity, and partly supported by their kind contributions. Some years before his death a few of his old
friends, who commiserated his misfortunes, subscribed
and purchased for him an annuity of £600 per annum,
which kept him in tolerable comfort.

In 1871 I happened to meet him at the house of a
friend. I told him I had been an original shareholder on
the Midland and North Eastern, and reminded him of
interviews I had had with him when he was chairman of

these companies. I expressed the regret I felt that he had lost the lawsuits he had had with the North Eastern Company. He said, "It was not so, but the litigations were interminable, and unless a compromise could be effected he saw no end to them."

He begged, as an old and considerable shareholder I would interest myself on his behalf. I told him I feared I had no influence, for except Mr. Leeman, I knew scarcely any of the directors, and, besides, it was not likely they would listen to a single shareholder. Moreover, I did not understand the questions at issue. Nothing more was said.

A few days thereafter he called at my house and begged I would see Mr. Leeman in regard to his claims, and afterwards frequently in the forenoon he called to explain his case. He sometimes shared our luncheon, and one day on descanting on his misfortunes to my wife he burst into tears. It was very painful, for I recollected, when as chairman of the companies, how, with an air of proud authority and confidence, he walked into the crowded meetings, followed meekly by his confiding directors, and how loudly and enthusiastically he was cheered by his shareholders.

I had several conferences with Mr. Leeman, who sympathized with poor Hudson's misfortunes. He had seen Mr. Thomson, the chairman, on the subject, but he was inexorable, and he thought I had better see or write to Mr. Thomson myself, which I accordingly did, and the following correspondence will explain the sequel.

[Letter from Mr. Mitchell to Mr. Leeman.]

" 66, Wimpole Street, London.
" July 14, 1871.
" MY DEAR SIR,—I have just returned from Edinburgh. I hope you have been able to do something for Mr. Hudson with your chairman.

" I am not going to defend Mr. Hudson, but he did good

service in his time; and he has suffered some twenty-three years of disrepute and poverty.

"The company is thriving beyond expectation, so we are in a position not only to forget, but give a generous settlement.

"Believe me, very faithfully yours,
"J. MITCHELL."

[*Mr. Hudson to Mr. Mitchell.*]

"37, Churton Street, Pimlico.
"July 21, 1871.

"MY DEAR MR. MITCHELL,—I am deeply obliged by your kind note, and for your recollection of my unfortunate case.

"Nothing has been done, except to-day the railway handed in the amended accounts amounting to £91,900. This the chief clerk received, and stated he should certify if he found the amount correct. Of course we did not bind ourselves to it.

"After he has made out his certificate, we shall take out a summons to vary it according to our view of it, which will be heard in open court before the Master of the Rolls.

"The company have, in the course of a few months, handed in a series of four different accounts by me for £122,500; second, for £114,700; a third, 101,500; and now one for £91,900.

"I believe at the last two meetings of the board nothing was said in reference to my affairs; so that, in fact, nothing is doing about them, and they are left to the dreary progress of the law.

"I find upon looking back to some old correspondence that the board offered to abate their demand by £23,000. Would they do this now? If so, I should be disposed to accept. The offer was made December 3rd, 1859. I think I could show legally and equitably that thirty, or at all events £27,000, should be allowed; however, I am ready to leave to any sound judging man to decide upon the different items. Nothing can be fairer. I feel I have strong claims on their consideration ; if they had not made such preposterous claims I should never have been in York Castle, or suffered other indignities.

"The reports of these committees were false and wrong, and thus I must suffer and bear.

"I am sorry to be so troublesome to you. It is not in my power to thank you sufficiently, but I trust the conscious feeling that you are serving an oppressed individual will be a sufficient reward.

"I am, yours sincerely,

"GEORGE HUDSON."

[*Mr. Hudson to Mr. Mitchell.*]

"37, Churton Street, Pimlico.

"July 22, 1871.

"MY DEAR MR. MITCHELL,—Since I wrote you yesterday, I have been thinking the matter over very much. I think it better to send you a list of my claims on the railway, that you may be in possession of the nature of them ; and I think when you have looked into them you will see they are grounded on, at least, equity and right, and my solicitors, as well as counsel, say that they are legally due to me. However, if we cannot come to some settlement we shall pursue them through the courts, and, if necessary, take them to the House of Lords ; but surely they will be inclined to adopt some course that may end the suit, which must be annoying to the directors as well as to myself. I shall be glad to give you any further information you may wish ; forgive my troubling you so much.

"I am, yours very sincerely,

"GEORGE HUDSON."

[*Mr. Mitchell to Mr. Thomson, Chairman of the N. E. Railway.*]

" 66, Wimpole Street,
" July 26, 1871.

" SIR,—I lately happened to meet Mr. George Hudson, and was sorry to learn from him that the North Eastern Railway Company were still litigating with him in regard to his accounts.

" On my expressing surprise at this, he suggested that perhaps I as an original shareholder of the company, who had a general cognizance of the circumstances out of which the litigation arose, might not be unwilling to see some of the directors with a view to bringing about an amicable settlement. I said I would be happy to be of any use to him, and accordingly after our meeting and frequent calls from him I saw Mr. Leeman twice, and I yesterday called for yourself about Mr. Hudson's affairs, but I found you were out of town.

" Of course as chairman of a great company, you must protect the interests of the shareholders; but I venture to think that consistently with that duty, you may be able to devise some means of putting a stop to this litigation. I understand that in 1854 a settlement was made, the terms of which he failed to implement on the day; might not the company revert to that settlement?

" The company might well act generously (seeing how flourishing under your able auspices it now is) towards one whose energy was formerly of such service to the railway interests of the country. Whatever were the faults and irregularities of that time, it is not my province to defend. I am very confident that if you could devise a means of ending these litigations, there is not a shareholder of the company but would be most grateful at the result.

" If the settlement I refer to cannot now be adopted, what would you say to referring the accounts, the amount of which I understand has been considerably reduced by a recent decision of the Chief Clerk in Chancery, to the arbitration of Mr. Clayton of Newcastle, a gentleman of undoubted integrity and knowledge of such accounts, or any other gentleman of position might be fixed on ? I have reason to believe that Mr. Hudson would willingly consent to such an arrangement.

"I shall be glad to hear that in some way or other the object I have in view in writing this letter may be served, and apologizing for the liberty I take in intruding myself on your attention,

"I am, sir, yours faithfully,
"J. MITCHELL."

[From Mr. H. S. Thomson to Mr. Mitchell.]

"Kirby Hall, York,
"July 31, 1871.

"DEAR SIR,—It is certainly very discreditable to the mode in which the judicial business of this country is conducted that the suit instituted by the N. E. Company against Mr. Hudson so many years ago should not yet have been brought to a close. But so it is; not so from any *laches* on the part of the N. E. Company, who have spared neither money nor pains in their endeavour to bring the suit to a speedy termination.

"Probably when Mr. Hudson persuaded you to write to propose arbitration, he did not inform you that a similar offer had been repeatedly made by him and as often refused.

"I must ask you to believe that the Directors of the N. E. R. Company have good reasons for the course which they have taken in this matter, and in which they will certainly persevere.

"I am,
Dear sir, yours faithfully,
"H. S. THOMSON."

[*From Mr. Mitchell to Mr. Thomson.*]

"Viewhill, Inverness,
"August 11, 1871.

"Dear Sir,—Having left London for the season, and being detained in Edinburgh, your letter only reached me the other day.

"I regret the decision of that letter, as a litigation prolonged over a period of twenty-four years is not only discreditable to our Law Courts, but I fear indicates a degree of persistence on the part of the company, which I should have imagined might have terminated before this time. Moreover the views set forth by the company's agents do not seem to be correct, inasmuch as the Chief Clerk in Chancery lately reduced the amount of the accounts by nearly £10,000. I learned since, on the authority of Mr. Hudson, that the new accounts are also in error.

"Now, as I said before, I do not venture to defend any of the irregularities of which Mr. Hudson is accused. The shareholders and the public by their fulsome adulation insisted upon his acting as an autocrat; he is now experiencing the fruits of that autocracy by suffering obloquy and obscurity. Had Mr. Hudson been wallowing in wealth there might have been a reason for this continued litigation; but you know that he has only been rescued from absolute want by the generosity of private friends.

"In reviewing his case we must not forget his services to the railway interests. You are aware that the Midland Companies were reduced greatly in value, torn by dissensions, when he effected an amalgamation, established harmony in working, vastly increased the property of the Midland, and extended its usefulness.

"In like manner he united various companies in the north-eastern district, comparatively valueless; and in fact projected almost all the lines and works which, under your auspices, have been so profitable to the shareholders. Had it not been for his perseverance the company would have been hampered by an atmospheric railway to Scotland. No doubt his projects were a little before their time; but they indicate his foresight of their value. For example, I recollect going to York to oppose his amalgamation of the Newcastle and Carlisle Railway at 6 per cent. which was subsequently adopted by the new directors at 7 per cent. In short, the great success of the N. E. Company is partly owing to his enterprise and ability, followed up by the energy and management of the present board—at this moment the Midland and North Eastern are the most flourishing companies in Great Britain.

"I think, therefore, when your board takes these facts into consideration they will see the propriety of compromising the matter by carrying out the original agreement of 1854, to which your board then agreed—it would not cost a farthing in the £1 to any shareholder; or if preferred by arbitration, as proposed, I am sure any shareholder of the company would give such a course a full approval.

"I hope you will lay this letter before the board, and, if thought proper, take the opinion of the shareholders at the approaching meeting.

"I am, dear sir, yours faithfully,

"J. MITCHELL."

[*From Mr. Mitchell to H. S. Thomson, Esq.*]

"Sept. 1, 1871.

"DEAR SIR,—I hope you will not think me very intrusive if I ask you if you consulted your board prior to the meeting on the 18th in regard to Mr. Hudson's matter.

"In these days of the influence of public opinion it appears to me that so lengthened a litigation should not be carried out without consulting the shareholders, or at any rate without the unanimous approval of the directors. With my limited information, proceedings in this matter look like persecution; and I am sure directors and shareholders are above any such feeling. But the lawyers sometimes pursue a case, when they get into it, with the keenness of our Highland sportsmen. As a measure of humanity, do settle it! The splendid success of the company under your able administration warrants the directors acting generously towards one who, whatever faults may be attributed to him, did the company great service in his time.

"The shareholders may feel very grateful for the wise administration of the directors by letting the public participate in the success of the company by reasonably reduced fares and increased accommodation.

"I hope all your neighbours will follow your example; it is the one way, in my opinion, to secure the permanent value of the property.

"I am, sir, yours faithfully,

"J. MITCHELL."

[*From Mr. Hudson to Mr. Mitchell.*]

"37, Churton Street, Pimlico,

"August 19, 1871.

"MY DEAR MR. MITCHELL,—I thank you very much for letter and enclosures. I am not at all surprised at Mr. Thomson's answer. Should you hear again from him in answer to your very excellent letter, I shall be glad to learn the contents. I am in great hopes that what we cannot obtain by your kind intercession we may obtain by law.

"It is rather amusing his complaining of the law's delays; had he presented correct accounts the suit could not have lasted long, the delay has been caused by his absurd claims. I am sure that I am within bounds when I say that we have already stock of £40,000, and we hope still to get rid of at least £20,000 more; the delay is easily accounted for. If your kind letter really gets fairly before the board, I think something may be done.

"I am leaving here on the 4th of September for Lowther Castle, Lord Lonsdale's. Any letter addressed to me either here or at that place will find me. I shall stay at Lowther till the 12th or 14th; and after that go to Mr. Taylor's, Chip Chase Castle, Rexham.

"I am glad to learn you are better; with my warmest and most grateful thanks and compliments to Mrs. and Miss Mitchell, I am, yours faithfully,

"GEORGE HUDSON."

[From Mr. Hudson to Mr. Mitchell.]

"37, Churton Street, Pimlico,
"November 30, 1871.

"MY DEAR MR. MITCHELL,—I am glad to have it in my power to report that I have arrived at a settlement with the railway company. It was at last brought about in this way. On my return home from the north, under the advice of Mr. Leeman, I had an interview with the board, which they at first refused, but at last agreed to meet me with a deputation, which consisted of Mr. Leeman and five others.

"After some discussion they asked me to make them an offer, which I did, and with the addition of five thousand, they agreed to recommend the board to accept; and after some opposition from Mr. Thomson, who, I believe, fought to the last, it was agreed the matter should be carried out and settled on this basis.

"Thus is ended a suit of twenty years, after an expense due of £10,000, which, if the same spirit had been shown by the board as was evinced the other day, might have been settled without a shilling cost. The fact is, they have got more than the law could have given had it been fought to its bitter end.

"I am sure I am very grateful for the interest and kindness you have shown for me in this affair. This result would not have been arrived at in all probability had your letters not brought Mr. Thomson to the serious responsibility he was incurring in his persecution of me.

"I hope you are better, with my warmest and best thanks, and kind regards to Mrs. and Miss Mitchell,

"I am, yours sincerely,
"GEORGE HUDSON."

Mr. Hudson, immediately on his return from the north, was fortunate at last to obtain a satisfactory settlement from the board as described in his last letter. Mr. Thomson, the chairman, otherwise an excellent and upright man, and an able administrator, opposed it to the last ; but evidently was unwilling to bear the odium of a discussion, which I threatened, of such a protracted lawsuit before the shareholders and public.

At any rate, the agreement was satisfactory to Mr. Hudson, but, alas ! it was of little avail, for whether from relief after the long-pending anxieties of his litigations, or from the excitement of his recent visit to his friends in the north, or from both causes combined, he was suddenly taken ill with heart disease, which was latent, and died on the 14th December, 1871.

Thus tragically ended a life of strange vicissitudes, of great usefulness, triumph, and renown, followed by ruin, indignity, and obscurity. His career warns all public men of the necessity of strict and honourable dealing with the affairs of public companies. It shows the emptiness of popular applause, and the worthlessness of fulsome adulation. The applause was mean and servile, for when affairs prospered every act was condoned ; but when the tide turned the discontented shareholders and speculators demanded a victim, and Mr. Hudson, as the most popular and prominent railway man of his time, was selected for the sacrifice.

During the long period of his obloquy he was never known to utter a complaint against individuals, although many who had been enriched by his different projects were the loudest and most vehement in the condemnation of his acts.

His sudden death prevented the agreement being concluded, and his annuity having lapsed, his widow and family were sunk in poverty, and received no advantage from the settlement which he had so thankfully welcomed.

II.

The Fisheries in the North.

As the fisheries in the North, with which I have an intimate acquaintance, are exciting great interest at present, I think it right to publish the evidence I gave before the Food Committee of the Society of Arts in 1869, as it contains my views of the great supply of fish from the shores of the northern counties and Hebrides; also as to the importance of the Central Fish Market now established at Smithfield with the view of supplying the population of the Metropolis with fresh and cheap fish. This evidence foreshadows the plan now happily in progress to secure that object, and the railway companies are now considering the possible reduction of the fares so as further to increase the facilities for the fish traffic, and to bring this excellent and wholesome food within the reach of the great mass of the inhabitants of London and the large cities in the midland counties of England.

Evidence of Joseph Mitchell, Esq., C.E., Member of Institution of Civil Engineers, F.R.S.E., F.G.S., before Food Committee of Society of Arts, in March, 1869.

Mr. Joseph Mitchell, C.E., of Inverness, and of 66, Wimpole Street, London, attended to give information to the Committee with respect to the supply and transport of fish from the North of Scotland.

Mr. Mitchell said he had, for 42 years, charge of the

roads, bridges, and harbours under Government in the seven northern counties. He was also 22 years engineer to the Commissioners of the Herring Fisheries, for building fishing harbours, and consequently was well acquainted with the whole coasts of Scotland and the Hebrides. For the last 15 years he had been engaged in constructing 280 miles of railway north of Perth, viz., the Central or Great Highland Railway, and the line bordering on the Moray Firth, from Keith along the shore to Golspie, in Sutherlandshire, and his attention was of late more especially directed to the fisheries, from wishing to promote the traffic of the railways he had constructed. The traffic by these railways would come into England from Perth by two routes: the east coast route by Edinburgh and Berwick; and the west coast route by Carlisle. In the summer of last year he drew the attention of the directors of the Highland Railway to the importance of the fish traffic as a source of revenue, and pointed out that the Moray Firth teems at all times with cod, turbot, haddock, flounders, and skate, and the shoals of herrings surpass anything on the coasts of Great Britain. The fishery was private enterprise entirely. Before the railways were made, the only way of realizing this harvest of fish was by curing. Cod and ling were pickled and dried, and forwarded to the southern markets. The herrings were cured and sent abroad, chiefly to the Baltic and Spain, and some to London, and of late years a very considerable trade has arisen in the curing (smoking) of haddocks for the London market, &c., but as yet only a very small portion of fish in the Moray Firth is sent south in a fresh state. Now that there are railways, he thought the fish might be sent south fresh, and thus realize a better price, and be of great value to the masses of the population in London and the southern cities. By the returns recorded in the report of the Fisheries Commissioners, there were caught in 1867, along the coast of the Moray Firth from Peterhead, and along the eastern shores of the counties of Ross, Sutherland, and Caithness, including the Orkneys, 348,748 crans, of which 216,000 were caught along parts of the Moray Firth which have access

s

more or less convenient to the Highland Railway. There are, therefore, about 36,000 tons of herrings caught, and it is estimated some 16,000 or 17,000 tons of other fish, making from 50,000 to 60,000 tons of fish annually caught in this locality, and very little of this, as yet, was sent south fresh. A cran or barrel consists of 700 herrings, making the total number of herrings caught in this district about 244,125,600. The catch of fish seems inexhaustible along the coasts of Scotland; the quantity appears progressive, for, according to the Fishing Board reports, the average cure for eleven years to 1820 was 183,980 crans or barrels.

				Barrels.
For 10 years to April 1830	...	...	350,049
,,	,,	1840	...	...	445,057
,,	,,	1850	...	...	615,722

For the ten years from 5th January, 1850, for Scotland and the Isle of Man (the collection for England having ceased at that date), the total cure was 613,654. For six years to 1st December, 1865, the cure was, for Scotland and the Isle of Man only, 683,526 barrels. In 1865 alone, the cure was 621,763 barrels; in 1866, 658,146; and in 1867, 825,589 barrels. These were the total quantities of herrings cured, as reported by the Commissioners, all over the Scotch coast, but the chief quantity was caught in the Moray Firth; and he gave these figures to illustrate the progressive increase in the catch of fish, showing that if the fishing is properly prosecuted the supply seemed to be inexhaustible. He knew that was disputed by some persons, but these figures were the actual returns from the Fisheries Reports. Now fresh fish in London was in a great measure the food of the rich, and that was plainly seen by the very small number of fresh fish shops met with. In all Mayfair there were not above six or eight, and fish at the West End was sold at the following prices:—Cod, 9s. 6d. to 14s.; shoulders, 4s. to 12s. 6d.; slices of crimped cod, 1s. 6d. to 3s. 6d.; haddocks, 1s. 6d. to 2s. 6d.; crimped skate, 1s. per lb. The prices in the Moray Firth were:—Cod of the best quality, 6d. to 8d., each

weighing 10 to 16 lbs.; haddocks, purchased over head, 1d.
to 2d. each, varying from $\frac{3}{4}$ lb. to 1 and 2 lbs. weight;
herrings, 20s. to 25s. per barrel, which, at the average
price in the London fish shops of 2s. per dozen, would be
£5 16s. 8d. per barrel. The prices in London were taken
from the daily list of a West End fishmonger, and were
quoted to show the difference. He saw no reason why
a large supply of the fish caught in the Moray Firth might
not now be supplied to London, and the other great English
towns. At this moment a train leaves Forres, a central
point on the Moray coast, at 1.50 p.m., on the arrival of
the train from Golspie, Inverness, and the north, and from
Lossiemouth, Burghead, &c., on the east, which could take
all the fish caught, and to be sent that morning. This train
reaches London at 9.40 a.m., 19$\frac{1}{2}$ hours from Forres; and,
of course, it would arrive some hours earlier at the towns
north of London. For that matter the train could be
increased in speed 1$\frac{1}{2}$ to 2 hours. Then again, fish caught
in the morning at the outports, such as Helmsdale and
Wick, and along the Caithness coast, could be brought
to the rail by six in the morning, and might be despatched
then, and arrive at most of the English towns about mid-
day. Now (continued Mr. Mitchell), the question arises,
How does it happen that, with prices so low in the Moray
Firth, and so high in London, and the time of transport
from the sea to London less than 24 hours, and, at the
present time, not more than from Ireland, Cornwall, and
even Scarborough, we do not send fresh fish from the
Moray Firth? He was answered by the railway manager,
that they carried all that came to them, and that it was
not his business to turn fish merchant; and no doubt that
was true. He was answered by fish-curers that they knew
their business better than he did; that often they had sent
fish to London, and if it did not arrive by early morning
it was put aside till next day, and so often sold at a loss.
He reminded the railway manager that he had got a
new instrument for the transportation of fish, and that it
was his duty, if he wished quickly to secure the traffic, to
make arrangements accordingly; that the able manager of

the Great Northern Railway, some 12 years ago, saw that
London was supplied with coals solely by sea from Newcastle and Durham, and that he contrived to take coal
from the South Yorkshire coal-fields, and even from Durham, at three-eighths of a penny per ton per mile; but this
was not done without a severe struggle, for the coal
merchants would not go out of their beaten track, whereupon he appointed clerks to take orders all over London.
The result was the coal trade on the Great Northern
gradually increased, so that, in 1867, that line carried
1,040,000 tons of coal to the Metropolis. The other railway companies followed his example, and he (Mr. Mitchell)
believed London was now half supplied with coals by railway, at from 18s. to 25s. per ton, some 20 or 30 per cent.
lower than before. He saw no reason why similar efforts
might not be equally successful in regard to fresh fish.
Herrings are cured in the north to the extent of, as he had
said, many hundreds of thousands of barrels. Now, the
barrel and curing cost 7s. 6d., a sum which would go far
to pay the transport. There could be no doubt, in his
opinion, that it would immensely benefit all parties if this
fish could be brought fresh to London, but it was clear
it could not go to Billingsgate. The wholesale salesmen
and fishmongers appear, like the coal merchants, to be
against any change. In his opinion, the demand for fish
in London was inexhaustible if people were sure of getting
the article. Why should not the northern fish-merchants
have agents in London, who could meet the trains and
take the fish at once within the reach of the consumers?
It should be the business of the London agent to secure
buyers. The whole should be done, and with the aid of the
telegraph ought to be done, so as to be as certain of
the market and consumption as they were certain of the
arrival of the railway trains. Of course, unless this was
arranged beforehand, a great supply would be a failure.
He thought the sales at Billingsgate, if Billingsgate is
continued, should be confined to the fish brought by the
river; and as to the fish brought by rail, the supply for
twenty-four hours could easily be known six or seven hours

before by telegraph; and Smithfield might be available for the concentration of the traffic and sale of fish as well as meat. Nothing could be more absurd than all the fish arriving at Paddington, going down by cart to Billingsgate, five or six miles, and the greater part being recarted four or five miles to the West End again. This carting he had no doubt was more detrimental to the quality of the fish than all the railway journey; and then, if it did not arrive by five in the morning, forsooth, it could not reach the customer till next day. One of the fishmongers stated that every hour the fish is out of the consumers' hand it deteriorates. Mr. Mitchell remarked that London contained upwards of 3,000,000 inhabitants, and covers an area of 118 square miles. Fish, of all articles of food, from its perishable nature, requires to be distributed over this area in the promptest manner, yet, at present, the whole supplies of London, besides the surrounding country, have to be concentrated at Billingsgate. He considered that, however convenient Billingsgate may have been before the period of the railways, it is not so now, for he believed at the present time two-thirds to three-fourths of the fish supply of London comes by railway, and, when there is a large supply, the passage to Billingsgate is blocked up for hours. Look at the mode in which fish is distributed at the present time. Trains arrive with fish from Ireland, Milford Haven, Cornwall, and Scotland, and they are taken from the railway stations by carts to Billingsgate, in some cases a distance, as I have said, of six miles, and then redistributed in carts all over the metropolis, six, eight, and ten miles. Surely the fish supply of 3,000,000 of people might afford profitable employment, not for one, but for three central markets. If you ask any of the fishmongers about this, they will tell you that more than one market will never answer, and that that market is Billingsgate. Well, the fishmongers are a most respectable class of men, and we are entitled to give weight to their opinions, guided by their personal interests and practical experience; but in my view, Billingsgate should now be confined to the sale of fish coming up the river, if retained at all. I fear matters will never alter, nor will fish become the food of the people, instead of being, as at present, almost exclusively the food of the rich, unless some public authority, in combination with the railway companies, will do as Mr. Seymour Clarke did in the coal trade—appoint agents all over London, irrespective of Billingsgate, for the immediate sale and distribution of fish as it arrives. Now, as to the time that fish will keep good, he had very good authority on that point. He consulted Mr. Anderson, an eminent and wealthy fishmonger in Edinburgh, who confirmed his (Mr. Mitchell's) views, that fresh fish may be sent from the Moray Firth with great advantage. Cod, haddock, and ling, by drawing the stomach, will keep, according to Mr. Anderson, for forty-eight hours, and in winter for four days. He recommended that they should be sent in boxes 2½ feet broad, 8 inches deep, and 3 feet long, with rope handles; and a few pieces of ice to fill up corners were a great advantage; and in the north ice could easily be got in any quantity with a little forethought. In fact, Mr. Mitchell thought that it only required arrangement and organization to add the great fishing of the Moray Firth to the fish supply of the other parts of the coasts of Great Britain. Indeed, fish from the Moray Firth may reach London, even by the present transit, as quickly as fish is now supplied from Ireland, Cornwall, and even from Scarborough. He had gone to Scarborough and to Liverpool, and corresponded with persons who were conversant with the transport of fresh fish from these distant localities, and the above was the result.

The Chairman remarked that one of the difficulties which was not easily to be got over was, if there were only one or two kinds of fish brought to a particular part, the dealers in fish who want a variety would not go to an isolated place for their supply. If the fish could be altogether brought by railway to a central spot such as Smithfield, he could imagine such a thing would work. With regard to the particular fish brought from the Moray Firth, such as cod and ling, it would be better for being kept a little time.

Mr. Mitchell—The Moray Firth and the Scotch coast had fish of every description except soles. Cod was, no doubt, better from being a day in salt.

The Chairman added, the great question was the distribution. They could hardly get people in the trade to alter their mode of getting supplies.

Mr. Mitchell observed, that no doubt was the difficulty. His object was to make it clear that fresh fish could be sent in good condition from the Moray Firth to London ; but he admitted the difficulty was how to get it distributed amongst the consumers, and yet the inhabitants of London would only be too thankful to take it. It was monstrous that the shores of Great Britain should teem with fish, particularly the Scottish shores, with ready means of transit, yet, he believed, three-fourths of the inhabitants of London never taste fresh fish. As he said, it was a luxury, the food of the rich.

The Chairman—The railway companies would require to be shown that it was their interest to encourage and facilitate this fish traffic, and they might have carriages constructed for the purpose of keeping the fish as cool as possible during the transit.

Mr. Mitchell said he had done his best in the north to draw the attention of the railway authorities to this subject, and since he had been staying in London he caused to be sent to him by way of experiment a cwt. of cod, ling, and haddocks ; they arrived in excellent condition. The fish of each kind were large. He was charged in the Moray Firth for the haddocks, 3d. each, for the cod 1s. 6d. each. Now the price list sent to his house by the fishmonger on the 23rd February was, haddocks 1s. 6d. to 2s. each ; Dublin Bay haddocks (and they are not much nearer London than the Moray Firth) were quoted at 2s. to 2s. 6d. each ; cod-fish 6s. 6d. to 15s. ; crimped haddocks from 7s. 6d. to 16s. 6d. ; crimped slice of cod 1s. 6d. to 3s. 6d. ; fresh herrings 2s. per dozen.

The Chairman asked Mr. Mitchell whether he was prepared with any propositions for getting over the difficulties suggested. Mr. Mitchell had suggested some arrangement with regard to Smithfield Market. He (the Chairman) understood the Corporation contemplated some alterations with respect to that market, and the fact that the great bulk of fish taken to Billingsgate was now brought by the railways instead of by water, might have some effect with regard to Billingsgate itself. Therefore any information with regard to fresh sources of supply of fish was important, as assisting the authorities to determine upon the future site of the central fish market, in the event of the removal of the present one.

Mr. Youl remarked it was important that fish should arrive in London very early in the morning; if not, the fishmongers would not distribute it. In order to enable the fish to arrive in time for the market, it would involve a great alteration in the trains coming from the north. Under the present arrangements it would seem the fish from the Moray Firth would not reach London till eight or nine o'clock, when the market of the day was over.

Mr. Mitchell thought the interests of the public were more important than the convenience of the fishmongers, and they deserved consideration. Although fish did not arrive in London before eight or nine o'clock a.m., or even ten o'clock, he saw no reason why it should not be distributed for dinner that day; besides, there was a large trade in fish from the Firth of Forth, which, for that matter, could arrive at any time in the morning. Mr. Mitchell's attention was first drawn to this subject by noticing that the moment the railway was open from Edinburgh by Berwick, and a new harbour at Dunbar, the great bulk of herrings caught in the Firth of Forth was sent south fresh in barrels and boxes, and more than double price was obtained for them, and the quantity sent was increasing every year.

Mr. Jenkins asked whether there was not a large supply of fish from Hull to the Midland Counties?

Mr. Mitchell—From Hull and also from Scarborough. The Scotch train came up in the evening from Scotland to York, and met the Scarborough train there, and at that place the train was marshalled to the different towns where the market was best for fish. It was delivered at Derby, Leicester, Leeds, Birmingham, and other towns. In fact, the London market was not reckoned by the fish-curers in the north so good a market as the towns in the Midland Counties.

Mr. Jenkins asked whether Hull was not a large depôt for the landing of fish from the German Ocean, and whether fish from that place would not reach the Midland Counties at early morning?

Mr. Mitchell replied that no doubt Hull would be the most central port, but he could not see any actual necessity for the London fish market being held so early as five o'clock in the morning.

The Chairman apprehended it was necessary to enable the dealers to distribute the fish over London.

Mr. Mitchell said, as far as he could gather, Billingsgate was at the present time one of the most inconvenient places in London for a market. It took four or five hours to bring fish from the Nore by the river, and it could come from Hull in that time. As regards the delivery of fish by railway, to which he understood some of the fish-dealers objected as irregular, he saw no reason why there should be irregularity with regard to the arrival of fish trains any more than with other trains. If fish waggons were attached to the passenger trains they would come as regularly as any trains in the country. There was a fresh-meat train started regularly every day from Forres, and it reached London in 36 hours. The meat trains kept time as regularly as the passenger trains, and it ought to be the same with fish.

Mr. Youl thought that the great evil at present was the length of time that the fish were now detained in the streets leading to Billingsgate before they could be unloaded in the market.

Mr. Jenkins inquired whether Mr. Mitchell calculated upon a new trade in fish, to the amount of 50 tons a day, having to contend with an already established trade.

Mr. Mitchell had no doubt the difference of price obtained would induce a great trade from the north of Scotland in the herring season. There would be a great difference in the returns to the dealers if the fish could be sent south in a fresh instead of in a cured state; the cost of curing would be saved, and the returns on their capital would be immediate.

Mr. Jenkins asked whether the rule did not always apply that there was a great difference at the fishing station and at the market some long distance off. For instance, herrings sold at £1 per thousand at the station would be sold for £3 per thousand 170 miles off.

Mr. Mitchell replied that was probably so.

Mr. Jenkins—And that the perishable nature of fish was an element in the amount of profit which the dealers required in transporting fish from one place to another?

Mr. Mitchell had no doubt it was so, according to present arrangements; but what he thought most to be considered was the public advantage and convenience, and not that of the fishmonger. He thought, by proper organization for the prompt delivery of the fish, it could be brought to the consumer in better condition, and, the area of consumption being enlarged, even if the price of the fish were less, the profit to the dealer would be more certain and greater from the increased quantity sold. But all this required a different mode of dealing from the present. In the herring season in Inverness, the whole community seemed to eat fish, and the odour of fish cooking pervaded the town as one walked about, such was the superabundant supply of herrings, which were sold at a very cheap rate. The only other mode of disposing of them was by curing, and as he had already stated that the barrels and packing cost 7s. 6d. each, when they were sent to the Baltic and other places abroad, it was a long time before the curers got a return for their capital.

Mr. Jenkins remarked that large quantities of herrings were received in this country from Howth, on the coast of Ireland, and he begged to ask Mr. Mitchell whether he did not think the fishers of Howth, who had no established trade for their herrings, could send over their produce at a cheaper rate than the Scotch dealers, who had already an established trade on the Continent and elsewhere?

Mr. Mitchell replied that they could not come quicker than from Scotland. The Scotch dealers would get better prices for the fish if they sent it fresh. The fish which cost, in the Moray Firth, 25s. per cran sometimes realized as much as 80s. or 90s. in the south. Even from the Hebrides, last spring, as many as 15,000 barrels were sent off, some in quick steamers to Liverpool, slightly strewed over with salt. When landed they were distributed to London and through the Midland districts. What was required, as he had already said, was an organization of the traffic, and for the distribution of the fish when it arrived ; the latter, no doubt, was the more important point. He thought there would be a difficulty in getting the fish into London so early as five in the morning from the Moray Firth. It would take from 12 at noon on the Monday till eight or nine on the Tuesday morning to bring the fish into the London terminus. He saw no reason why the wholesale fish market should not be held at nine o'clock as well as at five o'clock in the morning, as the dealers would then have ample time for the distribution of the fish from all quarters. It only required the alteration of existing habits, and he believed no one would suffer from it.

Mr. Youl remarked that the meat market was held at an equally early hour of the morning, which he apprehended was necessary for the requirements of the trade.

Mr. Mitchell questioned whether there was any absolute necessity for it. He added that the railway was now being extended from the Highland line at Dingwell to the West Sea, opposite the Island of Skye, and would be a direct communication from the whole Hebrides, and thus would lead to further large supplies of fish, available for the southern markets in a fresh state.

The Committee, having thanked Mr. Mitchell for the information he had given them, then adjourned,

INDEX

'n' indicates a footnote; ws indicates Writers to the Signet

ABERDEEN, 158, 189
Ackergill Tower, 130
Allport, James, 237n, 238
Anderson, Peter, 159–60, 180
Athole, John 4th Duke of, 195n
Athole, George 6th Duke of,
190–5
Athole Brose, 192n
Athole Highlanders, 194, 195n

BALMER, Thomas, 34
Bank agents ruined, 65
Barrogill Castle, 131
Belford, Andrew, 69
Belligerent muster of clan, 50
Ben Nevis, 24
Black Watch (42nd
Highlanders), 2
Board of Trade, 186–7
Bouch, Sir Thomas, 210
Brassey & Falshaw, 180–5, 220–5
Breadalbane, Marquis of,
152–3, 156
Bruce, Major Cumming, MP, 161
Bruce, Hon Thomas C., 196,
198, 202
Burgoyne, Sir John, 173–4

CAITHNESS, 127–39
Caithness, John 11th Earl of,
134–7
Caithness, James 12th Earl of,
137

Caithness, Alexander 13th Earl
of, 131
Caithness, James 14th Earl of,
137, 221–4
Caithness, George 15th Earl of,
131, 137
Caledonian Bank, 5, 16, 65–72
Caledonian Canal,
20, 24, 114, 120, 172, 189
Carr, Dr, 230–1
Castle Grant, 51
Cawdor Castle, 56–8
Chalmers, Rev Thomas, 98
Chisholm, Alexander W, MP, 142
Churches, building of, 4, 140
City of Glasgow Bank, 71
Clark, John, 67–70
Clearances, 84–8, 104–13
Coach Service to London,
169 and Vol I
Cock of the North, The, 30
Colchester, Lord, 207
Commercial travellers, 75–6
Commissioners of Roads and
Bridges, 129, 204–9
Cowlairs Tunnel, Glasgow, 150n
Crawshay, W., 237n
Cullen House, 52
Cumming, Sir Alexander, 190–1

DAVIOT House, 4
Deer forests, 109, 122

Delane, John T., 217
Dempster, George, of Skibo, 148
Destitution, 86, 120
Dingwall, 189
Disruption of Church of
            Scotland, 97
Droving of Cattle, 79 *and* Vol I
Duff, family of, 36–8
Duff House, 38, 41
Duffus, Lord, 130
Dunbeath Castle, 132–3
Dunrobin Castle, 92, 95, 100,
            103, 146–7, 215–19
Dunsmure, James, 73–4

ELGIN, 159
Ellice, Edward, MP, 123, 199
Emigration ship, conditions
            aboard, 111–12
Entails, 14, 16, 43
Extravagance of Chiefs, 107, 114

FALSHAW, James, *see* Brassey
Famine in Highlands, 39, 48
Ferries, 78–9
Fife, Earls of, 36–43, 183
Fish, transport of, 252–8
Fisheries, Scottish Board,
            73–4 *and* Vol I
Fishing and fishing vessels,
        86, 90, 118–20, 129–30, 213
Flagstones, Caithness,
            134–5 *and* Vol I
Fleet Mound, 89, 126
Forres, 202
Fort Augustus, 17
Fort George, 54
Fowler, Sir John, 211–12
Fowlis Castle, 218–19
Fraser Clan, 8–21
Fraser-Tytler, Col Wm, 190
Free Church of Scotland, 98
Funerals, 6, 142–4 *and* Vol I

GAME laws, 82, 109
Giles, Nettan, 220, 222

Glasgow, 76–7, 150n
Glendinning, J., 76–7
Glengarry, 123
Glenquoich, 123
Gordon Castle, 31
Gordon, Dukes of, 24–35
Government control of railways
            urged, 166–7n
Grant, Mrs Anne of Laggan, 106
Grant Clan, 44–53
Grant, John of Glenmoriston,
            160
Grant, Sir John Macpherson,
            160
Grant, Patrick, ws, 69
Grant, General Sir Patrick, 197
Gunn, George, 93, 97, 103, 215
Gwynne, Captain, 17

HARBOURS,
    89–90, 130, 169, 223 *and* Vol I
Highland and Agricultural
            Society, 131
Highland Honours, a dramatic
            toast, 133 *and* Vol I
Highland Railway,
        5, 16, 42, 48, 125, 140
Highlanders, authors opinion
            of, 106
Horne, James, ws, 138
Hudson, George, 229–51
Hudson, Mrs, 233n
Hutcheson, David & Co, 212

IMPORTS, adverse effect of, 118
Inns, improvement of, 75, 92
Inspectors of roads, 207–9
Invergordon, 189
Inverness Gas & Water Works,
            169
Inverness-shire Militia, 47
Investments in railways,
        229–30, 232–3n, 235n

KEITH Station, 184–9
Kelp, 107n, 118

Kirkwall, 140–1

LAND ownership, 116
Land, value of, 36
Late harvest of 1877, 111n
Law of Primogeniture, evil
            effects of, 117
Lawsuits,
        14, 19, 46, 81, 144–6, 224
Leech, John, 192n
Leeman, George, 242, 250
Leslie, James, 173
Loch, George,
            215–16, 220–1, 225
Loch, James, MP, 78, 83–94,
            98, 100–5, 146–7, 215
Locke & Errington,
    154–6, 159, 161, 164, 174n, 180
London fish markets, 252–63
Lord Lieutenants, powers of, 18
Lord Provosts of Glasgow, 75
Lowland agricultural counties,
                        115
Lumsden, Sir James, 75

MAIL Coach routes, 90
Marshall, William, composer, 26
Matheson, Alexander, MP,
            190, 196, 211
May, Sir Thomas E., 204, 207
Macadam, John L. &
            MacConnell, 128, 174n
Macdonald, General Godfrey,
                        113
Maciver, Evander, 93, 216
Mackenzie, Rev John, 96
Mackenzie, Sir William, 211
Mackintosh, Aeneas W. of
            Raigmore, 18, 190
Mackintosh Clan, 1–7
Maclean, Neil, 69
Maclean & Stileman, 221–4
Macpherson, a military family,
                        58
Macpherson, Cluny, 2
Macpherson, Captain D., 69

Mechi of Essex, 177
Menzies, Fletcher, 151
Menzies, Sir Neil, 151
Merry, James, MP and
            Ironmaster, 19, 21–3
Military recruitment, 120n
Mitchell, Dean & Co, 185
Mitchell, J. & Co, 213, 225
Mitchell, John, 207
Mitchell, Joseph,
        69, 164, 199, 202, 206–8
Monro, George, 65, 68
Moyhall, 2–7, 67
Mulben railway accident, 187
Murray, Kenneth, 218–20, 224
Musical instruments, 47, 51

NESS River flood of 1849, 171
Nicol, Dr J. I., Provost of
            Inverness, 150
North of Scotland Bank, 65–6

O'LEARY, Professor, 169–70
Orkney Islands, 139–41, 222–3
Orr, Sir Andrew, 75

PARKS, Captain of HMS Cuckoo,
                        169
Paterson, Murdoch and
    William, 165, 199, 202, 213,
    224–5
Perth, 152, 154, 157
Poor Law, 88
Potato Blight,
            48n, 169 *and* Vol I

QUEENSFERRY, 74

RAILWAY Mania,
        157–9, 162, 166, 234–5
Railways—Scottish : Aberdeen
    Railway Co, 168; Caledonian,
    154, 167, 180; Edinburgh &
    Glasgow, 149–50n, 154; Elgin
    & Lossiemouth, 151; Great
    North of Scotland, 163, 168,

179–83, 190, 195; Highland, 5, 16, 42, 48, 125, 140; Inverness & Aberdeen Junction, 184; Inverness & Nairn, 181–3; Scottish Central, 151, 152n, 153–4, 157, 167; Skye Railway, 210–13; Sutherland & Caithness, 213–26

Railways — English: Brandling Junction, 237, 239; Lancaster & Carlisle, 180; Liverpool & Manchester, 94; London & North Western, 94, 180; Midland, 229–32, 236, 239; North Eastern, 240, 242, 245; York, Newcastle & Berwick, 239; York & North Midland, 231–2, 236–7, 239

Railways and the aristocracy, 152, 160–1, 190

Railways, premature opening, 185–7, 197

Reay Country, 90

Reform Bill, 49

Regiments, Highland, 89 *and* Vol I

Rendal, J. M., 174–5

Rickman, John, 208

Roads and bridges, 83, 89, 92, 115, 120, 126–9, 139, 204–9 *and* Vol I

Ross, John, 69

Ross, Colonel John G., 69

Sale of estates, 18, 19, 33

St John's Masonic Friendly Society, 72

Scott, Hope, 210

Scottish Chamber of Agriculture, 101

Scrabster, 223

Seafield, Francis 6th Earl of, 160, 178

Seafield, John 7th Earl of, 183, 195

Sellar, Peter, 85–7, 99–100

Sheep Farming, 93, 99, 107, 114–15, 120–1 *and* Vol I

Sheridan, R. B., 192n

Sinclair, Dr Eric of Freswick, 132–3

Sinclair, Sir George, MP, 131–2

Sinclair, Sir John, MP, 127, 131

Skinner, General, 55

Skye, Isle of, 110, 113

Smith, James of Deanston, 160

Smith, Robert, 69

Smuggling, 35, 60–2

Society of Arts Food Committee, 252

Sport, 123–4

Stafford, Marquis of, 82–4, 90, 94, 215

Steamer services, 139–40, 211–12

Stirling, John, of Kippendavie, 154

Sutherland, Elizabeth Duchess-Countess of, 80–2, 94–6, 146

Sutherland, 1st Duke of, 82n, 94, 215

Sutherland, 2nd Duke of, 83n, 98

Sutherland, 3rd Duke of, 215–24

Sutherlandshire, 78–106, 146–8, 214–20; Clearances, 84–8, 104–6; Clergy, 93, 96–9, 105; Estate Factors, 93, 97; Pauperism, 86; Land reclamation, 100–1; Schoolmasters, 98

Tacksmen, 81–2, 93, 105, 216

Taymouth Castle, 155–6

Telford, Thomas, 208 *and* Vol I

Tenure of land, Clansmen's claim, 88

Thurso, 213, 225

Thurso Castle, 131–2

Thompson and Forman, 237

Thompson, Harry S., 245–51

Tilt Glen, 192

Timber floating, 51, 161n

Trail, James, Sheriff of
         Caithness, 134

UNION, Bill for Dissolution of, 45

VICTORIA, Queen and Prince
     Albert first visit to Scotland,
103, 121, 308

WALKER, James, 153–6

Waterston, Charles, 68–71

Weir on River Ness, 172

Wick, 213, 223, 225

Wood, Sir Charles, 174

YOUNG, William, 85, 89, 100